AF848536

Liberalising the Accounting Curriculum in University Education

This book presents the views of accounting educators, accounting education policy-makers, and accounting practitioners from across the world on the challenging topic of liberalising the accounting curriculum within university education. Accounting is a relatively new subject within universities and has been absorbed into a high level of education without any real attempt to do so within the traditional ethos of a liberal arts education.

In this collection, the logic of teaching using the liberal arts is described and contrasted with the practical vocational training approach of teaching which has formed the foundation of accountancy courses for many years. A proposal to change this established practice, by integrating the liberal arts into the university accounting curriculum, is followed by a series of short chapters which address the relevance, validity and worthiness of the proposed approach. Comments and counter-arguments are then discussed before further chapters illustrate how the proposed change may be achieved in a variety of different contexts – ranging from that of the global financial crisis to the inclusion of ethics and sustainability within the accounting curriculum.

This volume will help accounting educators to improve the design of their accounting degree programmes by moving away from an excessive emphasis on technical skills towards a broader consideration of a liberal contextualisation of the accounting curriculum.

Chapters 2 to 16 of this book were originally published as a special issue of *Accounting Education: an international journal.*

Alan Sangster has 30 years' experience as a university accounting teacher. Having worked in six universities in the UK and the University of Sao Paulo in Brazil, he is now Professor of Accounting at Griffith University, Australia, and Editor of *Accounting Education: an international journal*. He has a PhD in accounting education, is co-author of the top-selling textbook *Business Accounting*, has published over 60 research papers and book chapters, and has presented his research at over 100 conferences, including many plenary presentations, worldwide.

Richard M. S. Wilson is Emeritus Professor of Business Administration and Financial Management at Loughborough University, UK. During his career, he has been a practitioner and professor across many disciplines and in more than a dozen countries. For 40 years he has been active nationally and internationally in educational policy-making on the interface of accounting education and training. He has published widely, is the founding editor of *Accounting Education: an international journal*; holds two Lifetime Achievement Awards (one specifically for his work in the field of accounting education); and is an Academician of the Academy of Social Sciences.

Liberalising the Accounting Curriculum in University Education

Edited by
Alan Sangster and Richard M. S. Wilson

Routledge
Taylor & Francis Group
LONDON AND NEW YORK

First published 2013
by Routledge
2 Park Square, Milton Park, Abingdon, Oxon, OX14 4RN

Simultaneously published in the USA and Canada
by Routledge
711 Third Avenue, New York, NY 10017

Routledge is an imprint of the Taylor & Francis Group, an informa business

© 2013 Taylor & Francis

Chapters 2 – 16 of this book are a reproduction of *Accounting Education: an international journal*, volume 19, issue 4. The Publisher requests to those authors who may be citing this book to state, also, the bibliographical details of the special issue on which the book was based.

All rights reserved. No part of this book may be reprinted or reproduced or utilised in any form or by any electronic, mechanical, or other means, now known or hereafter invented, including photocopying and recording, or in any information storage or retrieval system, without permission in writing from the publishers.

Trademark notice: Product or corporate names may be trademarks or registered trademarks, and are used only for identification and explanation without intent to infringe.

British Library Cataloguing in Publication Data
A catalogue record for this book is available from the British Library

ISBN13: 978-0-415-65980-2

Typeset in Times New Roman
by Taylor & Francis Books

Publisher's Note
The publisher would like to make readers aware that chapters 2 to 16 in this book may be referred to as articles as they are identical to the articles published in the special issue. The publisher accepts responsibility for any inconsistencies that may have arisen in the course of preparing this volume for print.

Contents

Citation Information

The following chapters were originally published in *Accounting Education: an international journal*. When citing this material, please use the original issue information and page numbering for each article, as follows:

Chapter 2
A Role for the Compulsory Study of Literature in Accounting Education
Roger Jeffrey Lister
Accounting Education: an international journal, volume 19, issue 4 (August 2010)
pp. 329-343

Chapter 3
A Commentary on "A Role for the Compulsory Study of Literature in Accounting Education"
Melvin Berg
Accounting Education: an international journal, volume 19, issue 4 (August 2010)
pp. 345-346

Chapter 4
Will Compelled Study of Literary Classics Engender Enrichment, Creativity, Curiosity, and Romance in Accounting Students? A Commentary on "A Role for the Compulsory Study of Literature in Accounting Education"
Russell J. Craig
Accounting Education: an international journal, volume 19, issue 4 (August 2010)
pp. 347-350

Chapter 5
A Commentary on "A Role for the Compulsory Study of Literature in Accounting Education"
Lisa Evans and Ian Fraser
Accounting Education: an international journal, volume 19, issue 4 (August 2010)
pp. 351-354

Chapter 6
A Commentary on "A Role for the Compulsory Study of Literature in Accounting Education"
Bryan Howieson

Accounting Education: an international journal, volume 19, issue 4 (August 2010)
pp. 355-359

Chapter 7
A Commentary on "A Role for the Compulsory Study of Literature in Accounting Education"
Robert Jelly
Accounting Education: an international journal, volume 19, issue 4 (August 2010)
pp. 361-363

Chapter 8
A Commentary on "A Role for the Compulsory Study of Literature in Accounting Education"
Fawzi Laswad
Accounting Education: an international journal, volume 19, issue 4 (August 2010)
pp. 365-366

Chapter 9
A Commentary on "A Role for the Compulsory Study of Literature in Accounting Education"
Barihan A. Nabil
Accounting Education: an international journal, volume 19, issue 4 (August 2010)
pp. 367-368

Chapter 10
Deriving Four Lessons for Accounting Educators: A Commentary on "A Role for the Compulsory Study of Literature in Accounting Education"
Fred Phillips
Accounting Education: an international journal, volume 19, issue 4 (August 2010)
pp. 369-371

Chapter 11
Making our Students More 'fit for Purpose': A Commentary on "A Role for the Compulsory Study of Literature in Accounting Education"
Alan Sangster
Accounting Education: an international journal, volume 19, issue 4 (August 2010)
pp. 373-376

Chapter 12
A Commentary on "A Role for the Compulsory Study of Literature in Accounting Education"
Henry Saville
Accounting Education: an international journal, volume 19, issue 4 (August 2010)
pp. 377-379

Chapter 13
A Commentary on "A Role for the Compulsory Study of Literature in Accounting Education"

Peter Scott
Accounting Education: an international journal, volume 19, issue 4 (August 2010)
pp. 381-384

Chapter 14
Rejoinder to Commentaries on 'A Role for the Compulsory Study of Literature in Accounting Education'
Roger J. Lister
Accounting Education: an international journal, volume 19, issue 4 (August 2010)
pp. 385-391

Chapter 15
Black Swan and the Corn Maiden
Jesse Dillard and Mary Ann Reynolds
Accounting Education: an international journal, volume 19, issue 4 (August 2010)
pp. 393-401

Chapter 16
Revitalizing Accounting Education: A Highly Applied Liberal Arts Approach
Timothy J. Fogarty
Accounting Education: an international journal, volume 19, issue 4 (August 2010)
pp. 403-419

Chapter 17
University Accounting Curricula: The Perceptions of an Alumni Group
Shirley Carr, Frances Chua & Hector Perera
Accounting Education: an international journal, volume 15, issue 4 (December 2006)
pp. 359-376

Chapter 18
Incorporating Sustainability into Accounting Curricula: Lessons Learnt From an Action Research Study
James Hazelton & Matthew Haigh
Accounting Education: an international journal, volume 19, issues 1-2 (February-April 2010)
pp. 159-178

Chapter 19
Impact of an Ethics Presentation Used in the USA and Adapted for Italy
Gheula Canarutto, Katherine T. Smith & L. Murphy Smith
Accounting Education: an international journal, volume 19, issue 3 (June 2010)
pp. 309-322

Chapter 20
Contextualizing the Intermediate Financial Accounting Courses in the Global Financial Crisis
Robert Bloom and Mariah Webinger
Accounting Education: an international journal, volume 20, issue 5 (October 2011)
pp. 469-494

INTRODUCTION
Liberalising the Accounting Curriculum in University Education

RICHARD M. S. WILSON
Loughborough University, UK

ALAN SANGSTER
Griffith University, Australia

Knowledge is a defining characteristic of a profession but, given the ever-increasing knowledge base, curricula in professional disciplines are becoming overcrowded (Paisey and Paisey, 2007). This is not a recent phenomenon: the accounting curriculum has long been considered overcrowded as educators follow the demands of the profession for more coverage of '*x*', whatever '*x*' happens to be at any particular point in time. In the U.K., for example, 25 years ago it was the teaching of computer programming. Today, it is accounting standards, and arguably highly-relevant subjects for students and their future employers (such as double-entry bookkeeping) are disappearing from syllabi and being relegated to appendices in textbooks. Others, such as accounting systems, e-business, and continuous monitoring, continuous auditing, and continuous reporting have never managed to get past 'first base'.

Similar issues apply worldwide with curriculum content being very much directed by what 'needs' to be learnt (normally based on external factors, such as the demands of the accounting profession) rather than by reasons of pedagogy relating to what may be done with, and within, the curriculum to develop reflection, critical thinking, and the ability to think 'outside the box' on the part of our students, and so better prepare them for lifelong learning.

One traditional means of developing these skills in students is through the provision of a Liberal Arts Education. The Liberal Arts represent a college or university curriculum aimed at imparting general knowledge and developing general intellectual capacities *in contrast to a professional, vocational, or technical curriculum*. In the medieval European university the seven liberal arts were grammar, rhetoric, and logic (the *trivium*) and geometry, arithmetic, music, and astronomy (the *quadrivium*). In modern colleges and universities the Liberal Arts include the study of literature, languages, philosophy, history, mathematics, and science as the basis of a general, or liberal, education. (*Encylopædia Britannica*, 2010).

This is not to be confused with *The Humanities*: grammar, rhetoric, poetry, history, and moral philosophy—the *studia humanitatis* of Renaissance Italy, which today has moved to comprise of literature, language, philosophy, the fine arts, and history.

However, the Liberal Arts curriculum is sometimes described as the study of three branches of knowledge (*Encylopædia Britannica*, 2010):

(i) the humanities (literature, language, philosophy, the fine arts, and history);
(ii) the physical and biological sciences and mathematics; and
(iii) the social sciences.

It is the first of these three branches that is the main focus of this volume on *Liberalising the Accounting Curriculum in University Education.*

Many writers over the past 16 centuries have expounded the merits of a Liberal Arts education. For example, Cardinal John Henry Newman (1801–1890), in a series of addresses published in various forms in the nineteenth and twentieth centuries, wrote of the emancipatory benefits of such an education:

> [The purpose of a Liberal Arts Education is to] open the mind, to correct it, to refine it, to enable it to know, and to digest, master, rule, and use its knowledge, to give it power over its own faculties, application, flexibility, method, critical exactness, sagacity, resource, address, [and] eloquent expression . . . (Newman, 1852, p. 148).

Furthermore, in a different address, many years before the Accounting Education Change Commission advocated 'learning to learn' in 1990 ("Accounting programs should prepare students to *become* professional accountants, not to *be* professional accountants at the time of entry to the profession . . . developing in students the motivation and capacity to continue to learn outside the formal educational environment"), Newman stated the benefits of a Liberal Arts education for lifelong learning:

> A habit of mind is formed which lasts through life, of which the attributes are, freedom, equitableness, calmness, moderation, and wisdom. . . (Newman, 1852, p. 127)

For a long time it was considered, and still is by many educators, to be extremely beneficial for someone to experience an education of this type and then to move on to train for a career after leaving university. Indeed, in the U.S.A., over 500 Liberal Arts Colleges exist for undergraduate study where, typically, at least half of the four-year curriculum is devoted to study of the Liberal Arts. Similar colleges also exist in Europe and the rest of the world, although they are more often at secondary school (high school) level rather than at undergraduate level, and singularly absent from higher education.

Looking more closely at the U.S.A., approximately a quarter of the 120 or 150 hours of study required of accounting graduates by the local state Certified Public Accountants (CPA) bodies are on accounting topics, a similar proportion on business-related topics, and another 25 per cent on liberal arts topics such as written communication, social/behavioural sciences, mathematics, biological/physical sciences, historical perspectives, arts and humanities. The concept of a broad educational foundation upon which the specialism of accounting is developed appears to be thriving in the U.S.A., but this is not generally the case elsewhere. Perhaps this is partly the result of the history of accounting education in different countries. The U.S.A. has a longer history of university accounting education than the other English-speaking countries of the world, and the structure of its accounting degrees can be traced back to a curriculum oulined by the American Institute of Accountants (now, the Certified Public Accountants) in 1938 which recommended a 120-hour curriculum, half in accounting (30 per cent) and business (20 per cent), and half in the Liberal Arts:

> The [accounting] graduate [of this programme]... will not have received training purely as a technician but a broad and liberal education in which an understanding of professional technique will be rooted deep in an appreciation of the broader social significances of his profession (Miller, 1938, p. 193).

Surely, this is the model of university accounting education to which we should all aspire - yet, despite many convincing claims for the benefits of a Liberal Arts education, there appears to be a growing groundswell of opinion that these colleges may be in decline and that the concept of a Liberal Arts education may be elitist and no longer as valid in the twenty-first century as it was previously.

For example, in January 2010, *Times Higher Education* devoted its cover feature to the state of Liberal Arts education (Reisz, 2010). In it, grave concern is expressed for the noticeable shift away from The Liberal Arts that has occurred over at least the past 30 years:

> Classical liberal-arts education has been under assault for several decades, by a congeries of forces seeking to undermine and demonize the best that has been thought and said. ... Our universities have brainwashed a generation of culturally illiterate zombies. ... The humanities and arts are being cut away. . .. We seem to be forgetting about the soul and therefore risk failing to inculcate core values of empathy and respect [in our students and] we face a worldwide crisis in education that . . . [is] likely to be . . . more damaging for democratic self-government than the global economic crisis of 2008.

Lending support to the first part of this thesis, a few months later one U.K. university announced that it was ceasing the provision of philosophy at undergraduate level (Lowe, 2010).

Business schools, by their very nature - given their professional/vocational focus, have never been hotbeds of Liberal Education, not even in their infancy in Renaissance Italy. There are some exceptions: in the U.K., for example: Keele University has an elective Year Two module on Accounting and Philosophy; the University of Northampton offers a joint degree in Accounting and Philosophy; and The University of Cardiff Business School offers undergraduate modules in Business History, Economic History, and Japanese History. In addition, many U.K. universities have joint honours degrees combining a foreign language with one of an array of different business school disciplines, including Accounting.

These are, therefore, uncertain times for the Liberal Arts and the undergraduate accounting curriculum is generally (other than for some minor examples, such as those given above) already full to capacity. Yet there will always be proponents of the integration of the Liberal Arts and this volume is no exception. It contains a *Forum* and six additional chapters that focus in different ways directly on the Liberal Arts.

The first chapter is the *Forum* in which Roger Lister proposes liberalising the accounting curriculum through the exposure of students to literature, echoing the claims concerning the use of literature in the curriculum by many voices from the past, such as the poet John Milton (1608–1674) and Edward Copleston (1776–1849), Provost of Oriel College, Oxford and Bishop of Llandarf, who wrote:

> In the cultivation of literature is found that common link, which, among the higher and middling departments of life, unites the jarring sects and subdivisions into one interest, which supplies common topics, and kindles common feelings, unmixed with those narrow prejudices with which all professions are more or less infected. The knowledge, too, which is thus acquired, expands and enlarges the mind, excites its faculties . . . and thus, without directly qualifying a man for any of the employments of life, it enriches and ennobles all. Without teaching him the peculiar business of any one office or calling, it enables him to act his part in each of them with better grace and more elevated carriage; and, if happily planned and conducted, is a main ingredient in that complete and generous education which fits a man to perform justly, skilfully, and magnanimously, all the offices, both private and public (Copleston, 1852, p. 198).

If a *Forum* is to serve a useful purpose, it should develop our understanding of the issues raised. There is no doubt that this *Forum* has done so. In making his case, Lister targets the generally acknowledged soft skills gap in accounting graduates, suggesting that literature is their *only* possible saviour from the vagaries of the labour market, and suggests a contentious, challenging, and thought-provoking way to make this come about.

When he first read an early draft of this chapter, one of the Editors commented to the other that it was one of the most interesting scholarly papers he had read in the past 30 years. It was never going to have an 'easy ride' against such a diverse group of Commentators, and it certainly did not. All the Commentators had something to add to the debate and a rich pool of advice lies within the *Commentaries* in this volume. Lister's *Rejoinder* adds much to the debate and leaves issues unanswered and opportunities beckoning that will test the strength of will of even the bravest among us.

We are convinced that all who have been involved in this volume have been enriched by the experience; and we are sure that anyone reading through it will not regret a moment spent in doing so. It will be an illuminating, sometimes frustrating, at times entertaining but, overall, rewarding activity.

The *Forum* consists of Chapter 1, 11 *Commentaries*, and a *Rejoinder*. Despite the unanswered questions and lingering doubts concerning the practicalities and appropriateness of what Lister suggests, a vehicle is proposed in the end of the *Rejoinder* that certainly merits consideration.

This is a truly international book. Professor Lister is based in England, the authors of the 11 *Commentaries* are based in eight different countries, and some of the authors of the other six chapters are from yet more countries. The overall geographic distribution of authors is:

Australia 2
Canada 2
England 4

France 1
Italy 1
Jordan 1
New Zealand 5
Northern Ireland 1
Scotland 1
U.S.A. 6

The first of the chapters that follow the *Forum* is by Jesse Dillard and Mary Ann Reynolds (both from the U.S.A.). It takes a social constructionist stance and proposes the use of story writing by students to develop a broader awareness of the world around them and to recognize issues they must be prepared to face which are not within their current view of the world.

It is a thought-provoking piece on how to extend the soft skills of our students through creative writing, a branch of the Liberal Art of Literature, which leaves the reader in precisely the same position as the students who were involved with the writing experience described in the paper. There is a sense of 'what?' It is as if something is missing. It is, but that is the point of the Black Swan in the title. Those who stop and think about what they have just read when they finish reading this chapter will find themselves mirroring the students' experience in searching for something they do not know and of which they have no awareness. It also echoes Lister's Oxford Don and his table.

The next chapter is by Tim Fogarty (from the U.S.A.). It presents an alternative approach to that suggested by Lister in the *Forum*, but one which echoes some of the suggestions made by the Commentators. It advocates a derivative application of the Liberal Arts to improve accounting education.

The underlying message of Fogarty's chapter is that there are other options available to accounting educators which do not necessitate the involvement of Liberal Arts faculty and which may be just as effective in developing soft skills in our students; we just need to identify what a Liberal Arts approach is capable of producing in terms of students' soft skills enhancement, pinpoint what causes this to happen, extract it, and embed it in an accounting vehicle rather than utilizing the Liberal Arts. Although set in the context of the U.S.A., the proposal is nevertheless relevant to accounting educators everywhere.

In soliciting the views on the university accounting curriculum of an alumni group at Massey University, Shirley Carr, Frances Chua and Hector Perera (all from New Zealand) were motivated by their concern that many of the problems associated with accounting education arise from inadequate attention being paid to the design of accounting programmes, and an inappropriate emphasis being placed on the stakeholder approach in examining education issues. Moreover, they argue that too much of the accounting education literature deals with students' perceptions of such issues as teaching quality rather than seeking views from other groups and focussing more on curriculum design.

Carr et al. found that it is no longer considered appropriate for tertiary education providers to adopt a one-size-fits-all approach, and some of their findings were at variance with the stance of professional accounting bodies in both New Zealand and the U.S.A. (including the relative proportions of accounting, business and liberal studies which should constitute an acceptable accounting programme).

In the next chapter, James Hazelton and Matthew Haigh (based in Australia and France respectively) focus on a very specific approach to liberalising the accounting component of a graduate programme by incorporating principles of sustainable development into a predominantly technical accounting curriculum. As they explain, their study was informed by Freirian principles of praxis and critical empowerment. Two projects were undertaken to implement their novel approach, and action research methods were used to assess the results of these interventions. In seeking to bring reflexivity with specific reference to sustainability into the accounting classroom, both projects showed some success. However, efforts to bring about permanent curriculum change were hampered not only by the strongly vocational orientation of the student cohorts, but also by the traditional technical focus of the professional accounting bodies on the one hand, and by competing education reform agendas (such as that relating to vocational skills) on the other.

Another innovative intervention can be found in the chapter by Gheula Canarutto (from Italy) and Katherine T. Murphy and L. Murphy Smith (both from the U.S.A.) The study on which they report deals with, firstly, the impact on their perceptions regarding ethics of Italian accounting students following an ethics presentation (adapted from a presentation developed in the U.S.A.) and, secondly, a comparison of the Italian results with previously published results from the U.S.A. In the light of the plethora of financial scandals and corporate failures in recent years, it is encouraging to know that liberalising interventions such as this can be effective in inculcating a positive view of the importance of ethical behaviour on the part of accounting students in different countries.

The final chapter highlights an imaginative approach to liberalising (and integrating) the accounting curriculum by focussing on the Global Financial Crisis (GFC) of recent years. It was written by Robert Bloom and Mariah Webinger (both from the U.S.A.), and looks at an innovation at John Carroll University.

Bloom & Webinger use the typical *Intermediate Accounting* two-year sequence (as taught across North America) as the vehicle for embedding the GFC within the curriculum, and then highlight the ways in which other disciplines (such as economics, banking and management) interface with accounting and finance. Whilst this approach is less liberal in some respects than that of Lister, it still has much to commend it in demonstrating the complex relationships which need to be recognised and understood if accounting curriculum designers are to fulfil the aim of enhancing the educational base of accounting practice.

We hope that the ideas in this book will stimulate readers to make liberalising innovations within their own institutions from which all parties might benefit.

References

Accounting Education Change Commission (1990) *Position Statement Number One: Objectives of Education for Accountants* (Sarasota, FL: American Accounting Association).

Copleston, E. (1852) in: J. H. Newman *The Idea of a University Defined and Illustrated: In Nine Discourses Delivered to the Catholics of Dublin.* Available at http://www.gutenberg.org/dirs/2/4/5/2/24526/24526-pdf.pdf (accessed 26 August 2012).

Encyclopædia Britannica (2010) Britannica Online. Available at http://www.britannica.com/EBchecked/topic/339020/liberal-arts (accessed 26 August 2012).

Lowe, R. (2010) Middlesex philosophy department moves to Kingston, *Enfield Independent*, 11 June 2010. Available at http://www.enfieldindependent.co.uk/news/8214584.Middlesex_philosophy_department_
moves_to_Kingston/ (accessed 26 August 2012).
Millar, H. C. (1938) A suggested program of education for the accountant, *The Accounting Review*, 13(2), pp. 191-197.
Newman, J. H. (1852) *The Idea of a University Defined and Illustrated: In Nine Discourses Delivered to the Catholics of Dublin*, Available at http:// http://www.gutenberg.org/dirs/2/4/5/2/24526/24526-pdf.pdf (accessed 26 August 2012).
Paisey, C. and Paisey, N. J. (2007) Balancing the vocational and academic dimensions of accounting education—the case for a core curriculum, *Journal of Vocational Education & Training*, 59(1), pp. 89–105.
Reisz, M. (2010) The Core Connection. *Times Higher Education*, 7 January. Available at http://www.timeshighereducation.co.uk/story.asp?sectioncode=26&storycode=409838 (accessed 26 August 2012).

PART I: The Lister Forum

A Role for the Compulsory Study of Literature in Accounting Education

ROGER JEFFREY LISTER

University of Salford, UK

ABSTRACT *Literature can make a multi-faceted contribution to higher education—especially in a highly vocational field of study such as accounting. Such fields suffer particular pressure to impart 'marketable skills' in response to student demand, governments, and the professional bodies. Literature militates against the threat of 'de-disciplining'. Literature hones and enriches expression. It reinforces original, creative, imaginative and multicultural thought. By adding a disciplinary dimension, literature encourages reflective consideration of ideas in terms of the difference which they make to other ideas. Studied holistically literature sets important issues into the context of human endeavour and choices. Not least literature is prophetic. The labour market will, in the long run, penalise those who lack the qualities which can be uniquely imparted by a study of literature.*

I Introduction

There are five main motivations for the present paper.

The first is Lord Butler's address over 40 years ago to newly-created Fellows of the P. D. Leake Trust. The writer was one such beneficiary and duly acknowledges the indebtedness. The purpose of the Fellowships was to broaden professional accountants by enabling them to take a higher degree in a relevant discipline. However, Lord Butler looked beyond 'relevant discipline'. According to the writer's note he said that 'if professions (were) to meet the heavier demands of the future, members of the professional bodies must have (had) the benefit of some liberal arts education as undergraduates'. Forty years on, such *cris de coeur* remain opportune and duly audible as cash-strapped universities seek to hawk 'marketable skills' (Graham, 2005; Wolf, 2007). The present paper asks: can the arts—in particular literature—fuel qualities and increase direct insight into our field in ways which will make our graduates truly 'marketable' people and less impoverished human beings?

The second motivation for this paper is increased interest in reflective learning. Its advocates seek to recognise with Confucius that 'study without reflection is a waste of time; reflection without study is dangerous'. How does literature further this purpose?

The third stimulus is Mary Evans' *Killing thinking* (2004). Evans identifies the danger of intellectual poverty inherent in vocational education: a threat of universities becoming at worst skills factories providing technical apprenticeships. Accounting and cognate schemes of study are particularly vulnerable to her concern. Imparting 'skills' is a task best left to institutions better equipped to provide the service leaving universities free to emphasise the stretching of intellects and empowering of imaginations with minimal box-ticking.

The fourth motivation is the writer's unhappiness with Joseph Badaracco's *Questions of character* (2006b) and his responses to an interview in the *Harvard Business Review* (2006a). His finely-informed work goes back as far as Sophocles' *Antigone* and forward to the 20th century. Across time and cultures he identifies and sharply analyses examples of judgment in world literature. Despite the undoubted didactic power of his work, it entails a truncated approach which is limited to one aspect of one facet of the literature which he examines. This is far less valuable than imparting each work to students as an aesthetic whole with leadership, judgement or whatever as an inseparable part of that whole. Time constraints can be accommodated by rigorous selection of microcosmic material.

The writer's fifth motivation comes from long-term financial forecasting. Literature is prophetic. The twenty-first century has witnessed new attempts to review and forecast long-term equity returns for decades and centuries past and ahead (e.g. Dimson, Marsh and Staunton (2002); Goetzmann, Ibbotson and Peng (2001)). It will be argued here that literature, whether in the form of individual works or movements, may be the first to pick up the scent of a *zeitgeist*.

The writer is not claiming academic high ground for literature over other arts disciplines. A zealous but narrow student of literature will be a foreshortened creature unable to set his thought into the context of the choices that society has to make. It is no coincidence that one of the greatest minds in European literature, Goethe (1749–1832), was an accomplished scientist and mining engineer. Far from being divorced from reality, poetry has been described as 'a reaction to what is contemporary and topical' (Weinstein, 1995). However this may be, it will be argued that literature is particularly well-suited to serve our purpose.

The following sections pursue the above five motivations and are entitled: II Case for literature; III Reflective learning; IV Crisis in higher education; V Whole use of literature; VI Literature as prophesy. Section VII is the conclusion.

II A Case for Literature

Literature is a deep well of experience for the social sciences. However, it is more than this. By harnessing imagination literature extends experience. It raises the heavens and deepens the hells of life. Literature achieves connections among the seemingly disparate, be it within literature itself, across the arts or across disciplines.

A contrast is frequently drawn between the useful and the valuable disciplines (Graham, 2005, p 181). The former help us 'to live longer healthier and more prosperous lives' while the latter 'make those longer, healthier lives worth living'. Graham assigns art, literature, music, philosophy and history to the latter category. The present argument is that literature serves both purposes and has particularly much to offer in accounting education.

Ambiguity

Why will literature produce better graduates in accounting as Lord Butler implied? One reason is that our discipline, with a view to organized decision-making, tries to reduce ambiguity. Whether seeking to report structured financial instruments, to define the market portfolio or to address old chestnuts like depreciation we tend to limit parameters. The aim is to provide managers with formulae for their objective, the cost of their capital or to express an asset or liability. We may pay lip service to chasms of ambiguity separating formulae from reality but hasten to set them aside. This inevitably leads to barely recognisable caricatures of reality. For example, the favoured definition of cost of capital - weighted average cost of capital - is unreal and impoverished. The present writer has written elsewhere (Lister, 2005, pp. 142–157) that 'we can't measure the parameters of any definition (of cost of capital) with useful accuracy. Attempts to adapt general cost of capital to the individual company and then to individual projects merely compound the unreality. If we seek wisdom in practice we find managers behaving in an untutored, inconsistent and incomplete way.'

Progress comes from embracing ambiguity. As do our best colleagues already, we should imaginatively look into ambiguity's richness. Leading research in finance has never been shy about breaking down interdisciplinary barriers. It is sufficient to mention physics, neuroscience, cognitive psychology and a range of branches of mathematics. Tirole's definitive new textbook (2006) built around contracting is an open invitation to students to consider a more imaginative and complex set of incentives, covenants and signals. Imaginative innovation may lead finally to the scrapping of balance sheets which cost billions to audit and publish, yet whose contents have precious little economic meaning.

What has all this to do with literature? Literature is a transcription of life into language but much more. As one of the most imaginative forms of expression it encourages our minds to range questioningly, creatively and originally. It sets out to be ambiguous with its multidimensional evocations and dissonances. We see the world more intensely and in new ways which make us ask questions. An Oxford don used to test his Scholarship candidates by asking them: What's under that table? Some would answer Nothing, some Air, some Security, etc., etc., etc., and so the interview would go on. Let us in our field take a rewarding break from trying to 'eliminate ambiguity'. Let us do the opposite and free our minds. If we read only one stanza of William Blake's *Tyger* (1794), Lord Butler and Mary Evans' words soon begin to make sense:

> Tyger, Tyger, burning bright
> In the forests of the night,
> What immortal hand or eye
> Could frame thy fearful symmetry?

Some works explicitly exploit ambiguity to challenge and excite the reader. For example, critic Henri Coulet (1967) says of *Manon Lescaut* (1731) by Prévost (1697–1763) (Preface, tr. the writer):

Manon Lescaut is a novel which is all the more intriguing because we can search it endlessly while remaining uncertain of its lessons.

The existential message of Stoppard's *Rosencrantz and Guildenstern are dead* (1964) relies significantly on its choice of language to convey bewildering ambiguity. Christina

Rossetti's poem *Goblin market* has been interpreted in emotional and political terms and even as a critique of the seeds of exploitative advertising.

One of the most effective uses of ambiguity is dramatic irony. This occurs when the audience understands an incongruity between a situation and the accompanying speeches, while the characters in the play remain unaware of the incongruity.

Drama is in this sense the direct opposite of the objective, consistent, *soi-disant* truths so beloved of us accountants. Drama is an unspoken debate among writer, audience and cast as all create and explore interpretations. 'Thirteen ways of looking at a blackbird' by Wallace Stevens (1879–1955) is an exercise in ambiguity. It epitomises the endless angles of vision on reality.

Les sanglots longs
Des violons
De l'automne
Blessent mon coeur
D'une langueur
Monotone.....

The present writer's offering below is intended to deal with vocabulary not meaning.

The long sobbing
Of the violins
Of Autumn
Wound my heart
With sustained
Yearning

Perhaps the extreme instance of 'ambiguity' is French symbolist poetry which borders on music to the point that it has no visual 'programme'. It stimulates questioning and wonder, and inculcates a love of and a respect for language. Its music would thoroughly discourage any student from writing clumsily and sloppily. Hear *Chanson d'automne* (1866) by Paul Verlaine (1844–1896):

Embracing ambiguity inevitably entails mould-breaking which should always be on the cards in any accounting issue. Exposure to iconoclasm - especially if students identify with the initial shock at the time of a work's appearance - can only encourage our students to look with a critical and open mind at instances of ossification in our profession. *The father* by Strindberg (1849–1912) which appeared in 1887 prophetically portrayed the crumbling of moral values held sacred for millennia. Mould-breaking, for example in the cause of self-realisation, typically comes at high moral cost. Consider *Prometheus* (1774) by Goethe (1749–1832) which plainly despises divinity. The hero seems to worship mankind itself.

(Zeus) you can't touch my earth,
my cabin that you did not build,
my hearth whose glow you watch
with envy. There's none more pitiful than you, Gods!
The breath of our prayers
is your paltry nourishment,
our meager altar gifts sustain
your dreams of majesty.
You'd starve
but for the foolish hopes
of children and beggars.

The same occurs in the music of Beethoven (1770–1827). His Choral symphony (1824) using the words of Schiller (1759–1805) gives bourgeois morality a thorough shaking. He portrays the pious and the wicked (Alle Guten, alle Bösen), the lowest animals and highest celestial beings going forward hand-in-hand united in joy. Who is excluded, weeping? Certainly not the wicked: only he who has failed to secure a friend or conquer a beautiful woman. We are far from the European Court of Human Rights. With equal disregard for conventional morality Goethe's hero Faust at the end of the Second Part (written about 1832, lines 11233–11281) burns down the home and chapel and sacrifices the lives of the aged Philemon and Baucis for the sake of consummate self-realisation.

Thomas Hardy (1840–1928) in *Tess of the D'Urbervilles* (1891) takes an unconventionally bitter view of providence. And the heroine of *Lady Chatterley's lover* (1928) by D. H. Lawrence (1885–1930) fulfils and understands herself and love by breaking down social barriers including that of marriage to her crippled impotent husband. For Lawrence morality is a side- or non-issue in characters' quest for a perfect male-female relationship. The obscenity trial (1961) evokes the opposition of the equally subversive Walt Whitman (1819–1892) to all forms of censorship. William Blake in his *Marriage of heaven and hell* (1793) is totally anti-clerical overturning religious dogma and blaming it for the grossest immorality. At the same time advocacy of morality in literature can be as disturbing as its immorality. Charles Dickens (1812–1870) set out to shake up the complacent urban middle classes in a work like *Great expectations* (1860–1861) with its implicit critique of law and the city.

Among the most morally challenging cases is the Satan of *Paradise lost* (1667) by Milton (1608–1674). Almost in spite of himself Milton turned the embodiment of evil into a leader who is a near tragic hero and who commands the reader's sympathy. Satan prefers to reign in hell tormented by his fall than serve in heaven. All our might-have-beens, all our remorse are in Satan's (line 619):

> . . . thrice in spite of scorn
> Tears, such as angels weep, burst forth.

Light years from accountancy? Far from it. Picture our students, refreshed by literature directing critical thoughts to conventional accounting. It is not surprising that some scholars consider the creation of new aesthetic forms to be the most productive human endeavour.

Cultures

We encourage our students to think globally about their future profession. They will need to transcend international accounting standards, international asset pricing models, tax harmonisation and international economics. They will need to empathise with different cultures, corporate and national. Failure to do this has been a significant cause of merger failure (Gertsen, Søderberg and Torp, 1998; Tienari, Søderberg, Holgersson and Vaara, 2005). A country or region's literature gives insight into character, thought-patterns, decision processes, *zeitgeist* and the very fabric of expression. This can only help us to anticipate and resolve conflict. We would have been less inclined, as consultants, to propose totally unsuitable models for Russia and her neighbours if we had studied *War and peace* by Tolstoy (1817–1875)—as fresh and relevant today as in 1869. This work points up the country's ruthless unmanageable history. Facile imposition of western-style free choice was doomed to bring much of today's corruption and anarchy.

Popular literature as well as 'high' literature can serve our purpose. At an extreme Tzung-Yu Cheng in 1993 used children's essays to examine linearity and circularity in Chinese thought-patterns. Indeed, Schiller in his *Über naive und sentimentalische Dichtung* (Of naïve and sophisticated fiction) (1800) suggested that naïve fiction with its 'edle Einfalt' (noble simplicity) could attain an intensity of expression beyond the reach of sophisticated works. Nearer home the exhausted, anarchic cynicism of late 1940s France is nowhere better caught than in songs of Georges Brassens (1921–1981) and other *chansonniers* of the time. Where did Brassens get his umbrella that same morning in his song entitled *Le Parapluie* (The umbrella)?

> J'en avais un volé sans doute, le matin même à un ami
> I had one, probably filched the same morning, from a friend

Not only stolen, but casually stolen, and from a friend. However, and anticipating the next section of this paper, if we had used Brassens simply to teach French 1940s *zeitgeist* to our students they would be missing so much. Yes we would give them a link to the times, but they would miss Brassens' sentence structures, his exquisite choice of phrase and the 'blue flower' of romanticism that distinguishes him from the more melancholic *chansonniers* of the time.

A further rather more obvious reason for cross-cultural attention is that our students' overseas counterparts will expect to hold broad, intelligent cultivated conversations. It is well-known that in some countries etiquette requires a substantial general conversation before nitty-gritty business. David Beckham and Arsenal's vicissitudes will not stretch beyond the fish course. Our managers' protagonists will have benefited from a more disciplined and broader education than their British counterparts. Parts of Europe retain the rigour and breadth of the Prussian educational tradition which imparted classical and modern literatures hand-in-hand with other arts, natural and social sciences. Such managers will expect to discuss Machiavellian management, the advantages and dangers of iconoclasm, an existential approach to decision-making, the lessons of Plato's *Republic* (c. 428–328 BCE) and the harm done to Thamesside by 1950s architecture.

Literature is an art-form among others. So why the present focus on literature? First, because it is the field in which the writer was trained and is most familiar; second, because it is a particularly articulate and imaginative vehicle for communicating and illustrating concepts. Nevertheless, while not the present focus, it is recognised that inspiration of the real world has come from all arts. There is a history-long tradition of the fine arts enriching and carrying forward utilitarian fields. Wedgwood and Royal Doulton porcelain broke the chains of *biedermeier* with the help of contemporary fine artists. Music humanises therapy. Poetry, rhetoric and the classics enrich politics. Yet the large majority of our 'relevant' graduates in accounting and other social sciences have known none of these things and are thoroughly culturally impoverished.

III Reflective Learning

The second motivation of the present paper is the burgeoning of work on 'reflection and reflective learning' (Cottrell, 2003). What is reflective learning and how does literature help us to exploit its offerings? It has been widely used by health professionals (Anderson, Claire, 2006; Moon 2004; Mamede and Schmidt 2004) and has been taken on board by educationists in our own field (Hay, Peltier and Drago, 2004; Peltier, Hay and Drago, 2005).

Reflective learning aims to integrate knowledge with other knowledges and to imagine future and alternative consequences. Links and connections lead to awareness of a bigger picture. Graduates must be able to consider ideas in terms of the difference these ideas make to other ideas and not only in terms of the difference which these ideas make to the world. Managers must be able to address imaginatively values and evolution. Peltier *et al.* (2005) argue that this runs counter to what universities have become.

In addition to identifying links, reflective learning encourages us to bring to bear on learning the full range of our own experience and preferences. An intellectual problem's correct place is in a 'container', a melting pot of ideas, knowledge and disciplinary approaches from which will emerge at least in the first instance a direction rather than a recipe, even worse a foregone conclusion. Reflective learning invites us engage in dialogue with ourselves; to explore alternative interpretations of and answers to questions. More formally this is referred to as a metacognitive stance in which we are critically aware of our own processes of mental functioning. It is a challenge to us as tutors to reward reflection and not be slaves to a model answer which we might have been obliged to send to colleagues, external examiners or professional bodies.

How can literature encourage reflective thinking? Literature is shot through with questions, doubts, internal and external conflicts and dialogues. Through literature our minds are free to range across time and space. Literature breaks the chains of chronology and encourages the mind to juxtapose origins, consequences and ends.

IV Crisis in Higher Education

The writer's third motivation is Mary Evans' critique (2004) of the impoverished state of higher education in Britain. The economic aspect of her argument is that, in our attempts to provide key 'transferable' skills which are supposedly 'useful', we may be misinterpreting the demands of the very labour market we are trying to court. The state invests less in technicians and artisans than graduates. Presumably something special is expected of them. What? The labour market judges graduates on what they are rather than what they know. But universities are in danger of being expected to serve 'the rational bureaucratic state of the 21st century' which is 'a small-minded offspring of Enlightenment rationality and the market economy' (p. 3). Evans berates 'mangled ridiculous prose' to which our field is prone.

How can literature help solve the malaise which concerns Evans? Let us look in a bit more detail at her complaint.

Cultural divisions among universities increasingly reflect society (p. 144). The competition for places at Oxford, Cambridge and London is no longer about a social elite. It is about a political and cultural elite. These universities are the only 'reassuringly significant' route into the dominant culture. It is no longer simply a matter of language as in D. H. Lawrence's poem *The Oxford voice*. With Halsey, Lauder, Brown and Stuart Wells (1997) and Bourdieu (1986) culture is for Evans a valuable commodity which its possessor can deploy and signal with words and meanings. The present writer submits that literature mitigates the harm of being outside the magic circle of institutions. And it matters. Look at Evans' sinister picture of the penetration achieved by the world of cultural privilege (pp. 145–146).

In contemporary Britain, there is a strong case for the argument that cultural divisions are becoming more distinct, and more closely linked to the distribution of social and economic power than at any time in the history of the past one hundred years.

Culture's humanitarian gloss is a façade which masks its hidden power (p. 148):

Culture in the twenty-first century is at once the great new form of social power and the continued mask of crude social and economic power.

Her argument happily leads to the more morally comfortable argument of Wolf (2007) - namely that 'education is an end in itself'. Like Butler and Evans Wolf is concerned about the 'skills agenda':

> Understanding is a form of wealth. Happiness is an end. The experience of beauty is an end. Knowledge is also an end, not merely a means to some other end—a better job, a more attractive mate or . . . a more productive economy.

Literature is important as an end in itself as well as being a way out of increasing cultural disadvantage.

V Whole Use of Literature

The fourth motivation of the paper: Badaracco (2006b) says that MBA students should learn literature. He uses his extensive knowledge of literature from a range of times and cultures to identify lessons in judgment. He proceeds to apply the lessons to contemporary business. He traces answers to a series of fundamental questions (ibid., jacket note):

- Do my deepest aspirations impel me forward through hardships, and do they engage others' aspirations and dreams?
- Will my moral code help me make the right decisions for my organization even as business conditions change?
- Do my role models provoke me as well as embody values I can emulate?
- Do I have the patience, courage, and tenacity that leadership requires?
- Can I set clear performance standards for myself and others–and follow through on them?
- Do I recognize the hidden hazards of success and the ways to avoid them?
- Can I make the difficult trade-offs needed to run my unit or business?
- Do I think through high-stakes decisions adequately despite relentless pressures on my time?

Notwithstanding the intellectual accomplishment of his analysis, it is a truncated approach to literature confined to one aspect of one aspect of each work. It is limited to character analysis and emphasises only one part of each character. In so doing he misses out on a major and relevant instructive opportunity: the opportunity to impart each work as an aesthetic whole with judgement or whatever as an inseparable part of that whole. Unfortunately, his truncated approach diminishes and violates the works. Hear him on the *Antigone* of Sophocles (496–405 BCE):

> If Sophocles teaches us that leaders cannot escape their flawed humanity, he also suggests that we can lower the risks of error and tragedy through sound reflection. . . . As *Antigone* strongly suggests, the best reflection involves dialogue with others. Solitary, self-designated geniuses are a prescription for disaster.

Of course, part of literature's genius is to enter the mind of the characters; but he is alluding to one part of the psychology of one of a suffocatingly entwined set of characters. And what of the magnificent poetry? What of the nature of tragedy as propounded by Aristotle? What of hubris, fate and free-will? What of the history of Greek tragedy and its influence on the whole of western literature? There is far more education in *Antigone* than a gouged-out vignette on leadership. Of course, leadership comes in, but as part of an aesthetic whole. A work of literature is a self-sufficient, complete being with a life of its own. To teach by amputating one of its limbs is tantamount to reducing it to a glorified bullet-pointed management manual. The perpetrator is guilty of the aesthetic crime called in German *zerdenken* for which there is no English equivalent except the clumsy 'thinking to pieces.'

Badaracco uses Sophocles' *Antigone* written 2,500 years ago. Our point is better illustrated in a modern existentialist reworking of *Antigone* (1944) by Jean Anouilh

(1910–1987). It is permeated with issues of leadership. This would please Badaracco. King Creon faces his rebellious 'employee' Antigone. She risks triggering an internecine Darfur by behaving heretically. Creon wearily confronts her idealistic heroic behaviour with the need to compromise in order to avoid national chaos. In similar vein *Les mains sales* (soiled hands) (1948) by Sartre (1905–1980) looks at the need to behave 'immorally'—to get your hands dirty, in order to keep a show on the road. The lesson of Anouilh's King Creon and of *Les mains sales* is, in the words of the UK's wartime leader Winston Churchill, the unavoidable need in the real world to 'KBO' which, politely, stands for 'keep beggaring on'.

But if we present these works as case studies of leadership we are depriving our students of a rich imaginative and instructive opportunity. Anouilh's *Antigone* and Sartre's *Les mains sales* are rooted in an overarching concept of an existentialist, godless, absurd cosmos in which the only meaningful behaviour is to 'say no'. Such works emerged during the upheaval of the Second World War. Half of Europe's population was being reified or eliminated as degenerate by a dictator who threatened to dominate the world. This context is vital to an instructive understanding of Anouilh, Sartre or Camus and many more besides.

Of equal instructive importance is Anouilh's studiedly casual language. It is depressed, laconic and a-heroic: *Antigone*'s chorus opens the play leaning in a dinner jacket and colloquially but chillingly foretelling the fatal conclusion. There is more education, aesthetic, social and economic in this holistic picture than in a truncated tale of leadership.

Badaracco notes that Shakespeare's *Othello* is replete with themes such as race, gender, leadership, social ferment and Machiavellian behaviour. A war-hero, he inspires confidence and more in his Venetian command. He adapts to his seniors, juniors, private citizens and newly-espoused Desdemona with consummate chivalry. However, students would lose so much if the play were simply used to illustrate and discuss him as a leader interacting with the led. Villain Iago's Machiavellian materialism needs to be related to decomposition of the high ideals of the Renaissance. The new economic tempter tells fatuous, old establishment 'gull'd Venetian gentleman' Rodrigo to succeed by 'putting money in his purse'. What is Iago's motive? Does he literally love Othello and act out of jealousy? Is Othello's new bride his rival? Is Othello an aging alienated man tormented by sexual self-doubt? Is it the sensual hothouse Cyprus—contrasted with civilised Venice—which provides the final and necessary setting which turns Christian leader Othello into an atavistic ritualist? Moreover, while Othello's murder of his wife is a pagan sacrifice it has a transcendent nobility which dwarfs other characters. Then the glorious language: a handkerchief precipitates Othello's fall. Shakespeare, with the power of a machine gun, throws it at us three times in a few words (Act 3, Scene 3).

Badaracco invites us to use *Death of a Salesman* (1949) by Arthur Miller (1915–2005) to contrast Willy Loman's fanciful dreams with economically efficient 'good dreams' which have their roots in daily life and 'drudgery'. Good dreams are the lesson of this play. Of course, it will help our students to think about this but only, to maximum intellectual benefit, in the broadest context of the play. For example, is Loman a tragic hero in the literary tradition or not? If not, why not? Let students see how style and structure are perfectly suited to theme. Presents, pasts, realities and fantasies flow and separate in 'mobile concurrences' like the interior monologues of the stream of consciousness literature, and like the starting point of some of the most creative thinking in management. The work is an invitation to reflective thought.

All can agree with Badaracco that one of the hardest challenges is resisting the flow of success. This is indeed 'one of the most perplexing themes in literature and leadership'. *Macbeth* (1606) addresses Badaracco's point. Nevertheless, let us see how a truncated approach leads to loss of educational opportunity. Macbeth's raw, amoral ambition combats his milk of human kindness. His wife goads him. This and a succession of victories help to bring him down as in the bitter truth of the reference to the witches: 'They met me in the day of my success' (Act 5, Scene 5). However, greater questions than resisting the flow of success are asked here. The subtle interdependence between freewill and destiny transcends a simplistic illustration of chapters of accidents in the book of success. Is Macbeth a victim of fate? Are the witches' ambiguous prophesies utterances of fate toying with its victim? However, did the witches merely exploit his character flaw by picking their moment? Underlying all is a transcendent question so often raised by Shakespeare. Is the universe a stable place which man with all the new science of his time can control? Or, medievally, is it at the whim of outside forces, be they the witches of *Macbeth* or the superficially cute fairies of *A Midsummer Night's Dream* (1600)? In addition, we have not even mentioned the language.

Badaracco's question about resisting the flow of success is classically addressed in *Le père Goriot* (1835) by Balzac (1799–1850). It contains one of the most famous quotations of French literature in its almost final words 'à nous deux maintenant!' (It's you versus me now!). The young hero Eugène de Rastignac casts down the gauntlet before Paris society which he intends to conquer. The novel shows the gradual falling away of his scruples. This is necessary for his success. Compromises include serial adultery and predatory financial behaviour. But beyond such a mere 'case study' is Balzac's ability to bring a place to life by his extremely detailed descriptions in which not a word is wasted; and his successful portrayal of the amoral materialism of contemporary Paris. However, what perhaps most transcends narrow questions of ambition, success and their drivers is Balzac's portrayal of the cosmic energy which, irrespective of morality, class, wealth or social position, flows through his larger-than-life heroes. Goriot is 'le Christ de la paternité' who attains sublimity in death. One of the most sympathetic characters is professional super-criminal Vautrin. Not surprisingly Balzac was an admirer of Swedenborg (1688–1772) and Beethoven. Indeed, one of his heroes whose forename is significant—César Birotteau—dies to the imagined melody of the Fifth Symphony, having pulled himself up from ruin: a truly Promethean way to go. Imagine what our students would lose from stopping at a story of ambition and compromise.

The Nun of the *Canterbury Tales* by Chaucer (c. 1345–1400) is an example of assertiveness and accomplished inter-personal relations—she knows how to dialogue with, adapt to and charm her fellow-pilgrims. Beyond this 'case study' of urbane accomplishment is the choice of detail and limpid language with which Chaucer subtly suggests vanity and coquettishness beneath a pious exterior. Her cloak was of the most elegant; she was ornamented with beautiful green beads; and her shining brooch of gold bore a letter A for *amor vincit omnia*, love conquers all! Chaucer also introduces us to the lawyer—the sergeant of the law—efficient, impressive, inspiring confidence and able to reel off centuries of case law; clearly top management material. He could be the first slide in an assertiveness course. However, the interesting bit is that in one line Chaucer shows us his hollowness:

> And yet he semed bisier than he was.
> We've all met them.

The *Kaukasische Kreidekreis* (1947) of Brecht (1898–1950) brings alive the clash among claimants on assets in times of instability, distress and social upheaval. Who should run the show? Those with a legal or traditional right, or those best able to do the job? The latter is the answer according to Brecht. However, to discuss this without reference to his contribution to theatre would be to miss the most stimulating instruction in the play. Brecht's method is to present issues as open questions. Towards this end he tries to stop us identifying with actors' emotions. Heroine Grusche's self-sacrifice in the play is not intended to inspire sympathy. It is the act of a 'praktisch veranlagte Frau' a practically motivated woman. Brecht's tool is the *Verfremdungseffekt*, a distancing effect. He interpolates songs and uses a chorus who comments on the action towards this end. The same was achieved by masks in classical Greek theatre, in the middle ages and today in some Asian countries.

Inattention to the language of literature deprives our students of vital lessons which would help guard against some of their (and our) worst writing crimes. Few of us can cast a stone in the face of accusations of inarticulate, rambling, repetitious and jargon-ridden writing. So lend an ear to the greatest writers' quests for the original, right word, expression, sentence and whole. Flaubert's (1821–1880) search for a single right word (*mot juste*) could take hours. The discipline of poetry and in particular of a prescribed form like the sonnet imposes the most rigorous economy of expression. Our greatest achieve a naturalness with not one wasted syllable. Read Shakespeare's No. 116.

Let me not to the marriage of true minds
  Admit impediments. Love is not love
Which alters when it alteration finds,
  Or bends with the remover to remove:
O no! it is an ever-fixed mark
  That looks on tempests and is never shaken;
It is the star to every wandering bark,
  Whose worth's unknown, although his height be taken.
Love's not Time's fool, though rosy lips and cheeks
  Within his bending sickle's compass come:
Love alters not with his brief hours and weeks,
  But bears it out even to the edge of doom.
If this be error and upon me proved,
  I never writ, nor no man ever loved.

One of the finest poems in European literature is only 24 words long. A child of five could understand its words. The language of poet-scientist Goethe's *Wanderers Nachtlied II* (1780) is so simple and perfect as to be untranslatable. Those who have tried woefully illustrate the truth of the French proverb *Qui traduit, trahit*, (whoever translates betrays). The present writer's offering below is intended to deal with vocabulary not meaning.

Über allen Gipfeln
Ist Ruh,
In allen Wipfeln
Spürest du
Kaum einen Hauch;
Die Vögelein schweigen im Walde.
Warte nur, balde
Ruhest du auch.
Enveloping all peaks
Is rest.
In all trees
You sense
Scarce a breath.
The little birds are silent in the forest.
Only wait a while, soon
You will be resting too

The sloppiest jargon-ridden project writer would think twice and be sobered after half an hour analysing the expression in one or more of these poems. Moreover, for teachers and researchers drowning in professional jargon and prolixity they are pure therapy.

Perhaps the biggest loss to students if literature is mined for messages is to ignore the literary movements to which a work belongs. This instructively increases insight into the works themselves and brings students into contact with movements which are not confined to literature. Some, like post-modernism, have been predictive industrially and managerially as will be discussed in the next section. What better encouragement to inter-disciplinary thinking than encountering a movement which, in Jervis' words (1999, p. 335), 'multiplies the margins and transitions: we all become betwixt and between, flows and circuits rather than fixed points in a moving world'.

A possible defence of Badaracco's approach is that, although he addresses only one aspect of literature, the bit may attract students into the real thing. This links with the argument that a crowded curriculum cannot accommodate serious study of literature beyond the recreational level. The writer submits that these arguments are dangerous and defeatist. The danger is that a single-aspect approach will encourage a fragmentary, cafeteria attitude to literature. And against the defeatism of the time constraint argument, the writer submits that a tutor can and should identify sources which are of manageable proportion while being microcosmic without being truncated. With careful selection these can be conveyed in a short space and it is hoped will be supplemented by students' voluntary reading for pleasure. Examples are:

Blake's poem the *Sick Rose*;
Chaucer's Wife of Bath in the *Prologue* of the *Canterbury tales*;
Goethe's Faust's expression of discontent in Act 1 of the play;
Hopkins' poem *Windhover*;
Molière's Philinte's speech on the human condition in Act 1 of *Misanthrope* (1666);
Psalms 100 and 150;
Shakespeare's Othello's 'it is the cause, my soul' with other speeches from Act 5;
Verlaine's poem *La lune blanche* (easier to latch on to in a short time than *Chanson d'automne* quoted above).

VI Literature as Prophesy

The fifth motivation: literature, the product of intelligent, sensitive and imaginative minds, may be the first to pick up the scent of short-, medium- and long-term change. Moore's analogy between a poet and a prophet (1971, p. 5) is not an exaggeration. Literature can be prescient and hortative. Besides being of general significance managerially this is of specific significance to the would-be predictors of long-term required returns who do not baulk at dealing in centuries (e.g. Dimson *et al.*, 2002; Goetzmann *et al.*, 2001). Rates of time preference and required risk premia are bound up with anxiety, sense of stability and sense of control. Literature can capture a crucial historical moment. This can be seen as far back as Sophocles' *Oedipus* (c. 429 BC) where the hero's emotions, self-discovery, gestures of freewill and independence catch the advancing humanism in the Greek society of his time.

Let us next picture ourselves at the beginning of the 1780s trying to appraise the probability of 1789's upheaval. In 1784 we attend the performance of Beaumarchais' *Mariage de Figaro*. It is received with tumultuous acclaim. We wonder how the tilts at inherited wealth and privilege got past the censors. For example, Arnould (1952) quotes Lytton Strachey on valet Figaro protesting at the Count's attempt to abuse his seigneurial right:

Lytton Strachey quotes

> Vous vous êtes donné la peine de naître, et rien de plus: du reste homme assez ordinaire! tandis que moi, morbleu! perdu dans la foule obscure, il m'a fallu déployer plus de science et de calculs pour subsister seulement.
>
> You took no more than the trouble to be born; for the rest you're just more or less a common man. Not me! At sea in the crowd I've had to use more brains and tactics (than you) just to get by.
>
> Lytton Strachey comments:
>
> In that sentence one can hear—far off, but distinct—the flash and snap of the guillotine.

A decade earlier the *Sturm und Drang* (storm and stress) literature of Germany which represented the birth-pangs of romanticism adumbrated upheaval in the form of individuals challenging the state. The movement advocated attention to native, Germanic folk literature at the expense of the classics. It voiced Faustian contempt for bloodless, conventional learning.

In 1899, two decades before the Russian revolution, Tolstoy (1828–1910) wrote the searing drama *Resurrection* the hero of which reviles his inherited wealth, plans to return land to his own peasants and points out the absurd injustices dispensed to alleged criminals including children. As for the established church, an atheist character in the play addresses religious uncertainty with 'when you feel (religious) doubt have a drink.' Maxim Gorky's drama *Enemies* (1905) likewise foreshadowed a cataclysm. Written in exile and banned in Russia, it portrays a restless society in which the bourgeois feel insecure and a proletariat squaring up to the attrition ahead. It is a bridge between Chekhov and the Russian revolution.

Indeed the guillotine was already audible half a century earlier in the form of the Enlightenment's plainly subversive works. Montesquieu (1689–1755), Rousseau (1712–1778) and Voltaire (1694–1778) used reason to criticise the authoritarian state proposing a new social order based on natural human rights including those of children. Montesquieu and Voltaire respectively in *De l'Esprit des Lois* (1748) and *Lettres philosophiques* (1734) looked—albeit not uncritically—to England as a model of free people worthy of emulation. Both held open discussion of scepticism and atheism designed to make any monarch relying on his divine right feel distinctly insecure.

Even earlier the *Tartuffe* of Molière (1664) shows a religious hypocrite destroying the fabric of a household. Although a comedy we are left in no doubt how tragically it could have ended. Despite Molière's apologia to the effect that he was criticising bad churchmen and not churchmen one can see in *Tartuffe*, one of the early precursors of the subversive Enlightenment. The establishment of the time would have good reason to worry at how Molière sets common sense and the bourgeois family at the heart of social stability, not the church or the king with his divine right. When things go wrong in the bourgeois family (as in the very sombre comedy of avarice *L'Avare*, 1668) potentially tragic instability ensues. Even seeming idealists like Alceste in *Le Misanthrope* (1665) are presented as clownish automata because they rock the social boat with their wish to destabilise urbane social intercourse. Significantly Molière was writing at a time of instability in the form of the Fronde of 1648 when the king's authority was already under challenge.

Woyzeck (1837) by Georg Büchner (1813–1837) portrays a world of unremitting misery for its brutalised proletariat. It was written decades before *Das Kapital* and followed his *Hessischer Landbote* (*The Hessian Courier*) (1834) which urged peasants to revolt. It bitterly and brilliantly portrays the reification of a self-subordinated being by the rulers. Clash among factions is the issue in the same writer's *Dantons Tod* (1835) on the death of French revolutionary Danton. The work was duly mauled by the censors. The 1848 upheavals are in the air.

Embodying Marx and anticipating Freud, *The father* (1887) by Strindberg (1849–1912) shows and adumbrates marriage as nothing more sacred or blessed than economic partnership. The play questions the significance of fatherhood to its very physical essence and thoroughly demolishes male supremacy. If this play disturbs even now consider its impact at the time! It is hard to equal the pathos of the final scene where the father, regressing to an infancy seeking a mother, is finally eased into his strait-jacket. A more sinister instance of prophesy is *Das neue Reich* (The new empire) (1928) by Stefan George (1868–1933) which clearly foreshadowed the efforts of National Socialism in Germany. *Waiting for Godot* (1956) by Samuel Beckett (1906–1989) belongs to works which challenged order and conveyed a sense of bewilderment and lack of social parameters. Institutions have collapsed in *Godot.* Killing time is the only worthwhile activity.

Post-modernism is an eclectic movement which is highly relevant to economic forecasting. A recent conspectus (*The Economist*, 2006) describes how it has influenced modern retailing including Selfridges, Virgin, Body Shop and Nike. It has inspired liberation marketing which appeals to us to rebel, to value and generally 'be' ourselves. The conspectus specifically refers to the movement's prophetic power:

> More surprising, perhaps, than the pomos' influence on the way business presents itself was the accuracy of their predictions and the perspicacity of their perceptions.

Post-modernism 'shatters the mainstream into a zillion different cultural shards', a mass market 'turning into a mass of niches' and mass culture breaking apart into 'millions of microcultures which coexist and interact in a baffling array of ways' (Anderson, Chris, 2006). Consumers demand unlimited choice and 'the technology to create their own products'.

However, with post-modernism as with the French Revolution, a quest for the seeds of the future in literature needs to go beyond founding texts like *Dialectic of enlightenment* (1944) by Horkheimer (1895–1973). The founding text may be the first formal statement of a movement but its roots, and hence its prophesy, may await us elusively but identifiably in precursors. This rewarding but difficult quest is particularly challenging in the case of post-modernism which, almost by definition, claims to be revisionist, rootless and revolutionary. However, post-modernism may be at the least indebted to the Dada movement of the 1920s (Locher 1999) and has been traced back to the 1870s (Hassan, 1988, p. 12).

Contemporary observers of the 1960s recognised the cultural prophesy and influence of the decade's literature. Consider again Evans (2004, p. 109):

> A number of key figures, and key literary movements, became part of the history of social radicalism... The writers were inspired as much by liberty, equality and fraternity as by the beauty of the English language. Once this genie was out of the bottle there was no stopping the re-writing of English cultural history... Within a space of about thirty years, a whole new social world appeared on the curriculum and on the library shelves.

VII Conclusion

Literature can make a multi-faceted contribution to education in accounting and cognate fields. It reinforces original, creative, imaginative and multicultural thought. By adding a disciplinary dimension it encourages reflective consideration of ideas in terms of the difference which they make to other ideas. It militates against the threat of de-disciplining in one of the most vocational areas in the whole university curriculum. Studied holistically it sets issues into the context of human endeavour and choices. Not least literature is prophetic. These benefits are strengthened by literature's ability to expose its readers and listeners to some of the most concise, articulate, powerful and sensitive expression ever uttered. The labour market will in the long-run penalise those who lack the qualities which can be uniquely imparted by literature. If we deny literature to our students they will be the poorer: no flowers will mean no gold.

References

Anderson, C. (2006) *The Long Tail: Why the Future of Business is Selling Less of More* (New York, NY, Hyperion).

Anderson, C. (2006) Introduction, *Pharmacy Education*, 6(3), pp. 215–228.

Arnould, E. J. (Ed.) (1952) Beaumarchais, *Le mariage de Figaro* (Oxford: Blackwell).

Badaracco, J. L. Jr. (2006a) Leadership in literature, *Harvard Business Review*, 84(3), pp. 47–55.

Badaracco, J. L. Jr. (2006b) *Questions of Character* (Boston, MA, Harvard Business School Press).

Bourdieu, P. (1986) *Distinction: A Social Critique of the Judgement of Taste* (London: Routledge).

Cheng, T.-Y. (1993) Is Chinese thought pattern linear circular or both, Working paper, Ball State University, Muncie IN.

Cottrell, S. (2003) *Skills for Success: The Personal Development Planning Handbook* (Basingstoke: Palgrave Macmillan).

Coulet, H. (Ed.) (1967) Prévost, *Manon Lescaut* (Paris: Garnier-Flammarion).

Dimson, E, Marsh, P. and Staunton, M. (2002) *Triumph of the Optimists 101 Years of Global Investment Returns* (Princeton, NJ: Princeton University Press).

The Economist (2006) Post-modernism is the new black, 23 December.

Evans, M. (2004) *Killing Thinking* (London: Continuum).

Gertsen, M. C., Søderberg, A.-M. and Torp, J. E. (1998) *Cultural Dimensions of International Mergers and Acquisitions* (Berlin: de Gruyter).

Goetzmann, W. N., Ibbotson, R. G. and Peng, L. (2001) A new historical database for the NYSE 1815 to 1925: Performance and predictability, *Journal of Financial Markets*, 4(1), pp. 1–32.

Graham, G. (2005) *The Institution of Intellectual Values* (Exeter: Imprint Academic).

Halsey, A. H., Lauder, H., Brown, P. and Stuart Wells, A. (Eds) *Education: Culture, Economy, Society* (Oxford: Oxford University Press).

Hassan, I. (1988) *The Postmodern Turn: Essays in Postmodern Theory and Culture* (Columbus, OH, Ohio State University Press).

Hay, A., Peltier, J. W. and Drago, W. A. (2004) Reflective learning and on-line management education: a comparison of traditional and on-line MBA students, *Strategic Change*, 13(4), pp. 169–182.

Jervis, J. (1999) *Exploring the Modern* (Oxford: Blackwell).

Lister, R. J. (2005) Cost of capital: the case for the prosecution, *Investment management and Financial Innovations*, 2(2), pp. 142–157.

Locher, D. (1999) Unacknowledged roots and blatant imitation: postmodernism and the Dada movement, *Electronic Journal of Sociology*. Available at http://www.sociology.org/content/vol004.001/locher.html (accessed 4 February 2006).

Mamede, S. and Schmidt, H. G. (2004) The structure of reflective practice in medicine, *Medical Education*, 38(12), pp. 1302–1308.

Moon, J. (2004) Using reflective learning to improve the impact of short courses and workshops, *Journal of Continuing Education in the Health Professions*, 24(1), pp. 4–11.

Moore, H. T. (1971) *Twentieth Century German Literature* (London: Heinemann).

Peltier, J. W., Hay, A. and Drago, W. A. (2005) The reflective learning continuum: reflecting on reflection, *Journal of Marketing Education*, 27(3), pp. 250–263.

Tienari, J., Søderberg, A.-M., Holgersson, C. and Vaara, E. (2005) Gender and national identity constructions in the cross-border merger context, *Gender, Work and Organization*, 12(3), pp. 217–241.

Tirole, J. (2006) *The Theory of Corporate Finance* (Princeton, NJ: Princeton University Press).

Weinstein, A. (1995) *Literature and Life*, a series of recorded lectures (Chantilly, VA, The Teaching Company).

Wolf, M. (2007) Education is a worthwhile end in itself, *Financial Times*, 1 February. Available at http://www.FT.com (accessed 15 March 2008).

PART II: Commentaries

A Commentary on "A Role for the Compulsory Study of Literature in Accounting Education"

MELVIN BERG

I read this paper (Lister (2010)) from the perspective of someone who has spent a working lifetime in 'a highly vocational field like accounting' and consequently seeks the 'value proposition.' Presumably, the author would view success as observing 'cash-strapped universities' change their accounting curriculum to include literature and employers enthusiastically hiring graduates with this broadened knowledge in preference to those who were originally considered to have the most 'marketable skills.' Unfortunately, the value proposition seems only to be stated in the negative—'the labour market will, in the long-run, penalize those who lack the qualities which can be uniquely imparted by literature'; our graduates will be 'less impoverished people'. A value proposition articulated in a positive way would improve the readability and impact of this paper.

The author clearly demonstrates that literature is 'the field in which the writer was trained and is most familiar' and sets the tone of disdain for those who did not follow a similar path. He articulates his belief that the 'large majority of our "relevant" graduates are . . . thoroughly culturally impoverished'. If the objective of this paper is to be convincing to a broad readership, including decision-makers at universities and major employers of accounting graduates, the author runs the risk of offending those who could implement the change that he seeks.

The author professes disdain for anything less than complete acceptance of his thesis—'a zealous but narrow student of literature will be a foreshortened creature unable to set his thought into the context of the choices that society has to make.' Change, if it comes, usually arrives in small increments. To express disdain for incrementalism increases the risk of affecting no change at all.

At the risk of making 'accusations of inarticulate, rambling, repetitious and jargon-ridden writing,' I would observe that the structure—five main motivations—seems inconsistent with a paper that I presume, perhaps inaccurately, is written to encourage change on the part of both universities and employers. These motivations seem very personal, particularly the writer's 'unhappiness with Joseph Bararacco'. A structure of problem definition, analysis and proposed solution would, in my view, be easier to follow and more convincing. Further, I found the relative imbalance of the five sections disconcerting. The sections 'Case for Literature' and 'Whole Use of Literature' numbed this reader with unfamiliar examples and unclear conclusions. The sections 'Reflective Learning' and 'Crisis in Higher Education' seem superficial and unbalanced when compared to the depth of the other sections. 'Literature as Prophesy' had the potential of a unique value proposition but again fell into the pattern of a series of examples and assertions which do not lead the reader to an agreement with the author. The 'Conclusion' ended with the negative tone picked up at the beginning—'no flowers will mean no gold.'

I must leave now—returning to my vocation. Alas, I have not been 'refreshed by literature directing critical thoughts to conventional accounting.' I must 'KBO', aware that I will unlikely to be able to 'hold broad, intelligent cultivated conversations' but comfortable in the fact that most of my domestic counterparts will be similarly afflicted.

References

Lister, R. J. (2010) A role for the compulsory study of literature in accounting education, *Accounting Education: an international journal*, 19(4), pp. 329–343.

Will Compelled Study of Literary Classics Engender Enrichment, Creativity, Curiosity, and Romance in Accounting Students? A Commentary on 'A Role for the Compulsory Study of Literature in Accounting Education'

RUSSELL J. CRAIG

University of Canterbury, New Zealand

> We have to get the word out. It is not over. People still want to read!
> Nashville librarian Donna Nicely (Patchett, 2009, p. W3)

Lister's (2010) proposal to expand the reading base of accounting students is relevant and timely. It should initiate much-needed dialogue and a 'critical re-examination of the orientation and content' of current accounting programs (Young and Annisette, 2009, p. 107). If Lister's proposal could be implemented successfully it would promote interdisciplinarity, encourage creativity and help make each accounting course 'a journey of curiosity' (Fogarty, 2003, p. 335, 339). Nonetheless, many accounting educators who have sympathy for Lister's proposal would probably shudder at the thought of implementing it.

Despite cautioning that academic accounting is a 'greedy and unrelenting mistress', Fogarty urges accounting educators to indulge 'in the romantic and obscure' (2003, p. 336). In accord with Fogarty's promptings, Lister's proposal does 'indulge.' However, regrettably, the case presented in support of his proposal is weak.

The overarching objective of university accounting educators should be to produce graduates and research of service to society; but how well is this objective accepted and achieved? Routinely, we produce graduates who are preponderantly adept in the mechanical minutiae of accounting but 'functionally illiterate' in their broader understanding of the world in which accounting operates. Clarke *et al.* (1999, p. 77, italics in original) drew upon a definition of cultural illiteracy as 'the absence of knowledge of the social, cultural, political, economic, environmental and scientific perspectives from which one can look at existence' to argue that '*cultural illiteracy* is nurtured in many accounting degrees.'

The argument that a crowded accounting curriculum should *require* study of literary greats (and not of history, politics, languages, sociology, science or geography—or other areas of the Arts such as dance, music and painting) is unconvincing. This is in contrast to the stronger case that has been made for teaching ethics through literature (Young and Annisette, 2009); and the case for developing depth of reading *within* the accounting discipline by requiring students to read the life's work and original writings of the great minds of the accounting discipline—scholars of the stature of Littleton, Paton, Hatfield and Chambers (Amernic and Craig, 2004).

Lister's argument that accounting students should be *compelled* to study literary classics to improve their expression, encourage 'reflective consideration', and redress their 'intellectual poverty', seems a curious mix of heavy-handedness and romanticism. Nonetheless, Fogarty (2003) reports the benefits of a similar reading initiative taken with the 'freshman seminar' at Case Western Reserve University, USA. This involved him in leading a class which engaged in critical analysis of a biography, short poems, short whimsical essays, and books on human functioning and creativity.

In assessing Lister's proposal, it is timely to reflect on whether the accounting academy has aged to become a gerontocracy, disinclined to move with the times. Are we insufficiently alert to the televisual 'social structuration and acculturation' of students (Buckmaster and Craig, 2000, p. 374)? Do we need to accept that students are more comfortable engaging with film (and by inference, television, and the Internet)—as these are media 'with which they had grown up' (Fogarty, 2003, p. 338)? If so, then perhaps Lister is suggesting students' attention should be directed to the 'wrong' Homer. Would students benefit more from studying 'masterpieces' in non-literary televisual media—for example, the irony, satire, imagery and ideology of *Homer Simpson*? Or should we regard print, in the form of *Harry Potter*-ism, as ascendant?

Forced study of any out-of-discipline subject is likely to result in classes of disengaged, poorly-performing students. Will Lister's proposal offend English as a second language (ESL) students? Should they be *compelled* to study (English) literary classics? Would they regard this as discriminatory and prejudicial?

Lister's argument that compelling students to write formal analytic essays on great literary works will improve their expository clarity is made poorly and, in parts, is incomprehensible. Although Lister (see Abstract) claims that such essays will 'hone and enrich expression', his case would have been more persuasive had his article manifested, very clearly, the benefits of studying the literary greats.

To the contrary, Lister's article suggests his study was far from enriching—unless the base level from which his expression has been 'honed' was a low one. Lister acknowledges rightly that we are all capable of 'writing crimes'—and the writer of this Commentary claims no exception. However, Lister's advocacy of the benefits of studying the literary greats he cites (Sophocles, Blake, Prevost, Stoppard, Verlaine, Strindberg, Goethe, Hardy, Lawrence, Dickens, Milton, Tolstoy, Schiller, Plato, Sartre, Shakespeare, Miller, Balzac, Chaucer, Brecht, Hopkins, Molière, Beaumarchais, Gorky, Montesquieu, Voltaire, Büchner, Beckett, and Horkheimer) is impaired by the quality of his written exposition. His case would have been stronger had he presented a 'classic essay'—a masterful exercise in rhetoric, skilfully crafted, full of passion and imagery, in which the language is rich, the words sing, the sentences and the argument compel attention, and the literary tropes are used sublimely and effectively.

If Lister's essay is meant to manifest such characteristics, it is a failure. One doubts whether any of the literary greats cited would condone Lister's appalling metaphors ('scent of a *zeitgeist*' and 'chasms of ambiguity'), hackneyed metaphors ('a melting pot of ideas', 'shot through'), crude colloquialisms ('on the cards'), confused word use ('filched' not 'fliched'), hyperbole ('impoverished state of higher education in Britain'), and general lack of discipline with regard to punctuation. Further, what are we to make of sentences such as 'Drama is an unspoken debate among writer audience and cast as all create and explore interpretations' or 'Shakespeare, with the power of a machine gun, throws it at us in a few words (Act 3, Scene 3)'?

Implicitly, or by omission, Lister seems to want readers to accept that 'cultural impoverishment' resides solely in accounting students—and not in their accounting instructors. If so, this is a brave, highly contestable stance. Clarke *et al.* (1999, pp. 77–79), for example, have drawn attention to 'an onset of cultural illiteracy' which is afflicting accounting academe. Perhaps, Lister should have insisted that the accounting academy be required to study the literary greats too? Such a requirement would not sit well with those academics who covet the quantitatively-based reductionism of the physical sciences, and who show contempt for qualitative research, normative perspectives and discursive analysis (including ethnographies, philosophical musings, and biographies).

Lister shuns discussion of the operational pragmatics of his proposal. Which English department in any modern university would be keen to teach the 'literary greats' to hordes of predominantly (stereotypically at least) left-brained, Philistine-inclined, grudgingly-present accounting students? English departments in liberal arts colleges routinely teach students from other discipline areas. Perhaps the implementation of the proposal would be more feasible in those types of institutions?

If we teach 'literary classics' to students, then we need to be more adventurous than adopting the fare suggested by Lister. His selection is intensely conservative and concentrated heavily on the European tradition of 'great books.' It includes few American writers, no women writers, no contemporary writers, no Anglophone writers (for example, those from Australia, Canada, India), and no writers of colour. In considering the literature to be assigned, we should be mindful of the potentialities of the readings suggested by Fogarty (2003) and Young and Annisette (2009)—and to this I would suggest students be directed to read masterpieces of 'writing economy', such as *Longitude* by Dava Sobel (1995).

Accounting educators should accept the challenge to 'break out of the embedded routines of their teaching life and try something dramatically different' and to 'assign greater importance to the cultivation of imagination in accounting education [by recognizing] literature's vast potential' (Young and Annisette, 2009, p. 107, 106). For those prompted to accept this challenge, Lister's proposal and the catalogue of literature he provides, merits some consideration.

References

Amernic, J. and Craig, R. (2004) Reform of accounting education in the post-Enron era: moving accounting 'Out of the Shadows,', *Abacus*, 40(3), pp. 342–378.

Buckmaster, N. and Craig, R. (2000) Popular television formats, *the student-as-consumer* metaphor, acculturation and critical engagement in the teaching of accounting, *Accounting Education: an international journal*, 9(4), pp. 371–387.

Clark, F. L., Craig, R. J. and Amernic, J. H. (1999) Theatre and intolerance in financial accounting research, *Critical Perspectives in Accounting*, 10(1), pp. 65–88.

Fogarty, T. J. (2003) Stranger in a strange land: an accounting academic teaches the freshman seminar, *Accounting Education: an international journal*, 12(3), pp. 335–339.

Lister, R. J. (2010) A role for the compulsory study of literature in accounting education, *Accounting Education: an international journal*, 19(4), pp. 329–343.

Patchett, A. (2009) The triumph of books, *The Wall Street Journal, 17–18*, January, W3.

Sobel, D. (1995) *Longitude: The True Story of a Lone Genius Who Solved the Greatest Scientific Problem of His Time* (New York, NY, Penguin).

Young, J. J. and Annisette, M. (2009) Cultivating imagination: ethics, education and literature, *Critical Perspectives on Accounting*, 20(1), pp. 93–109.

A Commentary on 'A Role for the Compulsory Study of Literature in Accounting Education'

LISA EVANS and IAN FRASER

University of Stirling, UK

We share the enthusiasm of Lister (2010) for literature. Original and fresh thinking is to be welcomed. We are less convinced by some of Lister's specific arguments for incorporating literature in accounting education.

Lister suggests that interdisciplinary links in education can foster marketable skills in graduates. Teaching literature, he argues, addresses the limitations of a technical, skills-based and vocational accounting education which, *inter alia*, seeks to reduce ambiguity. Literature, however, exposes students to ambiguity, and engaging with ambiguity encourages innovative, creative and original thinking.

We believe that the suggestion that accounting aims to reduce ambiguity is simplistic. Ambiguity is intrinsic to (even) mainstream accounting. Accruals, provisions, asset lives and realisable values, as well as concepts such as materiality, fair value, fair presentation and substance over form are all ambiguous and require judgement. Students learn that different accounting policies and assumptions lead to dramatically different results. Contemporary accounting standards (arguably) involve a principles-based approach, not one based on unambiguous rules. Students engaging fully with these issues will not see accounting as merely a technical skill, but will recognise and be equipped to deal with its complexities.

Additionally, students are introduced increasingly to critical and interdisciplinary accounting research, which achieves many of the objectives desired by Lister, widening students' horizons and broadening their education. This goes further than Lister's suggestions, exposing students not only to literature, but also to other disciplines – including sociology, economic and social history, politics and law – pertinent to a rounded education. It even experiments with 'new aesthetic forms' (p. 9); as, for example, in the poetry published in *Critical Perspectives on Accounting* or the 'Literature and Insights' in *Accounting, Auditing and Accountability Journal*. Thus, far from being merely technical skills-based education, accounting curricula already draw on different 'knowledges' and encourage reflective thinking and interactive learning. This may indeed go some way towards equipping graduates with the knowledge and skills required to bridge 'cultural divisions' (p. 12). However, we are sceptical as to the extent that this, or a literature education, could be 'a way out of increasing cultural disadvantage' (p. 13). Indeed, it might be argued that to compete with graduates from the 'elite' institutions, and the social background that this may imply, requires superior *technical accounting* skills.

Lister further argues that exposing students to world literature will help to prepare them for the cultural complexity of international business: "A country's or region's literature gives insight into character, thought-patterns, decision processes, *zeitgeist* and the very fabric of expression" (p. 9). We agree that understanding other cultures is essential for international cooperation, and that literature may play a valuable role. However, some of the benefits claimed by Lister may well be lost in translation. Instead, greater emphasis on foreign *language* education is likely to create a better basis for appreciating cultural complexity than, to use Lister's example, the reading of *War and Peace.*

Lister next takes issue with a recent paper by Badaracco (2006), which promotes the use of literature in management education. Lister's view is that Badaracco's approach misses an opportunity to 'impart each work as an aesthetic whole' and as an educational opportunity to convey also other skills, such as good writing. Examples of simple and clear style in world literature are presented, but here Lister acknowledges the difficulties of translation: 'whoever translates betrays' (p.19). It seems, then, that inevitably much of the discipline and beauty of good writing may be as lost in translation as the cultural subtleties referred to above.

It is surprising that Badaracco is singled out for criticism, but that no reference is made to earlier papers on the use of literature in management or accounting education (Czarniawska-Joerges and Guillet de Monthoux, 1994; Czarniawska and Rhodes, 2006; Stone, 2001; Phillips, 1995). Perhaps Lister might also accuse this work of encouraging fragmentation, but we are surprised that it is not acknowledged.

Lister does not explain whether he advocates the incorporation of stand-alone literature modules in an accounting programme, or rather the inclusion of literature elements within existing accounting modules. Both raise practical considerations. Given the increasing complexity of our subject, the demands of professional accreditation, and the desire to incorporate interdisciplinary and critical elements, we cannot, simply write off curriculum and time constraints as 'dangerous and defeatist' (p. 20).

How could a literature module in an accounting degree, or a literature component in an accounting module, be delivered and, more importantly, assessed? If it was to be delivered by accounting academics, would we be likely to identify suitable individuals? Most importantly, how could we convince our stakeholders (students, professional bodies, employers) that such innovations are worthwhile or more so than the incorporation of disciplines (e.g. law, economics, foreign languages) clearly pertinent to accounting education?

Our reservations are reinforced by some major issues that remain unaddressed. If there is a clear logic for importing literature into accounting degrees then it appears that similar arguments are applicable to other academic disciplines: for example, engineering, law and medicine. Indeed, given the attempts – with varying amounts of success – to incorporate reflective and critical elements in accounting education, as well as the judgment and subjectivity that is in any event intrinsic to accounting measurement, it may be that education for some other professions may be more embedded in a functionalist paradigm (see e.g. Riahi-Belkaoui, 1996) than is accounting and perhaps, therefore, more in need of the creative and 'mould-breaking' elements which a focus on literature might bring. This is not to deny that accounting education would benefit from such innovation; merely that

Lister's paper does not argue convincingly for the incorporation of a literature element specifically in accounting education rather than in (technical and vocational) education generally.

Perhaps there is potentially a wider argument here for the incorporation of a (perhaps preliminary?) liberal arts element in the university education of those whose intention is to train for the professions. This is not such a radical idea as it may appear to some: in the past Scottish tradition, divinity or law degrees were typically preceded by a general arts degree incorporating such courses as moral philosophy or logic and the study of a foreign language. Indeed, foreign language study may have particular advantages in realizing Lister's objective to enhance the cultural awareness, and ultimately the marketability, of accounting graduates. Of course, implementing such a model would have financial implications – and certainly so at a time of global financial crisis. The necessary time may not appeal to our frenetic world. A pre-university baccalaureate along continental European lines may be a (possibly) more attractive alternative.

It is unclear whether Lister is arguing for a focus within accounting degrees on literature *per se* or on literature dealing specifically with accounting or accounting-related themes. It appears that the former is the case although the paper does not make this explicit. Lister does not indicate that he regards the latter as a viable alternative despite the fact that there is a surprisingly rich variety of such literature. While many authors (including Shakespeare, Dickens and Trollope) make references of varying extent to accounting, there is a limited but varied literature that focuses on accounting, and accounting-related themes, in much greater depth. This ranges over a variety of cultures, historical eras and geographies. Examples from English literature include Chaucer's *Canterbury Tales* (see Parker, 1999; Buckmaster and Buckmaster, 1999), Dickens' *Hard Times* (see Fraser, Gallhofer, Haslam and Sydserff, 2006), Somerset Maugham's autobiographical *Of Human Bondage* (see Boys, 1994) and Bruce Marshall's *The Accounting* (also published under the title *The Bank Audit*, see West, 2001). Maltby (1997), Jackson (1992), or Evans (forthcoming) provide relevant examples relating to continental European literature.

It is not difficult to envisage an accounting course or module being constructed around such a selection of literature, perhaps reinforced by consideration of the relevant historical and professional contexts. Such a course might be 'packaged' primarily as accounting *history* albeit significantly grounded in appropriate literature. Some degree elements along these lines, indeed, are one possible prescription to meet the central concerns of Lister (with which we have much sympathy). The benefits of studying history are recognized widely and include both those which are perhaps of more immediate relevance to professional work (such as the ability to assess evidence) and those which have a more general humane element (such as enhancement of moral understanding). This approach might easier meet the concerns – of students, educators and professional stakeholders – as to irrelevance, lack of time and cost, which may greet calls for the general literature education suggested by Lister. A study of accounting and finance in the speculative climate of Victorian Britain, utilizing such texts as Trollope's *The Way We Live Now*, for example, suggests obvious parallels with our contemporary financial state. At the same time this type of innovation in accounting education might go at least some way to addressing Lister's concerns as to the lack of reflection, creativity and imagination in accounting education.

References

Buckmaster, D. and Buckmaster, E. (1999) Studies of accounting and commerce in Chaucer's Shipman's Tale, *Accounting, Auditing and Accountability Journal*, 12(1), pp. 113–128.

Czarniawska, B. and Rhodes, C. (2006) Strong plots: popular culture in management practice & theory, in: B. Czarniawska and P. Gagliardi (Eds) *Management Education and Humanities*, pp. 195–218 (Cheltenham: Edward Elgar).

Czarniawska-Joerges, B. and Guillet de Monthoux, P. (Eds) (1994) *Good Novels, Better Management. Reading Organizational Realities* (Chur: Harwood Academic Publishers).

Evans, L. (2009) A Witches' Dance of Numbers': Fictional Portrayals of Business and Accounting Transactions at a Time of Crisis, *Accounting, Auditing and Accountability Journal*, 22(2), pp. 169–199.

Fraser, I. A. M., Gallhofer, S., Haslam, J. and Sydserff, R. (2006) *Hard Times*: Carlyle and Dickens on an accounting in the name of social progress. paper presented at the *Interdisciplinary Perspectives on Accounting Conference*, Cardiff.

Jackson, M. W. (1992) Goethe's economy of nature and the nature of his economy, *Accounting, Organizations and Society*, 17(5), pp. 459–469.

Lister, R. J. (2010) A role for the compulsory study of literature in accounting education, *Accounting Education: an international journal*, 19(4), pp. 329–343.

Maltby, J. (1997) Accounting and the soul of the middle class: Gustav Freytag's Soll und Haben, *Accounting, Organizations and Society*, 22(1), pp. 69–87.

Parker, R. H. (1999) Accounting in Chaucer's Canterbury Tales, *Accounting, Auditing and Accountability Journal*, 12(1), pp. 92–112.

Phillips, N. (1995) Telling organizational tales: on the role of narrative fiction in the study of organizations, *Organization Studies*, 14(4), pp. 625–649.

Riahi-Belkaoui, A. (1996) *Accounting, A Multiparadigmatic Science* (Westport, CT, Quorum Books).

Stone, D. N. (2001) Accountant's tales, *Accounting, Organizations and Society*, 26(4–5), pp. 461–470.

West, B. P. (2001) On the social history of accounting: the Bank Audit by Bruce Marshall, *Accounting History*, 6(1), pp. 11–30.

A Commentary on 'A Role for the Compulsory Study of Literature in Accounting Education'

BRYAN HOWIESON

University of Adelaide, Australia

> We know by one's reading
> His learning and breeding . . .[1]

Lister (2010, p.) poses this question: 'Can the arts—in particular literature—fuel qualities and increase direct insight into our field in ways which will make our graduates truly 'marketable' people and less impoverished human beings?' As an educational ideal, the short answer must be 'yes'! What teacher would not prefer his/her students to be articulate, mature, inquisitive, and enriched by the experiences of life's journey? But is this what business people and business students want? My experience of both would suggest that Lister's love of literature is not shared by all. Many might see it as a distraction rather than as a benefit. Consider the words of Holliday (1913, p. BR34):

> There is a theory that 'readin' rots the mind.' This idea, here in our quotation given its most felicitous expression, is not without considerable merit. Much reading hath made men mad. The consequence of excessive reading, any pathologist you meet on the street will tell you, is to incapacitate one for business. No successful man of affairs would employ as a traveling salesman one who betrayed signs of deep reading.

I offer this quaint example to demonstrate that, despite its laudatory objective, Lister's paper rests on a number of assumptions (both implicit and explicit) that are not beyond challenge and which reflect that author's clear love of and prior study of literature. Before I proceed further, I should note that I do not have the formal training in literature that Lister has—but I am not beyond a love of 'culture'. My home is bursting with beautifully bound Folio Society editions and my music collection ranges from the Abbess Hildegard of Bingen, to Vaughan Williams, to Blossom Dearie! However, I am an educator in accounting and have been so for nearly 30 years and across every possible level and type of student.[2] I use that experience in this Commentary.

First, I think it is important that we determine what Lister means by 'literature' because whatever is seen to fall within that category serves as the basis of his model for what is the legitimate subject of beneficial study. Lister (2010) does not actually define what he means by the term but his examples would suggest that he is referring to what might commonly be called 'the classics'; it is certainly not what might be labelled 'pulp fiction' or the product of mass media. There is more to this than merely a 'face off' between Jane Austen and Barbara Cartland. Lister assumes that those that have not been exposed to the classics (that is, our graduates)[3] are 'thoroughly culturally impoverished'! Although these perceptions of business students might be popularly held (and, indeed, have probably always been held by preceding generations about youth generally), I do wonder what is the hard evidence that such students are 'culturally impoverished'. Such sentiments also run the risk that they can be viewed as 'elitist' or 'patronising'—is the 'problem' that today's graduates just may not share the same culture of Lister and me? Even if the majority of modern business students have not explored the 'classics' (which I doubt), they may well still be exposed to the types of 'eternal questions' reviewed in Lister's paper via contemporary culture and contemporary media. As the 'human condition' provides commonalities in the experiences of all of us, the type of reflection and other benefits alluded to by Lister can be, it seems to me, achieved through other vehicles rather than solely through literature. Some may deplore the television programme '*Big Brother*' but the constant controversy generated by such shows suggests that many have reflected about the conduct of the participants and the program's promoters.

A second area of discussion concerns the demand and supply sides to Lister's proposal. The supply side is virtually ignored—do accounting and business educators possess the desire and competence in literature that Lister enjoys? I doubt it. I have found that most of these educators shy away from a subject like ethics, believing (incorrectly) that they have no competence in the discipline—it is only supposition, but I expect that many would have a similar reaction to the use of the classics because they trained as accountants, not literature teachers. Accounting educators aside, there are a number of demand side issues. Is there an expectation among business students and their future employers that they will do a business degree to study literature? In my experience, the answer is an emphatic (and sometimes hostile) 'no'. One reason for this response is that people understand that their exposure to literature is not limited to enrolment in a business degree—indeed, if the lessons of literature are their primary desire, then enrolment is possible in a Bachelor of Arts degree programme with an English major. More importantly, students and employers expect their studies and skill development to be contextualised[4]—in common parlance, they want to see the 'relevance' of what they are studying to their conception of their discipline or profession. For many people, the word 'relevance' has pejorative overtones—but I believe that the objectives that Lister desires from a study of literature can be achieved by other models that are grounded in the context of the students' discipline.

Lister suggests that the value of a study of literature to accounting (and business) students includes exposure to a tolerance for ambiguity, the development of original and creative thought, a multicultural perspective, the ability to reflect, and even the chance to foresee the future. This comes from literature's communication of life's great questions but here, I think, lies the difference between Lister and myself. Although we would be in full agreement that the benefits above are essential, his library, I suspect, is largely fiction whereas I prefer to read fact. 'Ah, so like an accountant', I hear you conclude dear reader, but is it not said that "fact is stranger than fiction"? My point is that, although Lister assumes that a study of the classics is the only way these skills and attributes can be obtained, I would suggest that they are equally, if not more, readily accessible to the average accounting student if placed within fact. We do not have to look far for examples—Enron or the sub-prime mortgage crisis. Here to rival any great novel are tales of greed and drama with widespread and catastrophic consequences in which accountants and accounting practices are central characters. The study of these 'stories' not only achieves the pedagogical objectives of Lister, but will be viewed by students as being 'relevant' to their chosen profession. Similarly, if we want students to develop original and creative thought and reflection about the key questions in accounting, then we need only ask them to read the accounting 'classics' from the so-called a priori period of accounting literature. I am thinking here of writers such as Chambers and Sterling among many others who used language with precision and whose arguments reflected their own broad reading and intellectual curiosity. This might have the added advantage, of allowing those who were rather fixated on accounting to see more clearly the links between the advantages of reading good literature and the practice of their chosen discipline. In addition, it could be argued that skills like 'reflection' and tolerance for ambiguity can be developed via the incorporation of topics like ethics into course activities and the proper use of case studies and other teaching methods. (I acknowledge that case studies alone are not enough.)

One should question the paper's comments on ambiguity for they show a misunderstanding of accounting practice. Lister (2010, p.) asserts,

> We may pay lip service to chasms of ambiguity separating formulae from reality but hasten to set them aside. This inevitably leads to barely recognisable caricatures of reality.... Imaginative innovation may lead finally to the scrapping of balance sheets which cost billions to audit and publish, yet whose contents have precious little economic meaning.

Although there is no doubt that financial reporting, for example, has its limitations and that, as a species, we probably prefer certainty to ambiguity, Lister's comments seem to ignore the realities of accounting practice; the need to live with uncertainty and ambiguity is very well acknowledged by accountants. One does not have to look too far for this—for example, accounting and auditing standards are replete with references to the need for accountants to exercise their 'professional judgement' and one of the qualitative characteristics of financial reporting in the accounting *Framework*, (namely, 'reliable'), explicitly recognises the need for unbiased 'estimates' in accounting. The debate as to whether financial statements represent 'economic reality' is certainly not a new one (see the literature of Chambers, Sterling and many others noted earlier) and capital markets research demonstrates that financial statements convey some, if imperfect, information to capital market participants.[5]

In short, accounting (and business more generally) is a mine rich with educational nuggets. The difficulty, I think, lies not with the ore in that mine but rather with how it is to be processed. For example, students can be exposed to the discomfort of ambiguity even through a technical problem such as, for example, calculating the amount of a provision for employee entitlements—this can be done unproductively simply as a mathematical calculation or, beneficially, if students are challenged about the assumptions and data they used to make that calculation. Unfortunately, it is the former mechanical treatment that tends to be promoted (and rightly criticised by Lister and others) rather than the more demanding alternative of challenging students. This brings me to my final set of observations—the practicalities of implementing Lister's proposal.

Lister is close to silent on the implementation issues associated with his proposal. Very little guidance is offered as to how such a study of literature is to be implemented. The Germans have a saying, 'It is not healthy to swallow books without chewing' and it is difficult to see how a sizable portion of an already crowded accounting curriculum could be given over to literature and still give it the attention it deserves. Perhaps a stand-alone course is the answer but this requires resources and, given the inflexibility of most degree structures, such a course would have to battle to supplant another. Insufficient attention is paid by Lister to considering the 'realities' associated with many accounting degrees in which classes of students numbering in the several hundred are common and there remains a serious shortage of qualified academic accountants to educate them. Apart from resourcing issues, there are also significant difficulties posed by the demographics of the student body. For example, in many countries (and Australia is an example) a very large proportion of the students come from countries where English is not their primary tongue. These students come to a Western style education with significant language limitations and different cultural expectations about what an 'education' entails, (e.g. an emphasis on rote learning and on calculations rather than on discussion and critique). For many of these students, the language in a textbook is a challenge, let alone more sophisticated literature. For instance, a colleague of mine recently had a tutorial question in which a forklift was featured—confusion about whether this asset was related to cutlery was only resolved when a picture of the forklift was drawn on the board. Let me be clear, I do not raise this example to denigrate the students concerned—they are hard-working and have far more courage than me in coming to study in a foreign language and culture. I merely raise the example to demonstrate the substantial challenges that the study of literature would pose for both educator and student in many universities.

Overall, I think that the key concerns that Lister raises about limitations in the education of accounting graduates are already well-understood and alternative models to the one presented in his paper have been discussed elsewhere addressing these concerns. (For example, many accounting degrees have been structured to ensure that students have the opportunity to study a major in non-accounting subjects if they wish.) One might be more persuaded if a description had been provided of how the proposals had actually been implemented in an accounting programme (preferably across a variety of class sizes and demographics). Unfortunately, the paper relies too much on Lister's hope that his own enthusiasm will be enough to excite this current generation of students. I hope that Lister is correct but I believe an actual demonstration of this would offer more comfort. With regret, the contemporary education environment does not encourage a *Dead Poets Society* but rather the romanticism of *Goodbye, Mr Chips*.

Notes

[1]Ambrose Bierce (1985/1911) writing under the pen name 'Jupiter Muke'.

[2]I do use a wide variety of 'readings' in my courses, not just textbooks, and not all of this is accounting-based. For example, in exploring the distinction between law and ethics I make use of Plato's dialogue *Euthyphro*.

[3]Indeed, it is worth noting that he also assumes that our graduates have no prior exposure to the classics, so what is happening in our secondary schools?

[4]If context is not important, why do universities persist in offering alternatives to the Bachelor of Arts?

[5]For space reasons I've not touched on the multicultural and prophetic qualities of literature discussed by Lister (2010). The former can be addressed by considering the development and implementation of international financial reporting standards—a tale rich in political jostling and cross-cultural conflict. I am less convinced about the prophetic role of literature as the examples provided are all *ex post facto*. Perhaps an example in accounting is the writing of Chambers who advocated an exit price based fair value accounting system—we have had to wait nearly 50 years to see this (partially) adopted by accounting standards setters.

References

Bierce, A. (1985/1911) *The Enlarged Devil's Dictionary* (Harmondsworth, Middlesex: Penguin Classics).

Holliday, R. C. (1913) Lang: His books, *The New York Times*, 26 January, p. x. Available at http://query.nytimes.com/mem/archive-free/pdf?_r=2&res=9C0CEFDF133BE633A25755C2A9679C946296D6CF (accessed 1 February 2009).

Lister, R. J. (2010) A role for the compulsory study of literature in accounting education, *Accounting Education: an international journal*, 19(4), pp. 329–343.

A Commentary on 'A Role for the Compulsory Study of Literature in Accounting Education'

ROBERT JELLY

Chartered Institute of Management Accountants, UK

The paper by Lister (2010) is of particular relevance to Academic Boards/undergraduate programme designers/course leaders/accounting educators as they balance the need to include an ever-growing body of technical content with the need to expose accounting undergraduates to a wider curriculum which encourages critical thinking, problem-solving, analytical skills and the other higher level cognitive skills identified in Bloom's (1956) *Taxonomy*, often referred to as the 'soft skills'.

Numerous stakeholders, standard setters, regulators and other influencers require these skills from today's accounting graduates—driven by employers, professional bodies, benchmark statements, and IFAC's international education standards.

It is both a stimulating and highly controversial paper, critical of current practice in both teaching content and the 'output' of today's accounting education—accounting graduates.

The main premise of the paper is that the study of poetry and other literature should be used as critical catalysts in expanding the minds of accounting undergraduates, with a bias on the part of the author towards a more 'classical education'. The assumption made is that accounting undergraduates are disadvantaged (although the disadvantages are not articulated in detail) as a result of the absence of these critical catalysts. References are made to a range of other research which generally (although not specifically) supports the premise and other assertions in the paper. From time to time Lister allows his natural passion for the premise to race ahead of the arguments supported in the research findings. The inherent danger in this approach is that the reader's support and interest in the paper is prematurely lost when, in fact, there is much to be gained in getting to the end of the paper and considering its findings, limited as they are without further research. There is a potential and an encouraging range of topics for future research, generated from the paper.

The paper is a valuable contribution to the dilemma faced by all academic programme designers specifically and accounting educators in general, in terms of how to expand the learning experience of accounting undergraduates beyond the technical content of already 'content heavy' degree programmes. In addition, there is a contribution here to a wider debate, which will undoubtedly grow in importance, following the recent and ongoing seismic shifts in the global economy, as to the role of a university education in contributing to happy, healthy, sustainable, equitable and prosperous societies. In academic subject areas such as accounting, with a history of strong influence (both positive and negative), by the Accounting Professional Bodies in existence (of which there are hundreds throughout the world) there are, as yet, unresolved challenges in balancing the needs of employers, professional bodies and a wider view of 'a necessary minimum set of competences' in the applied aspects of the subject area on the one hand, with the necessary theoretical underpinning and the need to 'learn how to learn' on the other. This paper will hopefully stimulate the asserted need to study subjects such as poetry and other literature in order to achieve important given ends, within the context of widely-accepted and applied benchmark statements in some university's national quality assurance regimes and IFAC's International Accounting Education Standards—which are notably silent on any detailed need to study such specific subjects as a means to achieving the ends—but are in agreement as to the specific objectives of the role of a 'general education' within the context of a wider 'accounting education'.

Is the road towards an ever-increasing global emphasis on technical subject content within accounting undergraduate education (requiring the need to study an ever-growing body of Audit, Financial and Ethical International Standards and legislation as examples), a one way street, or will the emphasis be reversed in the interest of more rounded accounting graduates?

The paper argues that the emphasis on an ever-increasing focus on technical knowledge, understanding and competence has been at the expense of a focus on learning *per se*. This is surely an argument which concerns all who have a stake in accounting education. The paper does make the unsubstantiated assumption that accounting students who are not exposed to the benefits and value of poetry and other literature in their undergraduate studies are in some way 'disadvantaged'. This assertion requires further testing. The role and reliance and/or failure of pre-university education in the areas of poetry and other literature—compulsory under most secondary school curricula, and certainly in developed nations if not in all nations—is not addressed. Nor is the best timing for such exposure to literature addressed. The role that the novel in particular can play in developing critical skills, problem-solving and decision-making skills has already been recognized and introduced in post-graduate management education, and hopefully this paper will encourage publication of parallel research in term of the benefits this introduction has played in enhancing the skills at issue and how these benefits can be measured.

Research sponsored by CIMA (2008) indicates that employers to date want graduates who are both competent in their chosen specialized area of study and who are broadly-educated individuals who can think critically, evaluate, analyse, synthesize and in general acknowledge that there is a world 'out of their (accounting) box' which they should access in solving problems and finding solutions. The novel (classical or modern) and poetry can assist in this objective to broaden learning. IFAC, in its International Education Standards, also recognizes that a broad 'general education' is a requirement in becoming a 'Professional Accountant'.

With the 'accounting academic pint pot' already full, in terms of accounting degree programmes, the paper raises many questions not answered: what content is to be removed to make room for a course of study in poetry and other literature? How is the study of poetry and other literature to be integrated into accounting programmes? How will students (the new 'customers' of higher education) respond to having to study these subjects? How will the impact of introducing these topics be measured in terms of their long-term perceived benefits? How is the study of poetry and other literature to be ranked in importance relative to the study of other equally important subjects such as ethics, psychology, sociology, philosophy and thus what weighting should the study be allocated relative to the total indicative study time?

Bringing these questions to the fore for accounting educators is the real strength of this paper. The paper as a result provides a welcome basis for future and it is, hoped, timely research into this area before the initiative is lost.

We must hope that whatever the response to this paper, if the assertions made are valid, then the proposition is not ignored. A brave Course Design Board may even consider a pilot—introducing a course in poetry and other literature (as part of a Critical Thinking module?) as an option in the honours year of an accounting degree. Then the market (student sign up and feedback) would be one measure of success of the proposals. Alternatively, does the essential reading list for management studies/decision-making/case study courses contain selected poems and novels?

Imposing the study of poetry and other literature surely seems counter-intuitive? For those accountants who love poetry or other literature or both, surely the love and benefits derived from the study come from something other than compulsion. In addition, who teaches the subjects? Moreover, which poems and which novels? Cultural diversity and moral relativity are also areas which require to be considered in the choice of poetry and other literature if we are to avoid all forms of educational imperialism.

The proposition in this paper is a controversial one for accounting educators but one which should not be ignored. The critical and sceptical response which hopefully will follow from this paper will be one which leads—at least in part—to more research in this area and more testing of the proposition by accounting educators. If this outcome is fulfilled then I am certain that Lister will consider his research objectives have been fulfilled.

References

Bloom, B. S. (Ed.) (1956) *Taxonomy of Educational Objectives*, Handbook 1: Cognitive Domain (New York and London: Longman).

CIMA and the University of Bath School of Management (2008) *'CIMA Future—the 2010 Chartered Management Accounting Qualification'*, International Stakeholder Research (London: The Chartered Institute of Management Accountants).

Lister, R. J. (2010) A role for the compulsory study of literature in accounting education, *Accounting Education: an international journal*, 19(4), pp. 329–343.

A Commentary on 'A Role for the Compulsory Study of Literature in Accounting Education'

FAWZI LASWAD

Massey University, New Zealand

The changing role of the accountant from a backroom number-cruncher to a boardroom financial-adviser requires the development of additional capabilities. Further, current accounting programmers have been criticized for focusing on content and ignoring the need to equip graduates with lifelong learning, professional and generic skills. Albrecht and Sack (2000) describe accounting education as broken and in desperate need of repair. They identify a number of problems with current accounting education that include a focus on content at the expense of skill development and not preparing students for the 'ambiguous' business world they will encounter upon graduation.

As knowledge is constantly changing, a key capability that is critical in the changing environment is the ability to learn. The development of generic skills (such as critical thinking, analytical and communication skills) in accounting programmes is essential for preparing graduate accountants for future job demands and careers as accountants. Developing such skills requires the broadening of the accounting curriculum to encompass a non-accounting content.

The paper by Lister (2010), the subject of this Commentary, is critical of the current focus of accounting education on developing marketable skills that make graduates 'job ready'. It advances an interesting proposition and makes a strong case for requiring the study of literature as part of university-based accounting study. It argues that the labour market will, in the long run, penalize those who lack the qualities that are uniquely imparted through the study of literature. It argues that the study of literature increases direct insight into the accounting field by encouraging students' minds to range questioningly, creatively and originally. Further, the study of literature increases reflective learning that would allow students to develop deep learning. The study of literature encourages critical thinking and the exploring of alternative interpretations and solutions to issues.

Lister's paper provides examples of literature and explains the insights that can be drawn which would help with the development of various skills. These insights were drawn by an accounting educator who has a strong interest in, and deep understanding and appreciation of, such literature. It could be argued that students who have minor (or no) interest in the study of literature, or who had a narrow exposure to such literature, may not be able to draw such insights.

Accountancy is a global profession and plays a vital role in the expanding international business environment. In such an environment, accountants will experience greater cross-cultural contacts. Lister argues that the study of literature enhances the understanding of other cultures, which is an important skill in the global business environment.

There would be little disagreement that accounting education needs to extend beyond the traditional focus on developing technical accounting skills. This focus may be influenced by the demands of current employers who expect graduates to be 'job ready'. This focus on current needs may meet the requirements of current and immediate jobs but it is likely to be at the expense of preparing accounting graduates for future careers.

There is general consensus that future careers would require strong communication skills, critical thinking and the ability to learn and adapt to the changing environment. However, there is less consensus on how to develop these skills. Lister argues that generic skills (such as critical thinking) are 'uniquely' imparted through the study of literature. It could be argued that such skills could also be imparted through exposure to other disciplines such as philosophy, sociology, languages and other liberal arts subjects. Therefore, there is a strong argument for expanding accounting programmes to include non-accounting and non-business education.

Although there is some agreement that accounting programmes need to expand to incorporate the development of wider skills, there are obstacles that would make it difficult to achieve this goal. These obstacles include a possible lack of interest on the part of students, employers and professional accountancy bodies where such skills may not be valued—or where it is believed that such skills are developed at the expense of accountancy knowledge and skills. The challenge for accounting educators is to achieve a balance between accounting knowledge and technical accounting skills and wider generic skills. Accounting programmes should include electives from non-accounting and non-business topics.

An alternative approach for accounting education is to adopt models used in other professions (such as law and medicine) where accounting education would be moved to the postgraduate level preceded by general education at the undergraduate level. This would ensure that accountants received a broader education with the opportunity to develop generic skills. However, this model would lengthen the educational requirements for accountants, which would result in considerable financial cost borne by students and taxpayers.

In summary, to enable accounting graduates to develop successful careers, accounting programmes should equip graduates with essential generic competencies such as communication skills, analytical and critical thinking. These competencies are best developed through exposure to non-accounting and non-business studies.

References

Albrecht, S. and Sack, R. (2000) *Accounting Education: Charting the Course through a Perilous Future.* Accounting Education Series, number X (Sarasota, FL, American Accounting Association). Available at http://aaahq.org/pubs/AESv16/toc.htm (accessed 12 November 2009).

Lister, R. J. (2010) A role for the compulsory study of literature in accounting education, *Accounting Education: an international journal*, 19(4), pp. 329–343.

A Commentary on 'A Role for the Compulsory Study of Literature in Accounting Education'

BARIHAN A. NABIL

American University of Madaba, Jordan

Lister (2010) comes in answer to a much-needed and overdue change in how both accountancy as a profession and accountants are to be regarded. This relates, therefore, to how accounting education needs to be addressed—not neglecting how students perceive the study of accounting, and what added value literature can give to accounting education.

I will concentrate on two issues which the paper discusses: accounting education in response to labour markets' needs, and accounting education in response to international markets' needs.

The labour markets continuously voice the need for accounting graduates with versatile skills and abilities to meet the dynamic nature of those markets. This call is not to be heard only in the West, but even more so in developing countries.

The educational systems in developing countries emulate western educational systems - but with a time lag that can range from 10 to 20 years. This problem is further compounded as we find businesses (such as financial institutions and some other industries) operating in international markets alongside western companies. The calls from such businesses in those countries are even louder and more desperate for all-round accounting graduates who can think, work, and contribute to their companies' success through a holistic approach to decision-making and problem-solving to mention but a few areas.

As Lister suggests, literature is a rich source for providing accounting students with skills such as reflective thinking and dealing with ambiguity and uncertainty. Courses offered to accounting students during their college years do not and cannot provide them with such skills due to their very nature.

Literature is an image of life with its endless complexities. Accountants need to take into consideration and incorporate different complexities—seen and unseen—into their decisions. These complexities do not only come from the setting or situation as in case studies used in teaching students but, more than that, literature delves deep into the complex world of man, depicting and exposing the psychological and mental processes thereby allowing students to gain understanding and insights into the characters of real-life persons during the course of their work.

Breaking interdisciplinary barriers prepares accounting students to address and deal with uncertainty and ambiguity which are intrinsic characteristics of markets, thereby preparing them to be better-rounded accountants who not only have to deal with figures (the technical aspect of accountants' work), but also with market situations, and with the players inside and outside their firms or companies (the holistic aspect of accountants work).

Accounting courses on accounting standards, best practices, financial planning, and forecasting, to give some examples, have not and will not be enough. Studying literature and other related disciplines encourages students to think about the complexities of the real-world situations that literature portrays and reflects—whether in totally imaginative situations or as a reflection of real-life.

Studying literature provides an holistic approach necessary to assessing situations, as can be seen in many literary writings, and not only basing opinions and decisions on any of the elements affecting a situation, as accounting students might believe.

A second issue related to what is discussed above and accentuates the relevance of literature as part of accounting education is a matter very much taking prominence nowadays and that is the issue of learning about other cultures. Literature is one of the best and easiest media to explain and portray the different cultures of different societies.

Not only do we need in our modern world to understand other cultures in an endeavour to bring peoples together. As important as that is on its own, there are the increased possibilities to travel and work in different countries with different cultures, and/or working for companies coming from different cultures.

Studying literature can be of great help in gaining insights and understanding not only of the customs of other cultures but, most importantly, the patterns of thinking of other cultures, the business etiquette practiced in each culture, and the set of values through which they conduct business. The importance of such matters cannot be over-emphasized when it comes to real-life situations.

I refer here to literature written by those belonging to the same culture and not as seen through the eyes of others - such as the literature written by some orientalists. As in such cases literature could be a hindrance rather than an aid to understanding other cultures.

Reference

Lister, R. J. (2010) A role for the compulsory study of literature in accounting education, *Accounting Education: an international journal*, 19(4), pp. 329–343.

Deriving Four Lessons for Accounting Educators: A Commentary on 'A Role for the Compulsory Study of Literature in Accounting Education'

FRED PHILLIPS

University of Saskatchewan, Canada

Lister (2010) evoked a strong reaction, which has prompted me to accept the Editor's invitation to write this Commentary. Although I am critical of the views expressed, readers who endure Lister's opaque writing will discover at least four lessons relevant to all accounting educators.

1. **Teach with passion.** If nothing else, I have been refreshed by the passion with which Lister expresses his views. Here is a writer whose enthusiasm is undeniable. One may not be excited by the ideas themselves, but the level of energy with which they are expressed is sure to engage an audience.
2. **Connect with your audience.** My initial engagement in Lister's (2010) paper faded quickly. I became struck by the irony that, although Lister was first trained in literature and is most familiar with that field, he has failed to apply a basic principle of communication: recognize the audience for your work. Few accounting educators possess the background needed to derive meaning from brief references to the works of Stoppard or Molière, yet Lister (2010) persists in referencing such works with seemingly little regard for the audience's comprehension of their points. Through the disengaging list of unfamiliar artistic works, I was reminded that an effective educator should first assess his students' level of understanding and then seek to build structures and deliver ideas in ways that connect with and extend their knowledge, interests, and abilities.

   Lister (2010) further distances himself from the reader by characterizing our field as a box-ticking vocation in which we pay lip service to chasms of ambiguity. With little evidence to support such bold claims, Lister goes on to imply that accounting educators have given up broader educational goals in the race to impart marketable skills, which apparently do not warrant the attention they have been given. One might see these characterizations as inflammatory tactics intended to spark debate, but I view them as Lister's lack of recognition that accountabilities rightly exist in accounting education. Students and accounting practitioners live in a world where their abilities are evaluated and rewarded or penalized each day. To suggest that accounting educators should turn a blind eye to these pragmatic concerns and to condemn educators for imparting useful, 'marketable' skills suggests that Lister (2010) is yearning for a day when we are not encumbered by the realities of life. But the inevitable fact remains that the accounting academy is and must be accountable for refining and imparting professional accounting knowledge, just as it is our responsibility to also develop problem-solving skills, ethical decision-making capabilities, and other competencies expected of professionals.

3. **Consider alternatives.** If accounting educators were to embrace the idea that the compulsory study of literature is appropriate, how should they implement such an initiative? Would one or more literature course be added to the existing requirements, possibly extending the time needed to complete the undergraduate programme? Or would the initiative replace other courses in sociology, psychology, philosophy, or economics? Perhaps, even more dramatically, would mandatory literature courses replace courses in auditing, taxation, or strategic cost management? Lister (2010) states that he is not claiming the academic high ground for literature over other disciplines, yet to impose one course at the expense of another requires just such an evaluation.

   Another issue relates to the proposal that the study of literature be compulsory. What value is created by imposing this constraint? A forgiving interpretation is that, by making the course mandatory, accounting educators can count on all students having completed a literature course and thereby design subsequent courses to build on these earlier courses. A less forgiving interpretation is that the compulsory constraint is needed to ensure that accounting students actually enrol in such a course. Many institutions already offer the option for business students to complete literature courses as electives, but the anecdotal evidence available to me suggests that the opportunity costs of forgoing other courses may outweigh the incremental benefits to be gained from literature courses.

   Three final considerations relate to whether the study of literature actually does reinforce original, creative, imaginative and multicultural thought; whether it does so more effectively than alternative innovations; and whether these achievements will transfer from literature to business. I very much doubt that the average business school student will be able to reach the level of insight envisioned by Lister (2010), such as being able to decompose the high ideals of the renaissance and meaningfully relate them to Iago's Machiavellian materialism. To convince readers otherwise, Lister (2010) should present empirical evidence on how well students with little prior preparation in literature can develop and apply the multi-dimensional thinking abilities purported as benefits of studying literature. A useful extension of this analysis would be to consider whether similar outcomes might be obtained through alternative means that are grounded in a contemporary business context. A great deal of research questions the extent to which students can transfer metacognitive skills and domain-specific knowledge across domains (for example, Dunbar, 2001; Gilbert, 1989; Glaser *et al.*, 1992; Hanson and Phillips, 2006; Kelemen, *et al.*, 2000; Paris and Glynn, 2004; Veenman and Spaans, 2005). Before asserting that the compulsory study of literature is a desirable curriculum change, Lister (2010) should present more compelling evidence of its educational effectiveness.

4. **Be wary of unintended consequences.** My final concern is whether the compulsory study of literature might yield unintended consequences. One unintended consequence is that, if students learn to admire literature as the 'most powerful and sensitive form of expression ever uttered', they may come to write in a manner unbefitting a business practitioner. I fear the day when accounting students write that 'the establishment of the time would have good reason to worry at how Molière sets common sense and the bourgeois family at the heart of social stability, not the church or the king with his divine right'.

In conclusion, Lister (2010) has presented a literary piece that contains important lessons for educators, but perhaps not the lessons he intended.

References

Dunbar, K. (2001) The analogical paradox: why analogy is so easy in naturalistic settings, yet so difficult in the psychological laboratory, in: D. Gentner, K. J. Holyoak and B. N. Kokinov (Eds) *The Analogical Mind: Perspectives from Cognitive Science*, pp. 313–334 (Cambridge, MA: The MIT Press).

Gilbert, S. W. (1989) An evaluation of the use of analogy, similie, and metaphor in science texts, *Journal of Research in Science Teaching*, 26(X), pp. 315 – 327.

Glaser, R., Schauble, L., Raghavan, K. and Zeitz, C. (1992) Scientific reasoning across different domains, in: E. de Corte, M. C. Linn, H. Mandl and L. Verschaffel (Eds) *Computer-based Learning Environments and Problem Solving*, NATO ASI series F, vol. 84, pp. 345–371 (Heidelberg: Springer Verlag).

Hanson, E. and Phillips, F. (2006) Teaching financial accounting with analogies: improving initial comprehension and enhancing subsequent learning, *Issues in Accounting Education*, 21(1), pp. 1 – 14.

Kelemen, W. L., Frost, P. J. and Weaver, C. A., III (2000) Individual differences in metacognition: evidence against a general metacognitive ability, *Memory and Cognition*, 28(X), pp. 92–107.

Lister, R. J. (2010) A role for the compulsory study of literature in accounting education, *Accounting Education: an international journal*, 19(4), pp. 329–343.

Paris, N. A. and Glynn, S. M. (2004) Elaborate analogies in science text: tools for enhancing perservice teachers' knowledge and attitudes, *Contemporary Educational Psychology*, 29(X), pp. 230 – 247.

Veenman, M. V. J. and Spaans, M. A. (2005) Relation between intellectual and metacognitive skills: ages and task differences, *Learning and Individual Differences*, 15(X), pp. 159 – 176.

Making our Students More 'fit for Purpose': A Commentary on 'A Role for the Compulsory Study of Literature in Accounting Education'

ALAN SANGSTER

University of Middlesex, UK

> *Zeitgeist*: **ideas and spirit of time:** the ideas prevalent in a period and place, particularly as expressed in literature, philosophy, and religion. (MSN *Encarta Dictionary*)

Lister, in his 2010 paper, questions whether The Arts—surely The *Liberal* Arts?—and, in particular, Literature (from the 'modern' as opposed to the classical Liberal Arts) can '... make our graduates truly "marketable" people and less impoverished human beings.' He proposes that we incorporate a separate liberal arts component into accounting degrees because students will become more questioning and more realistic in their perceptions and more capable of handling ambiguity. I have some problems with this, not in the concept but in its application. Firstly, Lister does not consider whether accounting belongs as a separate discipline in the undergraduate curriculum. He assumes it does. I would argue that it does not, and will address this point later in this Commentary.

Then there is the question of how The Arts (what Lister calls 'Literature') are to be incorporated into accounting degrees. It is difficult to dispute the benefits if we teach students about reality through allegory, rhetoric and logic. However, accounting is vocational and therefore, by definition, not part of a liberal arts education—and it never has been. Accounting should therefore, logically, be taught at a different level (or, perhaps more sinisterly, in a different place) from the Liberal Arts.

In contradiction to this position, Lister suggests that we should include 'literature' as a *separate* component of accounting degrees. Surely it would be more logical to use The Arts to teach accounting rather than simply adding The Arts as a separate component in the way that (at least in the UK) we used to treat computing and statistics in our accounting degrees. Having unintegrated components in those subjects was not a success, so why should we believe that the Arts as an unintegrated component would fare any better?

Another issue is that The Arts are already included in accounting degrees. Over 20 years spent in external examining and validating degrees in the UK and Ireland across both the old (classical) and new (vocational) sectors of our university system inform me that this is so. The majority of accounting students in the UK and Ireland leave university with a degree in accounting and some transferable skills in logical reasoning and the ability to recognise and deal with ambiguity (at least at a basic level). Those more capable of understanding the literature they have read, such as Hines (1988), graduate with a healthy distrust of accounting information in so far as its being 'socially acceptable truth' rather than 'accounting truth' is concerned.

Many of us perform the equivalent of Lister's Oxford don, often using the accounting body of the social constructivist literature. In so doing, we deconstruct the myth of accounting truth before the eyes of our students while at the same time empowering them to better understand a business world where accounting 'truth' is pervasive. I cannot envisage anyone who uses Ruth Hines's (1988) article in their teaching accepting that students would be better served by directing them towards such allegorical literature as Dante's *Inferno* or *Pilgrim's Progress* or *Robinson Crusoe* or *Gulliver's Travels* or *Animal Farm.*

Teaching accounting ethics also raises awareness and enlightened understanding, as does reading literature on accounting regulation, and on social and environmental accounting—all topics typically taught towards the latter stages of our accounting degrees. Is this not precisely what Lister is suggesting that we ought to be doing? If so, why do we need an unintegrated liberal arts component in our accounting degrees? We do not, although many accounting degrees of which I am aware would benefit from greater integration of the Liberal Arts, including accounting history, in order to increase the critical thinking skills of our students.

Our students need to be taught to validate and understand reality as they *and others* see it. Or, as Lister puts it, to embrace ambiguity. However, do they need to be taught this out of context, without any accounting content? Accounting has enough ambiguity without looking elsewhere. Lister mentions Shakespeare in relation to ambiguity, but not in an accounting context. Why not? Shakespeare wrote about accounting, particularly in *The Merchant of Venice*. Bady (1985) published an excellent article on the arithmetical and accounting ambiguity of the play that a sixteenth-century audience would have understood because of its direct relevance to accounting and business. Surely that article would be more relevant to accounting students than reading Shakespearean speeches and sonnets or Psalms 100 and 150.

Accounting as a university subject is as vocational as medicine. Consideration of a range of undergraduate medical courses shows that medical students typically study medicine and very little else apart, perhaps, from some sociology and some psychology. They learn how to solve medical problems. Typically, every skill they acquire through their degree is integrated into their learning of medical subjects. Why should accounting be any different?

Instead of the abstract non-integrated inclusion of the Liberal Arts in the accounting curriculum as proposed by Lister, why not consider the history of the teaching and learning of accounting and see whether there are lessons that can be learnt from it which may help us make accounting graduates more marketable—more fit for purpose?

History tells us that accounting as we know it started being taught in business schools in Renaissance Italy as part of the overall business curriculum. Liberal Arts were not taught in those business schools, although the works of Dante and Aesop were commonly part of the foundation element of the curriculum and arithmetic was the core subject. Merchants, stonemasons, architects, engineers, artists: they could all learn accounting as part of their education. In order to succeed in business, they had to know how to use arithmetic, algebra and geometry in their business, which is why the business schools were established in the first place. With the growth of business and increasing use of agents and joint ventures, merchants also needed a reliable system of accounting, and so accounting found its way into the business schools' curriculum. Pacioli's (1494) *Summa Arithmetica* was the first known printed business school textbook to contain accounting but, by the 1520s, accounting textbooks were appearing with increasing regularity as the importance of a sound accounting system to business increased (Sangster *et al.*, 2008).

Accounting began to appear as a university (as opposed to separate business schools) subject in nineteenth-century Italy and in the rest of the western world in the twentieth century. It slowly evolved into an academic discipline (Ragioneria) rising from within the business curriculum. Then, in 1926, Gino Zappa issued a manifesto that declared accounting was not a separate discipline but rather that it was at the core of the discipline of business (Economia Aziendale) formed by combining organisation studies, management studies, and accounting studies (Costa and Torrechia, 2008). Accounting is a social science that served the needs of business and should be taught from that perspective. The Zappian school of thought became dominant in Italy but has taken its time to migrate.

If the goal is to make accounting graduates more 'marketable' (i.e. more fit for purpose), surely this is where to start: stop teaching accounting for accounting's sake, teach it for the sake of business, as a part of the discipline of business taught in the context of management, economics, and finance. Teach accounting as a social science, within a business context to students who have knowledge, awareness and understanding of that context by virtue of the other subjects they are studying. Slowly but surely, the accounting profession is beginning to push us, in the UK at least, in that direction. For example, the latest (2009) requirements for exemption for accounting graduates from the examinations of the London-based Chartered Institute of Management Accountants make it highly unlikely that any accounting graduate will gain maximum exemptions. The same cannot be said for graduates of business studies.

This is the direction in which we ought to be going if we are to make our graduates better prepared for the workplace, not a blind pursuit of broadening of awareness through literature with no direct relevance to accounting or to business.

However, one thing that Lister's (2010) paper does well is to highlight the point that accounting knowledge without the ability to deal with ambiguity, to reflect, and to be critical is insufficient. This is indisputable, but there is no need to do so in isolation of accounting and business. Does it matter that one accountant's finance lease is another's operating lease or that one accountant's net book value is another's accumulated depreciation; or that depreciation using rates adopted by the Government for tax relief on non-current assets produces meaningless asset values in the balance sheet? Yes, and we need our students to understand this. What Lister suggests will help, but it is not the solution.

Yet, I found this paper well worth reading: it makes me think; it makes me want to understand its message; it makes me reflect on its content, to assess critically whether it makes sense, whether it has a message worth learning. We *can* make greater use of the liberal arts to enrich the student experience. If accountants could all think out of their tunnel-shaped boxes, we might have avoided the recent instances of accounting reality falling apart. I agree with Lister, we need to make our students more 'fit for purpose': I would just do it differently.

References

Bady, D. (1985) The sum of something: arithmetic in The Merchant of Venice, *Shakespeare Quarterly*, 36(1), pp. 10–30.

Costa, M. and Torrechia, P. (2008) Value and accounting between history and theory: the Italian case. paper presented at the 20th Accounting, Business and Financial History Conference, Cardiff, UK, 11–12 September. Available at www.cardiff.ac.uk/carbs/conferences/abfh2008/costa.pdf (accessed 28 February 2009).

Hines, R. (1988) Financial accounting: in communicating reality, we construct reality, *Accounting, Organisations and Society*, 13(3), pp. 251–261.

Lister, R. J. (2010) A role for the compulsory study of literature in accounting education, *Accounting Education: an international journal*, 19(4), pp. 329–343.

Pacioli, L. (1494) *Summa de arithmetica, geometria, proportioni et proportionalita* (Venice: Paganino di Paganini).

Sangster, A., Stoner, G. N. and McCarthy, P. (2008) The market for Luca Pacioli's Summa Arithmetica, *Accounting Historians Journal*, 35(1), pp. 111–134.

A Commentary on 'A Role for the Compulsory Study of Literature in Accounting Education'

HENRY SAVILLE

International Accounting Education Standards Board, Former Chair

Lister, in his 2010 paper, puts forward an interesting proposition and one with which I felt an instinctive empathy—although, ultimately, I did not think the case was a compelling one.

I think there were two main reasons why, at the outset, I found the case appealing:

- being an accountant myself who did not follow the straightforward 'relevant graduate' route, I always feel that there is merit in the arguments supporting a broadly-based education and training environment; and
- this instinct based on my own experience has been reinforced by a lifetime working in the profession, including an extended period with responsibility for recruitment and training matters in the office in which I was based. This extended practical exposure to the realities of the quality of students joining the profession reinforced an awareness of significant deficiencies in the education process leading to that point—and, in particular, to the 'soft skills deficit'.

Given the above by way of introduction, why then was I not ultimately persuaded as to the merits of Lister's case?

In large measure I find that Lister has defeated his own proposition within his Introduction, and, in particular, towards the end of that Introduction where he says 'The writer is not claiming academic high ground for literature over other arts disciplines.' But it seems to me that this is exactly what Lister is doing by postulating that there is a need for the *compulsory* study of literature in accounting education.

At an earlier stage in the Introduction, Lister makes a point about 'the arts' in general, and then particularises literature as having a pre-eminent capacity to '... fuel qualities and increase direct insight ... which will make our graduates truly "marketable" people ...'

Why should it not be reasonable to expect that a similar case for compulsory study could be made for other arts and humanities disciplines? One might argue that history, music, or philosophy—to name but a few—could all achieve the same result as literature in terms of producing '... more "marketable" and less impoverished human beings.' If proponents of these other disciplines could sustain their respective merits, what then for the education and training of accountants?

In seeking to support the case for literature as the means to the educationally well-rounded accountant, Lister draws on the example of Goethe as being not just a literary giant but also '... an accomplished scientist and mining engineer.' The example might be apt—if all accountants were geniuses of similar capability to Goethe. The system in general, however, is not geared to work with geniuses but with individuals of sound, not (normally) exceptional, academic ability or intelligence.

I join with Lister in bemoaning the 'cultural impoverishment' of many of those professional accountants whose route to qualification may have been based initially on a 'relevant' degree. However, this is a reflection of a general approach to education that seems to encourage a narrow interpretation of what it is necessary for a graduate to study in any particular field.

In so far as accountancy-relevant degrees are concerned, one of the specific problems that have developed over the past 30 years or so has been the massive growth in the volume of technical material supporting the profession, which has served to create substantial congestion in accountancy syllabi at all levels. I suspect that Lister will say it is the typical response of an accountant lacking in a breadth of vision to assert that the system, as currently structured, simply could not accommodate the luxury of adding in a course such as that envisaged. Lacking in vision or not, it is a fact that, in my own experience, the struggle is continually to revise and exclude existing technical elements to ensure that those essential new elements can be accommodated. I can hear Lister's phrase '... dangerous and defeatist ...' reverberating in my ears as I write these words; my response is that those charged with delivering a satisfactory system must discharge their responsibility with a degree of pragmatism and, not infrequently, an element of compromise, and cannot afford to rest on the moral high ground.

On some of the other particulars, I also find myself in agreement with Lister. There is no doubt that literature could be a very useful tool in helping develop reflective learning, and there is equally no doubt that reflective learning epitomises many of the attributes that one would wish to see developed in professional accountants; but I return to my refrain—literature is certainly not the only way to develop these attributes, and may arguably not even be the best way.

Further on in his paper Lister deals with what he calls 'the whole use of literature' and condemns the use of a '... truncated approach to literature ... misses out on ... the opportunity to impart each work as an aesthetic whole with judgment or whatever as an inseparable part of that whole.' Unarguable—but is the shortcoming a fatal flaw or is it simply the pragmatic response of one who accepts the benefits to be gained from the study of literature but who is prepared to direct the study in ways whereby the student will get much of the benefit?

I continue to ask myself: why, if my instinctive initial reaction was sympathetic to the author's proposition, am I unhappy with so much of the detailed rationale of the arguments being put forward? I think the answer may be that I agree with the desired output from the proposition—namely, the creation of '... truly "marketable" people and less impoverished human beings', rather than with the proposition itself.

My problem lies primarily in the impracticality of the proposed solution—but I also have a concern that Lister's assertions may not stand up to the test of comparison to alternative arts and humanities disciplines.

If the deficiencies exist that Lister's proposition is intended to address—and I accept that they do—then surely the problem lies with failure at an earlier stage of the whole education process, where a narrowness of focus is introduced at too early a stage. Apart from anything else, why should it only be accountants who need to benefit from a study of literature, or other aspects of the arts/humanities field? Why would other professionals not equally have benefited from similar exposure? If this more general application is appropriate, then it reinforces the suggestion that the appropriate place to deal with this deficiency is to introduce it at an earlier stage in the education process on a universal basis.

If this was the case, then students coming in to the universities—to whatever course—would come with the advantage of a broad arts and science based secondary education that would fit them not just for a technical education but also to take advantage of the opportunity to prepare for their working lives in the broadest possible way, and not simply through the acquisition of technical skills.

Part of the problem here lies in the fact that employers want to recruit graduates who are instantly useful (i.e. trained in the technicalities) whereas many tertiary institutions believe that their responsibility lies less in the realm of vocational education, which should be left to professional bodies and the like. Those in the tertiary sector who feel the sector should be less a 'degree factory' and focused more on developing the well-rounded graduate are struggling in the face of government policy that wants to continually broaden the base and accessibility of university education; they are also faced with the anomalous and self-contradictory position of many employers who complain about the output from tertiary institutions on the one hand, and at the same time demand that those same institutions deliver graduates with the highest possible level of technical skills and knowledge—and the maximum availability of exemptions from professional bodies' examinations. These two requirements do not sit comfortably together.

In summary, I have sympathy with Lister's objective in wishing to develop graduates who are truly '... less impoverished human beings'—I just do not think that it is *case proven* that the compulsory study of literature is the best or only way to achieve this end.

Postscript

Having now read again both Lister's (2010) paper and this Commentary I am tempted to wonder whether the author is not practising an early April Fool's Day prank. It occurs to me that the use of Goethe as a yardstick is so extreme as to border on the unbelievable; similarly to hold up the need to '... impart each work as an aesthetic whole ...' also seems to me, on further reflection, to be scarcely credible.

I wonder ...

Reference

Lister, R. J. (2010) A role for the compulsory study of literature in accounting education, *Accounting Education: an international journal*, 19(4), pp. 329–343.

A Commentary on 'A Role for the Compulsory Study of Literature in Accounting Education'

PETER SCOTT

De Montfort University, UK

Lister's (2010) paper is a timely contribution to the debate surrounding the kind of skills our students should be developing during their time at university, together with the kinds of skills that will be valuable to their employers when they graduate and enter the world of work.

The Leitch Report of 2006, into the role that education and skills can play in improving the competitiveness of the UK economy, has led to fears of higher education becoming a technical training camp for business and industry rather than fulfilling its mission to educate and empower the individual (Fearn, 2008). Students today are pragmatists—they see universities as a route to a well-paid job rather than valuing the intellectual development and the opportunity to study that universities provide (Fearn, 2008). Their approach to their studies is to direct their effort at those subjects to which marks are awarded rather than to enjoy the intellectual challenge of investigating a new area which, although it will not be assessed, would enable them to develop their minds as they strive to understand new concepts and ideas. Yet technical knowledge is worthless without intellect and the ability to think beyond the boundaries of that technical knowledge. This failure to move on will cause the repetition of today's mistakes tomorrow when fresh and original approaches are needed to resolve problems and cast aside rather than continue with today's discredited solutions.

Lister considers the role that a study of literature can play in producing graduates with these skills, skills that employers are looking for—and, in this respect, several valuable conclusions emerge.

Lister starts off his case for literature by considering ambiguity and the way in which our disciplines seek to reduce ambiguity. This is a well-chosen area. Much of what is presented in accounting degrees does suffer from the limitations described in this section; much is hedged round with caveats about the applicability of the techniques and mathematical models we use in our teaching, and there is too little exploration of which other techniques (or completely new approaches) might be used to solve the problems thrown up by current solutions and methods. Future managers need full exposure to this ambiguity in order to equip them with the skills to manage in an ambiguous, constantly changing world.

Part of this problem may lie in the perception that accounting is somehow a *scientific* discipline providing scientific accuracy in the measurement of events. However, accounting might be seen to be much more an art than a science, a way of presenting a picture of reality but a picture nonetheless that could have been portrayed in myriad different ways if the words and images chosen had been different, if the slant given to the words and images had been nuanced even slightly differently. Students cocooned in the accounting classroom with the well-tried and tested approaches in front of them are not exposed to this ambiguity, but are lulled into a comfortable complacency that fails to engage them in questioning these approaches. Yet what awaits them in the world of accounting when they reach the workplace? A significant number of judgements have to be made each and every day, all of which have to be based on nothing more than the evidence available: do the facts bear out what the auditors are being told? Do the accounts as presented provide a true and fair view? What shades of true and fair are there? What are the words we are hearing or reading saying to us? Can we read between the lines to see the true message of turbulence and uncertainty that lies beneath the smooth and comforting finish imparted by the words? These are the skills with which the modern accountant needs to be able to live and work in an uncertain world, a world that Heraclitus saw as being in a constant process of change—as true (if not truer) today than when he formulated the idea in the late sixth/early fifth century BC. Indeed, without this exposure to ambiguity and the idea of an ever-changing world, our merely technically proficient students might well seem to fulfil Heraclitus' view that 'most people ... go through life like sleepers, experiencing the world with little understanding, each lost in a private vision' (Nussbaum, 1999, p. 687).

Exploring the layers of meaning in literature, returning again and again to the same words to discover new meanings, new ideas, new pathways and new ways of looking at the same thing, is an excellent way in which to prepare students for this world of ambiguity, uncertainty and constant change. In a world of rapid change—change that is occurring at an ever-increasing pace—the ability to grasp the *Zeitgeist* and to develop thought and ideas quickly and effectively is essential in order for business to develop new approaches to remain competitive and ahead of their rivals, a skill that employers will value highly.

Literature, too, provides readers with a much greater grasp of culture and other worlds, a point emphasised in Lister's second area of concern. As is rightly pointed out, in a global economy, an appreciation of other cultures is fundamental in the business world in order to appreciate the different approaches to business and to life, and to integrate fully with others. The lack of foreign language skills among the English-speaking peoples is a well-aired issue. But what of the lack of language skills relating to our own language? 'Despair over home students' grasp of English' trumpeted the *Times Higher Education* in a recent issue (Gill, 2008). This is not a new worry, however, as *The Guardian* newspaper headlined 'Student spelling and grammar at "crisis" levels' (Smithers, 2003) and the inability of students to express their thoughts and views effectively is a constant source of frustration for university tutors.

When our students enter the world of work, the ability to write well and present a concise and clear case is one of the prerequisites of the true professional—not just for passing examinations, but for phrasing letters, reports, presentations and in talking with clients to convey the exact meaning intended with the requisite precision. Ashton

(2009) reports that 'UK businesses lose £6bn a year because of poorly written letters' and that 'bad writing is clearly a money and time drain'. Presentation of professional work is vital in ensuring that there is no lack of clarity in presenting the intended meaning. The study of literature will help in this regard, reading the words of acknowledged masters of language and exploring how they chose the right word for the situation or to express a thought, thinking what other words they might have used and seeing how inadequate and inappropriate those other words would have been in that given scene or narrative.

So much for the active benefits, but there is also the passive accumulation of better vocabulary and an appreciation of how language is constructed grammatically to present the intended meaning. Without these skills in language, our students will be excluded from the dominant culture as Lister rightly suggests and will be unable to interact with their colleagues from other countries with their much broader educational achievements. When a spelling or grammatical error or a poorly expressed idea could lead to a multi-million pound legal claim, it is quite clear that an ability to express themselves clearly and precisely is an absolute must for all members of the profession and is a skill that we should be facilitating from an early age.

The ancients considered the pursuit of practical skills at the expense of artistic and cultural studies to be the result of character flaws, and this unbalanced approach to their education made for unbalanced leaders who would inevitably end up damaging or even betraying their cities—good education was associated with virtuous behaviour while poor or unbalanced education was associated with moral failings (Duff, 2008). Our students are studying accounting with a view to joining a profession. This profession presents itself as having high ethical standards and expects high ethical standards from its students and members. While Lister does not emphasise this point, literature presents a variety of characters, some good, some bad, some amoral. From this cast of thousands, our students can observe ethical and unethical behaviour and observe real ethical debates and the resolution of ethical conflict presented in meaningful scenarios rather than in contrived professional ethical dilemmas. They can learn how truly ethical individuals do not just abide by a written code but how they develop a much deeper appreciation of what it means to be an ethical being as well as an ethical professional.

A recent report suggests that 'Victorian novels helped us to evolve into nicer people, say scientists' (Sample, 2009)—so these same novels can help our students evolve into not just nicer people but better informed, more ethically attuned, more cultured individuals with a much greater appreciation of the world around them and with a better perspective on both the past and on our own and other nations' rich cultural history.

Does it have to be literature? Studying *foreign languages* will inculcate linguistic precision and love of language as well as providing a certain amount of literary study from different cultures (not to mention the ability to communicate effectively with overseas colleagues and others). *History* will enable students to develop analytical skills as they sift and weigh the evidence, piecing together a view of what happened and why it happened as it did from the conflicting sources of evidence, as well as developing an extensive ability to express their thoughts in clear and precise language. *Philosophy* will encourage deep thought and the careful dissection of arguments to expose the fallacies or truths at their heart while developing students as ethical beings. Arts subjects clearly provide skills that employers are looking for—if this was not the case, why do professional accounting firms employ so many arts graduates as well as accounting, finance or business graduates? Surely it must be because they are 'truly marketable people and less impoverished human beings', the kind of thinking, well-rounded, fully educated and empowered individuals that business (and society) require for the challenges that lie ahead.

References

Ashton, R. (2009) Writing can be a powerful tool that can add to your bottom line, *Accountancy Age*, 22 January, p. 13.

Duff, T. E. (2008) Models of education in Plutarch, *Journal of Hellenic Studies*, 128, pp. 1 – 26.

Fearn, H. (2008) The class of 2020? *The Time Higher Education Supplement*, 27 November, pp. 32–37.

Lister, R. J. (2010) A role for the compulsory study of literature in accounting education, *Accounting Education: an international journal*, 19(4), pp. 329–343.

Gill, J. (2008) Despair over home students' grasp of English, *The Times Higher Education Supplement*, 11 December, p. 11.

Nussbaum, M. C. (1999) Heraclitus, *The Oxford Classical Dictionary*, 3rd ed (Oxford: Oxford University Press).

Sample, I. (2009) Victorian novels helped us evolve into nicer people, say scientists, *The Guardian*, 15 January.

Smithers, R. (2003) Student spelling and grammar at 'crisis' levels, *The Guardian*, 1 March.

PART III: Rejoinder

Rejoinder to Commentaries on 'A Role for the Compulsory Study of Literature in Accounting Education'

ROGER J. LISTER

University of Salford, Salford, UK

The writer is indebted to commentators on Lister (2010) for their observations. In order to respond within the confines of a *Rejoinder* he takes the liberty of distinguishing three categories of observation and of devoting most space to the second category.

1 *Commentaries* which add significant value and are self-explanatory. Such good wine needs no bush.
2 *Commentaries* which offer significant criticisms and point to significant omissions.
3 Observations which are vacuously intemperate or which allege omission of points which appear clearly in the paper.

Summary of the Argument

In company with Scott (2010) and Fearn (2008), the writer fears least education in our field becomes 'a technical training camp for business and industry rather than fulfilling its mission to educate and empower the individual.'

All too many of our students will face a rude awakening if through 'pragmatism' they direct their efforts at those subjects 'to which marks are awarded rather than to enjoy the intellectual challenge of investigating a new area which, although it will not be assessed, would enable them to develop their minds as they strive to understand new concepts and ideas' (Scott, 2010). Such 'pragmatists' are in particular danger of ending up as middle-aged mediocrities in the job-line. Success will belong to their intellectually richer counterparts who strive to think beyond the boundaries of technical knowledge. The solution is to promote, assess and reward broader striving.

The writer advocates literature for this purpose but its use must not be confined to selected aspects of literary theory that can be construed as germane to accounting method. Such selectivity and fragmentation deprives students of the unique benefit of studying a literary work as a whole. In answer to Evans and Fraser (2010), we must not be enslaved by the cognate and its parochialism. It would be an educational sin to allow a student to walk away from *Merchant of Venice* associating it with 'arithmetical and accounting ambiguity' (Sangster, 2010) rather than its myriad richer messages.

Popular Literature

The writer respectfully points out that, contrary to Howieson (2010), the paper already points to a role for popular literature. The writer enthusiastically accepts that a popular song of Edith Piaf and a film with Rowan Atkinson can be as relevant as a poem by Housman. Many of our students already approach Craig's (2010) *Homer Simpson* and *Harry Potter* with the zeal of a set text! The TV series *Lost* (2004 and ongoing) instils a state of inner reflection and reflective learning. Tony Hancock's TV work *Missing Page* duly demolishes simplistic predispositions about 'truth' as does Sidney Lumet's film *12 Angry Men* (1957) which roots out the irrational, atavistic roots of a jury's so-called thought-out verdicts. Judge Azdak's all too brief golden age in *The Caucasian Chalk Circle* (1947), by Brecht (1898–1950) has echoes in the first part of *Atonement* (2001) by McEwan (1948–) with its false judgement about another person's guilt.

There is the Promethean in the defiant Edith Piaf (1915–1963) who performed the song *Milord* in 1959 to confound rumours that she was ill or even dead, and whose live performance of *Je ne Regrette Rien* (I regret nothing) in 1960 at the Paris Olympia is iconic. Great poets know already how to use the popular. Whitman (1819–1892) draws his metaphors from ordinary things of nature like grass and the noiseless patient spider. He lauds ordinary and voiceless people like the prostitutes, slaves and sick with whom he associated.

The Giants of Accounting Thought

Literature is particularly fitted to render the services sought by the writer. It pushes out the frontiers of what it is possible to think. It reinforces original, creative, imaginative and multicultural thought. It encourages reflective consideration of ideas in terms of the difference which they make to other ideas. Studied holistically it sets issues into the context of human endeavour and choices. Not least literature can be prescient and hortative. These benefits are strengthened by literature's ability to expose its readers and listeners to some of the most concise, articulate, powerful and sensitive expression ever uttered. Commentators argue that some of these qualities can be found in the finest writers in accounting but the writer respectfully submits that even the greatest of these would not set their mastery of language, imaginative expression and eloquence beside the greatest writers of all time.

It is true that other disciplines have much to offer—not least ethics, history and philosophy. Language—native and foreign—as a study surely inculcates linguistic precision and love of language but, as generally taught, has less imaginative content than literature itself. Literature is a transcription of life into language but much more. Literature is memorable, provocative, sometimes iconoclastic, inspiring and widely accessible. As one of the most imaginative forms of expression it encourages our minds to range questioningly, creatively and originally. Literature's artifice generates greater reality. This is where the writer differs from Howieson's stated preference for non-fiction. If utilitarian justification is insisted upon, George Eliot (1819–1880), quoted by Wood (2008, p. 129), describes literature as 'a mode of amplifying experience and extending our contact with our fellowman beyond the bounds of our personal life'.

As pointed out by Jelly (2010), the writer's suggestion can contribute to the role of a university education in contributing to 'happy, healthy, sustainable, equitable and prosperous societies.' Loss in translation has to be lived with but excellent modern translations of tough nuts like Thomas Mann preserve cultural integrity and significance.

Ambiguity

It is accepted that the need to live with uncertainty and ambiguity is very well acknowledged by accountants and that accounting and auditing standards are replete with references to the need for accountants to exercise their professional judgement and arrive at unbiased estimates. However, borrowing Evans and Fraser's own critical adjective it is simplistic to compare the ambiguity of 'accruals, provisions, asset lives and realisable values ... materiality, fair value, fair presentation and substance over form' with the fundamental ambiguities of literature as elegantly crafted for example in Herman Melville's (1819–1891) *Bartleby* and *Billy Budd.* Both sit well with Pynchon's *Against the Day* (2006) and its story of unrestrained corporate greed, false religiosity, moronic fecklessness, and evil intent in high places.

To graduate with 'a healthy distrust of accounting information insofar as its being "socially acceptable truth" rather than "accounting truth"' (Sangster) is no substitute for what literature can offer. Time constraint should not oust literature's rich instructive opportunities—nor should 'the demands of professional accreditation.' The preference among some accounting firms and industrial employers for top arts graduates is an amber light. Saville (2010) refers to the 'soft skills deficit.'

In response to an earlier referee's suggestion the writer reminds himself that ancient universities of Europe had it as a large part of their purpose to promote reflective engagement with the culture, religions and professions of the society in which they were engaged (Graham 2005, Essay VII).

Some of the *Commentaries* imply that instruction in the benefits of literature is a matter for schools. This misses the point that the benefit of literature in the senses described by the writer to young adults differs profoundly from school lessons. It is possible to harness towards fresh creative thinking course-members' maturing experience of lived history, culture clashes, relationships, alienation, conflicts, success, failure, decline and bereavement—to name but some of the things which resonate with maturity. Indeed, some university teachers of literature of the writer's acquaintance feel the need to undo the harm of examination-orientated box-ticking which is literature to all too many school students.

Implementation

Several commentators point to the need to go on to suggest how the ideas of the paper should be implemented.

With or without literature, delivery of interdisciplinary accounting is a challenge involving dialogue across social science, arts, other sciences, and information-providers. For example the library—better named academic information service—is increasingly a place where we forge interdisciplinary links.

A further issue is whether we have the right to impose literature on people who chose to major in accounting. Students must fully take on board the fact that accounting, finance and business courses, whilst being among the most vocational, are also among the most interdisciplinary requiring literacy in disciplines such as mathematics, law, behavioural sciences and obviously economics; even better if they are exposed at an adult level and in an adult manner to literature.

Table 1. Course outline

Theme	Examples of works[a,b,c]	Example of vocational counterpart[d]	Leisure[e]
1. Special gifts of the different literary genres: drama, narrative and poetry	Initial reference to some of the works to be used later		
2. Rigour, economy and freedom of expression	Hemingway's *Old man and the sea*; Hopkins' *Windhover*; Goethe's *Wanderers Nachtlied.*	Prolix, trite, jargon-ridden prose in academic, professional and in-house business writing	Room with a view
3. Richness of meaning	Blake's *Tyger*; Wallace Stevens' *Thirteen ways*; Eliot's *Prufrock.*	Simplistic expression	Court jester
4. Human personality	Character(s) in Chaucer's *Prologue*; Maugham's *Razor's Edge.*	Empathy in personal relationships	Winslow Boy
5. Reification	Pynchon, *Against the Day*; Büchner's *Woyzeck*; Fritz Lang's film *Metropolis.*	Danger of de-humanizing 'human resources'	An Inspector Calls
6. Vulnerability, disorientation and decline	Miller's *Death of a Salesman*; Kafka's *Trial*; Tony Hancock's *Missing Pages.*	Human impact of corporate crises	Breakfast at Tiffany's
7. Alienation (tribal, class, gender and other)	McEwan' *Atonement*; Updike's *Terrorist*; Kafka's *Metamorphosis*; Frisch, *Andorra*; D H Lawrence's *Oxford Voice*; Ayckbourn's *If I Were You.*	Cultural conflict (e.g. in merger)	Big Fat Greek Wedding
8. Tolerance	Lessing's *Nathan*; Lacratelle's *Silbermann.*	The value of tolerance	My Fair Lady
9. Case for reason over emotion and *vice versa*	Sidney Lumet's film *12 Angry Men*; Azdak in Brecht's *Chalk Circle.*	Danger of rationalised predisposition in decisions	To Sir with Love
10. Distortion of truth	Orwell's *1984*; Huxley's *Brave New World.*	Propoganda, spin	I'm All Right Jack
11. Ambiguity, moral and other	*Lost*, the TV series; Milton's Satan in *Paradise Lost.*	Facile, hasty, herd- and halo-driven approbation and condemnation in ethical decisions	Spy Who Came In From the Cold

12. Conflict and compromise	Anouilh's *Antigone*; Sartre's *Les Mains Sales.*	Idealism, pragmatism, reconciliation in imposition of models.	La Strada
13. Leadership	Badaracco's *Questions of character*; Brecht's *Caucasian Chalk Circle.*	Corporate leadership	Inn of the Sixth Happiness
14. Power	Golding's *Lord of the Flies;* Barrie's *Admirable Crichton.*	Exercise of power	Oliver Twist

[a]Time allocated to the course will likely not exceed one lecture and one seminar weekly—seminar enrolment being broken down to groups of eight to thirteen. For this reason one work or two complementary works will be chosen for each week's focus. It is hoped formal contact hours will be supplemented by course members' reading for pleasure.

[b]Some of the choicest opportunities are presented by works not written in English. Except where there is a widely-agreed English title, foreign titles have been used in this paper to facilitate access to translations.

[c]The writer is persuaded that older, timeless classics best provide instruction, perspective and context. Furthermore they tend to be less arcane, less dependent on epistemic and exegetical background, and previous knowledge. Alternatively, some educators may prefer more modern works and examples are accordingly given here.

[d]Column three indicates that each theme has one or more vocational counterparts but, as stated above, this must not be pursued at the expense of presenting a work as an entity. It is entirely counter-productive to reduce a work to an amputated, bullet-pointed management manual.

[e]It is hoped that the films suggested here will substitute for some TV pap game shows and inane soap operas.

Failure to achieve due personal contact with large groups causes obvious tutorial problems and the more sinister danger of reification of students. A literature course can help rather than hinder. One of its benefits is to inspire discretionary reading and discussion of distinct experience outside the classroom towards a multi-cultural community.

Who would teach it? The writer accepts that it may first be necessary to grow teachers from among our arts-educated colleagues. It is hoped that in contradiction to Phillips (2010) teaching in the right hands will make it unnecessary to eschew works on grounds of initial shock at the unfamiliar. Would incrementalism be better than wholesale adoption of the writer's suggestion (Berg, 2010)?

> Measuring-line by measuring-line, a bit here and a bit there so that they would go and stumble backward and be broken. (*Isaiah* 28, 13.)

The writer submits that incrementalism would destroy itself, thus kicking the whole idea into the rough. For example, taking parts of works or selecting bits of literary theory which seem cognate to accounting loses most of the benefit of literature. Instructors with such a 'pragmatic response' in the face of increased technical content in accounting (Saville, 2010) will not be directing 'the study in ways whereby the student will get much of the benefit.' They will be disembowelling an opportunity.

The suggestion that the present idea is untested in practice is partly true. However, note that Badaracco (2006) explicitly uses literature to teach students of business [albeit in a highly contestable manner] as the paper argues. Note also that in very many universities in the USA students of business subjects including accounting are required to take a course outside their discipline.

A scheme for 14 weekly sessions wherein each course-member attends one presentation and one seminar might look as follows.

References

Badaracco, J. L. Jr. (2006) *Questions of Character* (Boston, MA, Harvard Business School Press).

Berg, M. (2010) A commentary on 'A role for the compulsory study of literature in accounting education', *Accounting Education: an international journal*, 19(4), pp. 345–346.

Craig, R. J. (2010) Will compelled study of literary classics engender enrichment, creativity, curiosity, and romance in accounting students? A Commentary on 'A role for the compulsory study of literature in accounting education', *Accounting Education: an international journal*, 19(4), pp. 347–350.

Evans, L. and Fraser, I. (2010) A commentary on 'A role for the compulsory study of literature in accounting education', *Accounting Education: an international journal*, 19(4), pp. 351–354.

Fearn, H. (2008) The class of 2020? *Times Higher Education Supplement*, 27 November.

Graham, G. (2005) *The Institution of Intellectual Values* (Exeter: Imprint Academic).

Howieson, B. (2010) A commentary on 'A role for the compulsory study of literature in accounting education', *Accounting Education: an international journal*, 19(4), pp. 355–359.

Jelly, R. (2010) A commentary on 'A role for the compulsory study of literature in accounting education', *Accounting Education: an international journal*, 19(4), pp. 361–363.

Laswad, F. (2010) A commentary on 'A role for the compulsory study of literature in accounting education', *Accounting Education: an international journal*, 19(4), pp. 365–366.

Lister, R. J. (2010) A role for the compulsory study of literature in accounting education.

Nabil, B. A. (2010) A commentary on 'A role for the compulsory study of literature in accounting education', *Accounting Education: an international journal*, 19(4), pp. 367–368.

Phillips, F. (2010) Deriving four lessons for accounting educators: a commentary on 'A role for the compulsory study of literature in accounting education', *Accounting Education: an international journal*, 19(4), pp. 369–371.

Sangster, A. J. A. (2010) A commentary on 'A role for the compulsory study of literature in accounting education', *Accounting Education: an international journal*, 19(4), pp. 373–376.

Sarton, G. (1962/1998) *The History of Science and the New Humanism (with Recollections and Reflections by Robert K. Merton)* (New Brunswick: Transition Books).

Saville, H. J. (2010) A commentary on 'A role for the compulsory study of literature in accounting education', *Accounting Education: an international journal*, 19(4), pp. 377–379.
Scott, P. (2010) A commentary on 'A role for the compulsory study of literature in accounting education', *Accounting Education: an international journal*, 19(4), pp. 381–384.
Wood, J. (2008) *How Fiction Works* (London: Jonathan Cape).

Part IV: Views on the Accounting Curriculum

Black Swan and the Corn Maiden

JESSE DILLARD* and MARY ANN REYNOLDS**

**Portland State University, USA, **Western Washington University, USA*

ABSTRACT *Our responsibility as educators is to encourage our students to engage their minds and imaginations in visioning for themselves ethical frameworks that will serve them well as they experience the chaos of living. We consider how to facilitate seeing and creating the world differently by reframing ideas and enlivening them through alternative media forms. Through their own investigations, actions, perceptions and engagements, students construct their own realities. We provide an example of how both students and their teachers can empower an emancipatory framing through the use of reflection, metaphor and story.*

Introduction

The challenge for educators is to peer confidently into the unknown. From chaos theory (e.g. Gleick, 1987), we understand that the new emerges from the old with little or no means for predicting its appearance. Black swans represent events that do not fit within the context of traditional paradigms and that constitute the unseen dilemmas that can destroy an organization, a group, a family, a reputation. Stories are imaginings of the future or a way of giving meaning to the past. Stories can also be used in sense-making as we attempt to differentiate the relevant from the non-relevant in a complex society. Sense-making is a critical activity for organizations (Weick, 1995) and for the individuals attempting to find their own identity and appropriate responses within them, and indeed within the society in which the organization is embedded. We propose storying as an activity that can lead to understanding and can shape behaviour.

The Story

> In a far-off valley villagers toiled and students sought. Seeking information about the universe they turned to the stories of the past. They called for the elders to teach. And One came singing, singing old stories of emergence and planting, and then of change, of strife, of

busyness, of new plantings of shy harmony and a time of quiet. It was into this time of quiet that the students had stumbled. So, they thought, quiet is the way, the way of the universe.

But, She Who Sings told other stories and drew pictures on the ground with coloured sand and cautioned of other ways and things unknown in the valley. The students only laughed. Though they enjoyed the songs, how could they make sense of stories of chaos and change? The valley was Quiet and had ever been so.

She Who Sings wrapped her hand-woven blanket around her, gathered her few things in her ancient basket and walked softly to the cave at the top of the hill. Sitting on a large flat rock she called for her friend.

Green Owl drifted silently down beside her and looked out over the peaceful valley.

"Why are you troubled?" he asked.

"I am afraid for the children. They see only Quiet and the Green plantings of their parents and grandparents. The children do not know how to vision difference or change. The cycles of change always come, and come in unexpected ways. How will these little ones survive?"

Owl looked out over the valley and in his far-seeing saw more than Quiet, and he knew the singer, Corn Maiden, was right. The edge of chaos was coming on the wings of the black swan, and the village knew only Quiet.

"Perhaps", he said, "perhaps we can teach the children to write new stories. You have sung to them the Past. Perhaps, they can imagine the Next. In their imagination they may see a Black Swan. If they can story it, they can understand it and dream a new dream. New dreams will create when the chaos comes."

"Can we not Tell them," She asked?

"No" he answered gently, "the story has power only if they find it themselves."

"Come then, we must tempt them to write." They rose from the rock and walked toward the Valley.

Storying

Kamuf (2007) discusses the confusion resulting from, 'crossing between calculation and narration, between count, account and recount,' (p. 252), and posits that our bottom line focus replaces thinking with counting. If accountants then cannot rely on numbers alone for sense-making and directions, Kamuf suggests finding, 'an opening in calculating, accountable logic to locate a space for other articulations between our account and our abilities, the space precisely of a free space or free play that can be taken in to account only in the figure of the unknown, the factor of uncertainty' (p. 253). It is precisely this unknown that students must engage as they visualize and construct their own future. Seeing the relevant elements and making sense for themselves can be a first step toward creating their better world. Storytelling can aid in anticipating change and, in doing so, precipitating change both within and without.

The use of storying (or storytelling) creates new understandings as students fashion their own desired behaviour. Gargiulo (2006, p. 5) cites the premise that through stories we enact our intentions, thoughts, values, or knowledge and proposes that the related key functions of stories include: empowerment of the speaker; creation of an environment; encoding information; and engaging thinking. Our responsibility as educators is to encourage our students to engage their own minds and imaginations to vision for themselves relevant ethical frameworks that will serve them in anticipating the chaos of living. Together, teacher and student, consider how to facilitate seeing and creating the world differently by framing ideas in different ways and sharing them through alternative media forms. As students, through their own investigations, actions, perceptions and engagements, construct their own realities, we can empower an anticipatory and emancipatory framing through the use of reflection, metaphor and story.

In the remaining discussion, we contemplate 'the story'. We consider how we might facilitate imaginings by, with our students, taking the time to listen to alternative rhythms and by tempering the calculable with the incalculable and unforeseeable. In doing so, we contend that a normative framing provides a useful departure point for responsible imaginings. First, we propose an ethic of accountability as a normative framing from which alternative stories can emerge. Following from this frame, we consider our responsibilities as accounting educators. We then discuss alternatives whereby we might better fulfil our responsibilities.

Imagining New Accounting Stories

Where then might we turn for guidance? Ravenscroft and Dillard (2007) discuss the use of moral imagination in teaching ethics in the classroom. Imagination has been used throughout history to shape meaning. Study of classic texts shows us where our society came from. The contemplation of science fiction can provide stimulation as to where our worlds might be headed. Through our imagination we can create new stories that inform our futures. According to Lakoff and Johnson (1999), metaphorical imagining provides *the* means by which humans engage in abstract thinking and conceptualizing a future. Stories are the metaphors of the future.

Study of contemporary literature can enable the understanding of 'others'. Young and Annisette (2009) argue that reading fiction can engage the moral imagination and thus be more effective than merely teaching models or frameworks. The value of literature is in shaping our society by enabling us to see more than our contemporary local circumstances. There is clearly importance in literature in understanding 'the other', and the usefulness of story in moving toward change or action. We then propose that an effective approach to engaging students in the discourse of ethics is to engage the moral imagination and allow the students to create their own stories. They can most effectively learn from their own engaged creation.

Thus, conceptualization enables one to perceive and act differently and can lead to the emergence of new understanding and new possibilities and choice. This ongoing iterative engagement with one's world could continue to inform ethical choice. Ethical choice and accountability is constructed on both the group and the individual level. Thus there is a responsibility to both teach the historical context of decisions faced and also to elicit creative action from individuals.

Before the discovery of Australia by the Dutch in 1697, the empirical evidence of Western Europeans confirmed that all swans were white. As Popper (1992) and others have pointed out, little can be confirmed and much can be disconfirmed. The black swan problem originated as a debate concerning the possibilities and limitations of induction as a means for scientific reasoning. In the common vernacular, a black swan refers to a rare and unexpected high impact event. Following the work of Mandelbrot (1982) appropriated by Taleb (2007), a metaphorical black swan: resides outside the scope of reasonable expectations in that little in the past suggests its possibility; has an acute impact; and posterior analysis can be constructed such that the event appears predictable and explainable. The practical implication is that what you do not know can be more relevant than what you do know. Our inability to predict (anticipate) high impact, outlier events follows from not allowing for the possibility of their existence, because they do not fit within the generally accepted parameters of possibility. They must be imagined, not rationally deduced.

Baskin (2005) notes the relationship between storying and cognition, and introduces the notion that, 'storying is a biological imperative for human beings, the psychological mechanism by which they can capture the coherent perceptions of an unknowably complex world required for survival' (p. 32). Further noting, 'internal story creation reduces the world's complexity to a state in which people can effectively choose actions, . . . acting on such internal stories helps create a spiral of experience, storying, acting and confirmation or contradiction of storying in experience, leading to knowledge. . .' (p.32). Removing some of the noise in the environment facilitates the ability to develop knowledgeable discernment and to focus on the 'difference that makes a difference,' (Bateson, 1979 cited in Baskin, p. 32). In a world of much aggregated numbers posing as meaning nestled securely in the nominal safety of the 'bottom line', how will our business and accounting students find their way?

Take for example the current banking crisis. As Nocera (2009) points out, risk management models used by the major investment banks did not take into account the possibilities of black swans. As a result, they could not foresee the possibility of a major liquidity crisis and, thus, were caught unaware and unprepared, leading to the demise of several major financial institutions and a major economic crisis. As this and many other situations illustrate, we ignore the possibilities of black swans at our peril. The inevitability of black swans requires that we be continually aware of the possibility of their existence. To do so requires that we think and imagine in creative and iconoclastic ways, visualizing futures not closely fettered by the past. Stated differently, we must story the future possibilities as a means of imagining and creating them.

Morgan (1983) takes the position that "the process of knowing involves a process of forming and transforming, and that in knowing our world; we also form and transform ourselves (p. 405). We can use this position to consider the creative engagement with the world through the use of metaphor to map from the familiar to the unfamiliar. Regarding metaphor, Llewelyn (2003) suggests that action leads to knowing and that it is through action in constructing our reality we define our contact with our reality. Lakoff and Johnson, (1980, and Lakoff and Turner 1989; quoted in Llewelyn, 2003) note that, 'Metaphor not only aids understanding it structures experience' (p. 669). Imaginings move out, independent of time and space to be reunited in one's experiences.

The Seeds for Imagining

Imaginings emerge from a set of preconditions. Call them seeds if you like, seeds planted in the minds of the children. Order begins to emerge as strange attractors (see, Johnson, 1995) appear organizing individual elements into coherent possibilities, possibilities that become imaginable. We propose these ideas as representing initial conditions, metaphors, or frames that might provide a context within which new, richer, more humane imaginings may emerge.

Our focus in the accounting curriculum centres on economic organizations, primarily publicly-traded, for-profit entities. Maximizing long-term shareholder value, long espoused as the primary responsibility of corporate management,[1] represents a dangerously limiting perspective (Kelly, 2001). The emerging ecological and social challenges necessitate planting new seeds that yield new, more imaginative stories. New seeds require richer soil.

Assuming that enhancing the human condition[2] characterizes our ultimate goal and that, currently, a participative governing structure provides the best available political vehicle for doing so, we assert that the societal purpose of business is to facilitate a democratically governed society grounded in justice, equality, and trust supported by a sustainable economic system. This premise provides the legitimating context for business as a social institution[3] and, as such, it represents a reasonable context for imagining new understandings and new accountings. Business organizations accomplish their societal mandate by providing goods and services and employment opportunities. In order to fulfil this mandate, society grants organizational management the right[4] to use certain of society's economic assets.[5] As a result, organizational management recognizes society's right to hold them accountable for the use of the assets. Thus, organizational management accepts its responsibility[6] to render their actions transparent and understandable. In acknowledging organizational management's responsibility to give an account, society accepts the responsibility to specify the means and criteria whereby organizational management is held accountable for acting in the public interest. This system of rights and responsibilities constitutes an ethic of accountability that should inform any accountability regime.[7] New imaginings are reflected in the reporting requirements and performance evaluation criteria and, as such, influence future behaviour.

Accountability systems represent the essential element in any legitimate systems of rights and responsibilities. The old stories do not address the cycles of change, change that comes in unexpected and powerful ways. The unexpected hovers just below the horizon. Change comes on the wings of the Black Swan. The children must plant new seeds, create new stories; imagine new 'knowings'. The Corn Maiden intuits the impending change and the requisite new plantings necessary for yielding the new 'knowings' required in the impending times of strife. The Green Owl brings understanding and wisdom to these new dreams.

An ethic of accountability requires that we move beyond both the traditional utilitarian 'good' and the deontological 'right' toward discerning an appropriate course of action within the context of a creative, ongoing conversation among all constituents. We propose that such should be the nature of the classroom dialogue. We next recount an experience incorporating storying as method.

Can we energize new thoughts by modelling storying? An example is found in an Accountability and Ethics class. The instructor modelled process by reading an introductory sentence, then showing a contemplative landscape view. Reflecting the thought process, the emergent story, 'Black Swan and the Corn Maiden', was read aloud. This story, recounted at the beginning of this paper, is a story calling for students to experience the writing of their own stories. The class was then given a possible introductory sentence, a thoughtful background picture was presented and participants were asked to start imaging their responses. The class was then given time to write. The objective of this experience, shifting into a different thinking mode, was evidenced as all shared their creative and unexpected responses with their colleagues. Following this experience, students wrote a five page personal ethics statement as the closing activity in this graduate level class. These responses were shared with their colleagues. These personal statements revealed personal commitment to ethical performance in their professional activities. The feelings that were demonstrated spoke to a level of personal engagement with the notions of ethics in context. The experience of personal storying seemed to shift writers into an expression of what rang deeply true for them rather than a logical reiteration of theories studied. The students engaged their own feelings and imagined their own moral response to ethical challenges that inevitably arise. As in any open and trusting community, the effective classroom depends on each participant being granted autonomy to imagine and create as well as being held accountable, which requires open and honest communication.

As new stories unfold, an open and legitimate dialogue concerning process and content emerges. The dialogue moves understanding toward:

- a broad base for conceiving alternatives;
- a framework for setting priorities;
- inclusive and comprehensive evaluation criteria; and
- a realistic conceptualization of implementation.

The importance of context is balanced with the prescription of general rules as well as the means by which the accountability and regulatory systems are implemented.

The societal function of the accounting profession is concerned with the integrity and accountability of financial and administrative systems and those who design, implement, and utilize them. As such, accountants, and the profession, must adhere to stringent standards of integrity, responsibility, and accountability. The public accounting profession is granted the right to act in society's stead and, in accepting this right; the profession accepts the responsibility for specifying, evaluating, and enforcing appropriate evaluation criteria, acting in the public interest in doing so. The academic accounting community has a responsibility to be actively engaged in, and facilitative of, the ongoing conversation surrounding an ethic of accountability and the associated public interest responsibilities of the constituents within the context of an ever- changing environment. This conversation must hold the imaginative possibilities for different futures as well as, and in light of, the constitutive events of the past.

A major responsibility of the accounting academy concerns education and educational innovation. The objective is providing the means for constructively addressing critical issues facing accounting and organizational management as they exercise their rights and attempt to fulfil their responsibilities. This requires a curriculum and mode of delivery that includes both an appreciation for the historical and current role of organizational management, accounting, and the accounting profession as well as an ability to envision new opportunities for socially responsible, and responsive, development.[8]

Educational innovation ranges from pedagogy and programme development to educational research, with some directly concerning the rights and responsibilities implicated in an ethic of accountability. This requires an appreciation of the depth and complexities of the issues facing the profession. We design the curriculum to transcend the production of accounting technicians[9] by explicitly addressing the societal role of accounting, integrating and enhancing technical competence with an understanding of the complex responsibilities of accounting to organizations, society, and the environment. Topics included are the philosophical and moral grounding of accounting and the ethical and social dilemmas likely to be faced in the practice of accounting as well as an appreciation of the development of the profession, its relationship to the public, and its role in society, especially as it is associated with imagining an accountability ethic. Innovative programs provide students with an appreciation of the situated societal roles of the profession as well as their own rights and responsibilities as accounting professionals. Organizational management as well as other stakeholders should recognize the interrelationships among economic, social, and natural systems. This includes recognizing the uncertainties faced in an emerging reality.

As accounting educators, we must also acknowledge our lack of creativity. We too must join our students in writing new stories in order to understand the world differently. For example, Staubus (2005) calls for us to expand our and our students' understanding and appreciation of the accounting profession's duties and responsibilities to the investing public. There is a paucity of creative theory and research that has resulted in a dearth of conceivable alternative courses of action. This has implications for both our teaching and research. Williams (2004) is more explicit, noting how as accounting academics we are being hoisted on our own petard. He points to the narrow discourse permitted in accounting as a contributor to the current auditing and accounting failures and claims we have not persuaded, or at times permitted,[10] our students to look outside the socially-constructed simplistic world view of Positive Economic Science (PES). As recent events make unfortunately evident (e.g. Nocera, 2009), a critical issue is providing an education experience not broad enough to recognize the possibility of black swans.

We note that, as educators, we have a particular professional responsibility to teach more effectively the future professionals, our students, to identify and engage with the ethical issues that are present and emerging. We must continually question how our students may best be prepared to engage the complexities around them. We are advocating imagination through creating imaginary worlds. We are calling for multiple imaginary worlds, not one dominant one, such as PES, that constrains our vision.

The question is informed in Morgan's (1983) *Beyond Method*, as he recollects that in Jung's view, 'humans meet themselves in the symbolic constructions that they use to negotiate their world.' Further, this is seen as paralleling Heisenberg's notion that, '... in science one confronts only oneself, since one is investigating the way one has engaged one's world. Many social theorists, like the quantum physicists, have long favoured the idea that what we see and experience as reality is something extracted from a more complex and fundamental domain' (Morgan pp. 388–389).

If we perceive social phenomena differently, perception will drive the way we engage with the world around us. Hines (1988, 1992) and others (e.g. Burchell *et al.*, 1980; Morgan, 1988; MacIntosh, 1985; Dillard and Reynolds, 2008) have discussed the social construction of reality by accountants. If action provides a means of knowing the world, then through our actions we construct our realities and engage with the world around us. Can this individual construction of reality be turned to advantage? Can this be utilized as a means of empowering individuals and encouraging responsibility and accountability? Can it be useful in opening our minds and attitudes beyond extant ways of thinking? Can we engage our imaginings such that we can create the possibility of a black swan? We believe we have no choice to do otherwise.

Conclusion

How do we successfully prepare to recognize the black swan? One possibility is to engage the imagination. We have offered an example in the opening paragraphs of this paper. We propose that students write their own story embedded within an ethic of accountability. Proposing that when their imaginations are engaged they will remember and thus more likely implement the notions that emerge from their own work.

What should students take away from their educational experience? As a result of their engagement, they could develop an expanded scope of possibility and understand the world differently. This understanding may enable them to choose to live their lives differently, to engage in the business professions differently. Thus, the possibility exists to change the understanding and practice of accounting in such a way that increases the welfare of all, rather than a privileged subset of society. In doing this, we as educators have changed as well. We see the world differently and thus may chose to live our lives differently, teach accounting differently, and increase the welfare of all.

Our challenge as educators is not just understanding the past but introducing our students to novel events, to possible future paradigms, and stimulating their imagination in such a way as to broaden the scope of possibility. For a moment, we, and our students, must stop calculating and consider the incalculable and the unforeseen. We must take a breath, step away from the irresistible logic of calculation and listen to alternative rhythms of the past, present, and future.

> Green Owl circled the meadow. He was undismayed by the soft tears of the toiling student. The fierce writing frown of her companion did not concern him. The soft voiced debate of the others did not concern him. He saw their storying. He saw them drawing pictures and scowling with the effort of New Thought. He smiled to himself as he saw them learning and storying their futures. The Little Ones would be well. They are emerging into new knowings, and thus, new beings.

Acknowledgement

The authors wish to acknowledge the support provided by the Center for Professional Integrity and Accountability, Portland State University.

Notes

[1]A position legally codified in the USA (Greenfield, 2006).

[2]This assumes that the human condition is inextricably connected to enhancing natural, social, and economic systems (Capra, 1996).

[3]This is true for any social institutions, not just within the economic sector.

[4]Rights represent privileges accruing to an individual or group.

[5]Here we would generally include financial, human, natural and technological resources.

[6]Responsibilities are the obligations accruing from the societal privileges granted through the rights bestowed.

[7]These ideas have evolved from Yuthas and Dillard (1999), Dillard and Yuthas (2001), Dillard (2007; 2008) and Niebuhr (1963).

[8]We are not implying that this is not currently being done, only that we must be ever vigilant in ensuring its inclusion and continued relevance.

[9]The professional certification examination process in the USA encourages the technical focus of accounting education wherein the student incurs a significant proportion of the training costs as part of his/her university training.

[10]This seems particularly the case in US doctoral programs (Fogarty and Ruhl, 1996; Schwartz *et al.*, 2005; Tuttle and Dillard, 2007).

References

Baskin, K. (2005) Complexity, stories and knowing, *Emergence: Complexity & Organization*, 7(2), pp. 32–40.

Bateson, G. (1979) *Mind and Nature* (New York: Dutton).

Burchell, S., Clubb, C., Hopwood, A., Hughes, J. and Nahapiet, J. (1980) The role of accounting in organizations and society, *Accounting, Organizations and Society*, 5(1), pp. 5–27.

Capra, F. (1996) *Web of Life* (NY: Anchor/Double Day).

Dillard, J. (2008) An ethic of accountability, *Research on Professional Responsibility and Ethics in Accounting*, 13, pp. 1–18.

Dillard, J. (2007) Legitimating the social accounting project: An ethic of accountability, in: J. Unerman, B. O'Dwyer and J. Bebbington (Eds) *Sustainability Accounting and Accountability*, pp. 37–53 (London: Routledge Press).

Dillard, J. and Reynolds, M. A. (2008) Green Owl and the Corn Maiden, *Accounting, Auditing & Accountability Journal*, 21(4), pp. 556–579.

Dillard, J. and Yuthas, K. (2001) A responsibility ethic of audit expert systems, *Journal of Business Ethics*, 30(4), pp. 337–359.

Fogarty, T. and Ruhl, J. (1996) The stratification of academic accounting in the US: the role of doctoral funding awards, *Critical Perspective in Accounting*, 7(5), pp. 509–528.

Gargiulo, T. L. (2006) Power of stories, *The Journal for Quality & Participation*, Spring, pp. 5–8.

Gleick, J. (1987) *Chaos* (NY: Penguin Books).

Greenfield, K. (2006) *The Failure of Corporate Law: Fundamental Flaws and Progressive Possibilties* (Chicago: University of Chicago Press).

Hines, R. (1988) Financial accounting: in communicating reality, we construct reality, *Accounting, Organizations and Society*, 13(3), pp. 251–261.

Hines, R. (1992) Accounting: filling the negative space, *Accounting, Organizations and Society*, 17(3–4), pp. 313–341.

Johnson, M. (1993) *Moral Imagination: Implications of Cognitive Science for Ethics* (Chicago: Chicago Press).

Kamuf, P. (2007) Accounterability, *Textual Practice*, 21(2), pp. 251–266.

Kelly, M. (2001) *The Divine Right of Capital* (San Francisco: Berrett-Koehler).

Lakoff, G. and Johnson, M. (1999) *Philosophy in the Flesh* (New York: Basic Books).

Lakoff, G. and Johnson, M. (1980) *Metaphors We Live By* (Chicago, IL: The University of Chicago Press).

Lakoff, G. and Turner, M. (1989) *More than Cool Reason* (Chicago, IL: The University of Chicago Press).

Llewelyn, S. (2003) What counts as 'theory' in qualitative management and accounting research? Introducing five levels of theorizing, *Accounting, Organizations and Society*, 16(4), pp. 662–708.

MacIntosh, N. B. (1985) *The Social Software of Accounting and Information Systems* (New York: Wiley).

Mandelbrot, B. (1982) *The Fractal Geometry of Nature* (New York: W. H. Freeman & Co).

Niebuhr, R. (1963) *The Responsible Self* (San Francisco: Harper Press).

Popper, K. (1992) *Conjectures and Refutations: The Growth of Scientific Knowledge*. 5th ed (London: Routledge).

Morgan, G. (1983) In research, as in conversation, we meet ourselves, in: G. Morgan (Ed.) *Beyond Method: Strategies for Social Research*, pp. 405–407 (London: Sage).

Morgan, G. (1988) Accounting as reality construction: towards a new epistemology for accounting practice, *Accounting, Organizations and Society*, 13(5), pp. 477–486.

Nocera, J. (2009) Risk Mismanagement: What Led to the Financial Meltdown, *New York Times Magazine*. Available at http://www.nytimes.com/2009/01/04/magazine/04risk

Ravenscroft, S. and Dillard, J. (2007) Imagining: toward using cognitive science in teaching business ethics, in: D. Fisher and D. Swanson (Eds) *Advances in Business Ethics Education*, pp. 167–190 (USA: Information Age Publications).

Staubus, G. J. (2005) Ethics failures in corporate financial reporting, *Journal of Business Ethics*, 57(5), pp. 5–15.

Schwartz, B., Williams, S. and Williams, P. (2005) US doctoral students' familiarity with accounting journals: insights into the structure of the US academy, *Critical Perspectives on Accounting*, 16(3), pp. 327–348.

Taleb, N. N. (2007) *The Black Swan, The Impact of the Highly Improbable* (NY: Random House).

Tuttle, B. and Dillard, J. (2007) Beyond competition: institutional isomorphism in US accounting research, *Accounting Horizons*, 21(4), pp. 387–409.

Weick, K. (1995) *Sensemaking in Organizations* (London: Sage).

Williams, P. F. (2004) You reap what you sow: the ethical discourse of professional accounting, *Critical Perspectives on Accounting*, 15(6–7), pp. 995–1001.

Young, J. and Annisette, M. (2009) Cultivating imagination: ethics, education and literature, *Critical Perspectives on Accounting*, 20(1), pp. 93–1–9.

Yuthas, K. and Dillard, J. (1999) Teaching ethical decision making: adding a structuration dimension, *Journal of Teaching Business Ethics*, 3(4), pp. 339–361.

Revitalizing Accounting Education: A Highly Applied Liberal Arts Approach

TIMOTHY J. FOGARTY*

*Case Western Reserve University, USA

ABSTRACT *This paper critically assesses the potential of the liberal arts to contribute to accounting education in the USA. I argue that the contribution that these disciplines can make through current institutional structures is quite limited and highly conflicted. A proposal is made to extract the essential skills that are believed to be produced by the liberal arts. These could be re-embedded in an accounting education that featured the classic professionalism model as a conceptual centerpiece. Consequences of such an approach are extended and limitations are recognized.*

The effort to reform accounting education has generated ideas and initiatives since the late 1980s and early 1990s when the international public accounting firms first voiced their concern (Arthur Andersen *et al.* 1989) and financed special entities tasked with the study of the problem (i.e. the Accounting Education Change Commission). A subset of these pedagogical proposals is collectively referenced as efforts to liberalize that which transpires in the accounting classroom. Since this time, many writers have pointed to a liberal arts education as the core of a preferred approach.

Much liberty has been taken with the definition and scope of the liberal arts over the many years than have been consumed with the accounting education reform project. Many such suggestions recommend the use of non-traditional materials more recognizable to the students of the humanities and social sciences. These include literature (Crumbley and Smith, 2000), history (Previts, Coffman and Tondkar, 1993), and religion (Gray, Bebbington and McPhail, 1994). Others focus more upon the instructional delivery methodologies, recommending vehicles such as the novel (McDermott, 2006) and videos (Martin, Evans and Foster, 1995). Others aspire toward a broad education of the college student by offering suggestions for the number and composition of courses taken in liberal arts disciplines by accounting students (e.g. Proctor, 2006; Willitts, 2009).

Although what constitutes a liberal arts approach to accounting education has no precise definition, its creativity has been impressive. The pursuit of intellectual breadth stands in distinct contrast to the technical and highly-specialized competence that has more routinely marked accounting education. The lack of coherence in the aggregation of these ideas may not be excessively troublesome, especially since accounting may also lack strong connectivity between its central constructs (Lucas, 1997). On its face, the liberal arts, as practiced more regularly outside the school of business, presents much that should be envied by accounting educators.

The impressive history of the liberal arts as the *sine qua non* raw material of the educated person has fallen on hard times in recent years. Some estimates suggest that US student enrollment in liberal arts majors has declined by 50% since the mid-1960s (Cohen, 2009). Such a long-run trend produces stronger evidence of change than the rather fleeting dip experienced by accounting enrollments during the aftermath of the dot com bubble (see Barsky and Catanack, 2000). Most commentators expect the current economic crisis to exacerbate student exodus, such that administrators will further retrench their liberal arts programs (Jenkins, 2009). Meanwhile, US business school enrollments, including those in accounting, are at historic highs (AASCB, 2009). These developments support Fusfield's (2009) claim that business itself is a new liberal art. In such an environment, a diaspora of liberal art content and methodologies to fields such as accounting would be no surprise.

The purpose of this paper is to examine critically the infusion of the liberal arts into USA accounting education. The paper concludes that such a development holds false promise for the improvement of accounting pedagogy, in part because it is excessively indirect, somewhat impractical and not scalable. Another approach that attempts to extract the best elements of the liberal arts is suggested. Implications for the future of accounting education are then drawn.

The Bold Promises of the Liberal Arts

Many writers associate the study of the liberal arts with personal development. Sometimes, such personal improvement through purposeful education is linked with the broader social agenda of civil participation (e.g. Cohen, 2009). The liberal arts work as a repository of the collective wisdom of the ages, sorting away the ephemeral from that has proven capable of surviving the test of time. Exposure is expected to bolster reflective thinking (Jenkins, 2009). How students use knowledge, reconstructing it for present purposes, is closely linked with the emergent self-concept (King and Baxter-Magolda, 1991). What results from the study of the liberal arts has been ambitiously described as a life worth living (Kronman, 2007). Key understandings from great minds about the nature of truth, beauty and goodness are certainly of value and need to be appreciated (Gardner, 1993). Not only do such investments enrich the quality of life, but they also provide what Pinsker (2009) calls intellectual scaffolding to sustain people through the challenges that life presents. This sort of personal maturation allows students to form their values in a more conscious way than they would without benefit of such a set of educational experiences.

An education motivated by personal development should aspire to produce an individual who is intellectually and culturally well-rounded. To the extent that more exploration is required, this agenda would call for a wider set of courses. Ideally, these experiences would then trigger a free spirit of inquiry over topics not covered by the formal curriculum.

The liberal arts, therefore, can be understood as a process of reaching beyond and expanding the current self (Weisbuch, 2007). Ideally, learning would be prioritized over teaching, and more customized educational experiences should be possible.

Personal development as the 'uber-objective' of education is difficult to dispute in theory. However, the practicality of its attainment can more readily be questioned. Students, perhaps reflecting their pre-university educational experiences, may not be prepared for personal development of this magnitude. Byrne and Flood (2004) show that reproductive understanding, a low level form of learning, predominates how accounting students appreciate their own studies. This conclusion is also supported by those who have sought to understand generational cohorts of students. The so-called *Millennials* now attending college, albeit bright and hard-working are characterized as not particularly self-reflective (Murray, 1997).

Personal development's main limitation as a viable objective is its very imperfect articulation with career aspirations. The nexus between personal growth and professional betterment has remained speculative (Cohen, 2009). With vocational ambitions being formed earlier and with unprecedented vigor (Howe, Strauss and Matson, 2000), personal development may be squeezed out as a important personal agenda. Self-selected pockets to the contrary (see Strassburger, 2010), the purposeful personal development journey seems particularly ill-fit to the age where most have to compete vigorously for acceptable economic positioning.

Perhaps personal development is too much to ask from the liberal arts. Focusing more exclusively upon cognitive skills, a distinct contribution to clear analytical thinking might be more manageable. Many believe that the liberal arts are particularly able to prepare people to discern the truth from language. As put by Pinsker (2009), a liberal arts education enables students to recognize when someone is speaking nonsense. Those educated in this way should be able to differentiate between deep knowledge and sound bites (Weisbuch, 2007). Training in logic and rhetoric would seem particularly appropriate in an era marked by the systematic manipulation of missing information (McKibben, 1992). The liberal arts can thus be seen as more capable of serving democracy than in aiding capitalism (Nussbaum, 2010).

Enhanced thinking ability subsumes the ability to adjust one's mental processing of changed conditions. Kelly, Davey and Haigh (1999) advocate a holistic accounting education steeped in the liberal arts to better facilitate this continuous cognitive flexibility. Changing one's position requires considerable degrees of critical reflection, as well as a meta-cognition awareness about the thinking process.

The contribution of the liberal arts to the development of more complex and supple thinking abilities is limited by a variety of factors. The rhetoric that would have us believe that this happens automatically within conventional curricula is overstated (Strassburger, 2010). Again, one could question how receptive students are to the process that this change would necessarily entail. For the most part, Millennials are much more wedded to conventional thinking and the social *status quo* than is the case with previous generations (Wilson, 2004). Perhaps more importantly, faculty members across the university find great convenience in focusing upon material that can be reduced to a singular correct answer. With the exception of law schools, education tends not to prioritize situations of high exceptionality and poor structure (Subotnik, 1987). Equally inconsistent is the tendency to think of critical thinking abilities as an *ex ante* predictor of good college performance (e.g. Kealey, Holland and Watson, 2005) rather than one of the most noble objectives of education.

Willetts (2009) traces how the liberal arts in general, and philosophy in particular, replaced religion as the basis for education in Western societies. This history serves as a reminder that ethicality and morality remain as a core dimension of this form of education. The liberal arts should expose students to differing points of view which can be judged and weighed for the purpose of taking a knowledgeable and principled position. This process may take on even more importance as technology makes more and more possible (Bok, 2005). The liberal arts, therefore, may be instrumental in moving people away from their indefensible initial reactions, and toward what Hannah Arendt (1971) called *representational thinking* wherein advocacy is more deeply appreciated. This competency would support democratic societies and consensus interpretations of the public interest.

Liberal arts subject matter typically offers students robust opportunities to take opposite sides of issues. Unlike the material sciences, these disciplines usually offer multiple reasonable positions. However, students need more remedial work before they can reach the point where such dialogues are beneficial. Too many lapse into agentic acceptance or advocate very predictable positions that do not do justice to the dimensionality of the issues. Many fail to appreciate that the study of the liberal arts, at a worthwhile level, is quite demanding, requiring difficult intellectual work (Jones, 2010).

The promise of the liberal arts is that general lessons can be extracted from their original contexts and applied to our world. Although the study of historical conditions and bygone circumstances can be rewarding, the prospect that present relevance exists creates a stronger lure for students. Continuous connections to the present would seem to be an essential element of the case for the incorporation of a liberal arts framework into a more present-minded curriculum. Lacking a serious commitment to such explicit applications, the liberal arts become a set of factoids in the hands of the uninitiated.

Many commentators suggest that the liberal arts have failed to establish their relevance. Part of this is the persistence of the attitude that making this connection is either unnecessary or unwise. The demand for useful knowledge is often dismissed as pedestrian and narrow, and short-sighted (e.g. Blumenstyk, 2010). The Ivy Tower view that the value of the liberal arts was a case so apparent that it need not be demonstrated provides great comfort for those within its embrace (Glenn, 2010). Progressively, however, the opinion that these areas of study are above economic (i.e. cost benefit) scrutiny has waned (Ewell, 2004).

Since the case that the liberal arts cannot be an island that is so valuable that it merits both our unquestioned allegiance and support, but instead must contribute to the causes of modernity, has not been made convincingly (Jenkins, 2009; Weisbuch, 2007), its elements cannot be clearly assessed. Whether such a case can be made without resort to nostalgic arguments about learning in less complex and troubled times also is uncertain. We doubt that the liberal arts can avoid reductivity in the effort to be timeless.

The strongest arguments in favor of the liberal arts would appear to be intertwined with a highly stylized set of approaches to learning that may be well facilitated by their content. For example, literature, by providing characters whose perspectives are partial and predictable, illustrates the relativity of truth in more robust ways than would be possible with an impersonal and falsely omniscient textbook. Along other lines, subject matter distant from the economic vortex may facilitate non-zero sum cooperative learning. The breadth of the liberal arts might further creative cooperative learning structures (see Johnson, Johnson and Smith, 1998). The liberal arts also mesh well with service and experimental learning, in that the community can be reconceived as a living laboratory by creative instructors. The rich legacy of the liberal arts also provides those students with the motivation to become self-styled learners with a very deep pool in which to swim.

All these possibilities suggest a potential coherence problem. The many ways in which the liberal arts *could* make a contribution threatens the distinctiveness that they *will* make.

Part of the problem might be curricular, in that students have no concentrated disciplinary or temporal exposure to these areas (Willitts, 2009). Unlike the systematic approach taken to non-liberal art major fields of study (see Gardner, 1993), universities usually allow a random selection of liberal art experiences to be amassed by students. Dziuban, Moshal and Hartmen (2005) assert this to be part of the reason that students come to understand the university as bricolage. Having apparently abandoned working toward any vision of what constitutes an educated person, we collectively marginalize the liberal arts with terms such as general education and distribution requirements. The potential of the liberal arts to make a difference to students largely remains nascent and unrealized when faculty are allowed to stay within their very small research-defined research niches (Strassburger, 2010).

For some, the intuitive promise of the liberal arts to enhance the education of people in other fields is sufficient. For others, the lack of systematic empirical evidence hampers belief. This section has shown that there are ample reasons to expect a strong impact from the liberal arts. However, there are also no shortages of constraints and limitations on such a relationship.

The Contested Terrain of the Liberal Arts

The application of the liberal arts to business education, on their own terms, seems problematic. This process becomes more troubled when one admits that the liberal arts exist in a specific societal context, and therefore, cannot be applied with full force on their own terms.

Education in the USA has become much politicized in the last few decades. As a critical mechanism of economic growth and national competitiveness, education is proving itself too important to be left in the hands of educators. The liberal arts, as the standard bearer of the historic university, finds itself in the difficult position of being neither able to live up to an expanded rhetoric about educating people (Strassburger, 2010), nor able to make them economically sustainable in the more mundane sense understood by students and their parents (Blumenstyk, 2010). With mere education serving as the answer to most problems, the liberal arts have migrated to a much more difficult position than they previously had occupied.

Much of the above dilemma resides in the expectation that job training and an education are simultaneously accomplishable rather than fundamentally incompatible. Most advocates of the liberal arts believe that the pursuit of the latter is the supreme objective (e.g. Ungar, 2010). These proponents do not take a consistent position on job training except to relegate it to a subordinate role. The latent belief persists that training should be borne by employees as an aftermath to a proper university education. Such a model would carve out a large role for the liberal arts by rejecting more short-run vocationally-motivated pursuits and being untroubled by the loose coupling between pedagogic prompt and distinct competency. The arguments that solid reading and writing abilities underlie all career hopes (Segal, 2010) and that a real education should prepare the person for all careers not just their first (Ungar, 2010) are useful here. Furthermore, the idea that human dignity is the ultimate economic value (Nussbaum, 2010) possesses some power.

A strong faction of various constituencies would propose an alternative balance between job training and foundational education. Those who see the university experience as an engine of social mobility would challenge the legitimacy of any study unconnected to a vocational pursuit. *Ceteris paribus*, this orientation would marginalize the role of the liberal arts. Prime proponents of a job training priority include employers (Blanthorne,

Bhamornsiri and Guinn, 2005) and alumni (Carr, Chua and Perera, 2006). Students play a more subtle role by stressing the importance of factual understanding (Byrne and Flood, 2004) and advocating against process-based grading (Berry and Ulstad, 2005).

While the tension between job training and a less economically-motivated education will continue to be waged, the scales have been tipped toward vocationalism for some time. Broad-scale trends toward the commodification of teaching and degrees (see Cayton, 2007) contribute toward the imbalance. Universities are being tied closer to the economic imperatives of the labor market and are less able to pursue the classic objectives of the liberal arts (Giroux, 1996).

In addition to examining the demand for the liberal arts, consideration of its supply is required. The academy consists of various groups of similarly-trained individuals who compete with each other for resources. These disciplines possess externally-derived status, but in part also depend on the ability to attract a sufficient volume of students. Here, the liberal arts, albeit high in external status, are vulnerable due to declining student enrollments (Cohen, 2009; Segal, 2010). As put by Jenkins (2009), this situation puts the liberal arts on the chopping block. Accounting, with a surfeit of students, finds itself in the opposite situation with nagging doubts about its disciplinary legitimacy (e.g. Demski, 2007). Arbitrage across the disciplines tends to be imperfect since we should expect each field to pursue its self interests. Therefore, attempts to build new competencies in-house often produce better results than contracting for these services. This means that legitimacy transfers are rare.

In addition to the disciplinary struggles within universities, conflict among schools also bears upon the supply of the liberal arts. Although the liberal arts have been well-represented across the academy, they flourished so well at smaller private universities that such entities became known as liberal arts colleges. Recently, the viability of such universities has been threatened by the disproportionate success of larger state-sponsored universities, as well as research intensive private universities (Baldwin and Baker, 2009). To some extent, students have voted with their feet opting more for educational models that featured rapid pre-professional exposure as opposed to the classic life of the mind (Glenn, 2010). The battle about the liberal arts incorporates the conflict between these education industry sectors with normative approaches that either exacerbate or mitigate current enrollment trends.

The proper role of the liberal arts in education also reflects social class politics. To a certain extent, the liberal arts intensive education as a prelude to a professional graduate degree represents a high-cost alternative that has recently been made more accessible by a more vocationally-focused undergraduate experience. How one draws the line of minimally acceptable quality tends to affect who can afford to participate. In other words, economic pressures may make a liberal arts experience unaffordable to the lower socio-economic classes (Cohen, 2009). The liberal arts may become a new consumable of distinction for those who can afford it (Cayton, 2009), even if its study is not inherently elitist (Nussbaum, 2010). Suggestions that the liberal arts approach to education merits more direct governmental support, and without such a subsidy still represents an economically smart investment for people in all socio-economic classes, continue to be made (e.g. Ungar, 2010) and mitigate its selective appeal.

Resetting Liberal Arts as Skills

This paper has argued that sufficiently deep exposures to the liberal arts are capable of producing a better educated person. Although the evidence is not strong, and therefore, some degree of faith is essential, this serves as a reasonable maintained hypothesis.

However, the way in which the liberal arts are delivered to students, whose main interests lie elsewhere, tends to undermine their value. As argued above, this conclusion is the joint result of the liberal arts not being designed for this purpose, the complexities of modern university curricula and the many distributional consequences of policy intervention.

The proposed solution is to extract the desired skills from their liberal arts context and reset them in business and accounting coursework. This substitutes a direct delivery system for a very indirect one. A purposeful direction replaces a happenstance one. Although the focus on skills should not substitute for everything that we should value about the liberal arts, this proposal attempts to transplant the core of that which is valued by business school constituents. Although this attempt may represent a colonization of that which is theoretically better on its own terms, it offers an expedient solution to a very trenchant problem.

Writers on the value of the liberal arts to the education of professionals are hard pressed to avoid the solid grounding of their arguments in the skills that student hone in the process of study. Gardner (1993), for example, enumerates many different types of intelligence which share their usefulness to the solving of problems or the fashioning of products. The literature varies only in the scope of the skills that are believed to be produced and cultivated, ranging from many (e.g. DeLa Harpe, Radloff and Wyber, 2000) to a small handful (Cohen, 2009) to singular ones (e.g. Proctor, 2006). The range of these skills-writing, communication, interpersonal intelligence, etc. dovetail neatly with that officially endorsed by the Accounting Education Change Commission (1990).

Little doubt exists that accounting education in the USA is deficient in the degree it imbues students with necessary skills. As a very content-oriented discipline, accounting's education problem has a long tradition (see Graham, 1939). Many studies have demonstrated the importance of skill levels to performance (e.g. Kealey *et al.*, 2005). As Bay and McKeage (2006) point out, traditional accounting educational environments in the USA do not naturally inculcate necessary skills in the absence of specific interventions. As a result, there seems to be a unlimited appetite in the literature for unique delivery techniques (e.g. Crumbley and Smith, 2000). Judging from the nearly complete absence of content suggestions in the literature, one has to assume that this component is well-covered relative to the skills gap.

The limited attention of curricula to competency formation is certainly not unique to accounting. More generally, the emphasis on factual mastery and the lecture format yield an education of limited value to all students (Gardiner, 1995), especially in an era of rapid change and instantaneous access. The liberal arts may provide a superior path to a skills-based education because the factual strata provide less inherent fascination for business students, and therefore, can be held in check. This might facilitate a focus on the deep learning that is believed to be a better objective of education (Jackling, 2005), as well as bring a more conscious approach (Paul, 2009) and a purposeful disruption of the ordinary (Hall, Ramsey and Raven, 2004). Again, without intervention accounting students will vary widely in the depth of their learning, even when such is operationalized by simple tasks such as reading assigned material (Phillips and Phillips, 2007).

Thus, we need to balance the disciplinary desire to pass salient knowledge down to subsequent generations, with the onlay of the skills necessary to appreciate those facts. Whereas the liberal arts offer ample practice at skills development, they are not ready to deliver the factual foundation that necessarily constitutes major fields of study. For example, that which makes a student an accounting student is the knowledge that enables a translation of economic transactions into accounts that conform to standards. The skills that are needed should not stray too far from this environment.

Meta-cognition is a very under-valued skill that needs to be cultivated in an accounting education which is informed by the liberal arts. In the tradition of double-loop learning (Argyris and Schon, 1978), insight about how we learn accelerates the simple mastery that is motivated by performance. Although limited by self-reported data, studies have shown that higher degrees of self-awareness are associated with stronger academic accounting performance (Christensen, Fogarty and Wallace, 2002; Schleifer and Dull, 2009). Interestingly, the promulgation of self-insight does not seem to be among those generic skills routinely claimed by the liberal arts. Nonetheless, its importance would seem sufficient to envelop as an important educational objective.

The liberal arts may provide their students with more opportunities to express themselves than does accounting. To the extent this is true; the liberal arts may facilitate the development of critical communication skills. As such, accounting education should more religiously undertake communication skill-building. Currently, we only possess rudimentary knowledge about the communication anxiety of our students (Gardner, Milne, Stringer and Whiting, 2005). Instructors also do not form a consensus regarding the standards of communication acceptability (Musgrove, 2006). Those willing to provide guidance that goes beyond content to reach the caliber of the communication's effectiveness greatly magnify the value of their classes (Ornstein and Sandowsky, 1997). Difficulties are numerous, and can be expected to occur, but ample guidance is also available (e.g. Stocks, Stoddard and Waters, 1992).

Many writers continue to advocate the case method as a pedagogical device that is sufficiently robust to convey the importance of skills within an appropriately factual context. The case approach, long since associated with legal education in the USA, remains an under-utilized resource in accounting education (see Knechel, 1992), even one capable of securing the contributions of accounting practitioners (Krause, 2005). Case studies, when used thoughtfully, enhance and burnish several important generic skills (Boyce, Williams, Kelly and Yee, 2001). They also force users to focus on the exceptions to the rule, as opposed to its less provocative textbook regularities (Subotnik, 1987). Although a large body of empirical studies has not yet been performed, evidence of the effectiveness of case studies exists (e.g., Ballantine, Duff and Lanes, 2008). In a sense, the case study provides a context which substitutes for the rich tableau of history and the humanities offered by the liberal arts. While this is not perfect, it provides a step in the right direction.

Whether the liberal arts have any advantage in the movement toward cooperative learning is unclear. As defined by Cottell and Mills (1993), cooperative learning features intense small group interaction as teams work toward a structured objective. As part of a learner-centric classroom, this approach encourages students to assist each other, since outcomes are purposefully non-zero sum. Glenn (2010) asserts that such interaction, marked as it is by individualistic structured designs and developmentally motivated purposes, lies at the heart of the liberal arts. Many skills come to the forefront in the creation and management of teams that would be beyond the reach of the instructor-dominated model (see Ravenscroft, Buckless and Hassall, 1999). The documentation of a more profound engagement by students (e.g. Holtfreter, 2005; Ballantine and Larres, 2009) makes the method worthy of the attention of accounting educators.

In sum, this section has illustrated the skills that could be extracted from the liberal arts (or are logical extensions thereof) and could be built as seamless components of accounting coursework. This effort would replace an indirect contribution with a direct one, using the case method or cooperative learning as a possible vehicle.

Professionalization as Context

Traditional accounting education, as we have come to know it in the USA, might not be the best designed vehicle from which skills can be organized and packaged. The way courses are defined and distinguished from each other emphasizes the technical content of their material and minimizes a sense of what can be done with information. A focus on skills is a difficult fit when the categorical emphasis resides on definitional and procedural mastery. Just as the liberal arts convey cultural, literary and historical contexts wherein the encouragement of skills development could take place, accounting education needs a better and more integrative delivery system.

The model of professionalism served as a means by which our understanding of specialized expertise could be organized. The aspirations of accountants to be professionals continue unabated (Melancon, 2002), suggesting the continued relevance of this status to their education. Unfortunately, our appreciation for the professional construct has declined and we have allowed its elements to become rhetorical devices toward other objectives (see Wyatt, 2004). Perhaps the effort to reclaim the model and its implications could work as a context similar to the liberal arts around which important skills can be organized.

Professionalization is a process of learning and socialization. The core of any profession is the unique and demanded knowledge base that its practitioners possess. How this information is deployed toward the solution of client problems can only be mastered over a lifetime and through the guidance of more experienced members of the guild. Thus, professionalism combines generic skills with the cultural specificity of practice.

By organizing around some conception of what it means to be a professional, accounting education can more effectively use what has been called problem-based learning (see Breton, 1999). This approach works against our tendency to silo knowledge and to deny the existence of interdependencies. This would discourage the use of reductionistic exercises and more likely identify the misconceptions that surprisingly persist through conventionally-managed courses (Gardiner, 1995). Problem-based learning elevates the skills that are needed from afterthought to an interwoven element of the process. Embracing the requisites of professionalism might also reduce the extent of reality shock (Dean, Ferris and Konstans, 1988) experienced by graduates as they take positions in practice. It is hoped that their appreciation of the industry as it currently exists, would serve as a better baseline than that which the liberal arts provides from which to eventually improve practice.

Professionalism enables an aspiration which accommodates, but is not limited to, the deep vocationalism of today's student. The classic model includes ennobling ideas of a social contract wherein service to the public interest is conceived. If nothing else, the perspective diversifies the modalities by which the young can be reached. Whereas decision usefulness and economic contracting have their place in accounting education (see Frecka, Morris and Ramanan, 2004), they underestimate the social and psychological aspects that could be identified in more robust pedagogical frameworks. Although learning for learning's sake might not be reached, a compelling conception of a meta-purpose might push us in that direction.

The acceptance of professionalism as a purposeful context brings education closer to the propagation of action learning possibilities. Learning by doing has been advocated by many (e.g. Paisey and Paisey, 2005) and is implicitly or explicitly endorsed by public accounting (Arthur Andersen *et al.*, 1989; PricewaterhouseCoopers, 2002). Although actual engagement with the world of practice is not essential, bridging the schism that has separated academics and accountants would have value (Skousen, 1977). The attempt to cherry-pick the selected materials of practice (e.g. Catanack, 2006; Phillips 2006) is much too tepid. Alternatively, care should be taken, lest the complexities of the real world mute the lessons intended (see Svetlik, 2007).

In that classic professionalism and that which is currently done under the mantle of professionalism are hardly synonymous, accounting academe can still function as the conscience of this occupational group. At the same time that a focus on the parameters of accounting work and its consequences can better identify requisite skills (see DeLa Harpe *et al.*, 2000); a realistic sense of ethics can be imparted. Discussions of what is right and wrong about accounting practice (see Ratliff, 2006) should find more connection with students than that which might be situated in philosophy or history, venues in which students often flounder.

Projecting the Consequences

The idea that steps should be taken that would bring skills to the forefront of an accounting education that is integrated by a concern for accounting professionalism could be expected to contribute to many outcomes. These include changing the quality of accounting education and altering the prospects of the main constituents and beneficiaries.

In general, students tend to value the competencies that they believed to be developed as part of their post-secondary education (Arnold, Loan-Clarke, Harrington and Hart, 1999). If more skills were identified and improved, higher student satisfaction would be likely. This could come from a mitigation of apprehensiveness (Miller and Stone, 2009), repetition of skill usage (Dallimore, Platt and Hertenstein, 2009) and novel pedagogies (Hwang, Lui and Tong, 2008).

To the extent that the proposed changes in emphasis will engage students in a variety of ways, a wider set of learning styles can be accommodated. With a content focus, the lecture remains the default teaching technique. As such, one learning style tends to be advantaged over others. Although non-traditional pedagogies also favor some learning styles over others (Ramsay, Haulon and Smith, 2000), the rebalancing of teacher behaviors may help service a broader spectrum of students (Brokaw and Merz, 2000).

Indirect benefits are inherently more speculative. Institutions that have more clarity about their desired outcomes usually fare better in mission-driven accreditation exercises. However, favorable outcomes in this domain require much more, and tend to require ample resources. That students continue to report that the primary reason that they selected or did not select accounting as a major field of study was the interest that they perceived in the topic (Violette and Pryor, 2005; Francisco, Noland and Kelly, 2003) suggests there are strong returns possible to curricular-wide reform efforts. The low level of formal teaching training received by US accounting faculty force them to self-train for these duties (Swain and Stout, 2000). Allowing them to enhance skills in the same environment as their students is both efficient and effective (Lavoie and Rosman, 2007).

Conclusions and Limitations

This paper has advocated a deep application of the liberal arts to improve accounting education. This requires that we identify what a liberal arts approach is capable of producing, extracting it for direct use in the accounting classroom, and re-embedding it in a professional context.

Ultimately, the ideas expressed in the paper will be judged by value-added criteria. Programs of study have to deliver that which is demanded by students and potential employers. For these purposes, much can be said in favor of the liberal arts. We might wish to be able to take solutions off a pre-existing shelf, but that would be the easy way out of a difficult situation. At the same time, they are ultimately unsuitable for indiscriminate importation.

This assessment of accounting and its position in the higher education industry pertains only to the USA. An appreciation of how differences might play out, even in a limited range of comparison, is beyond the scope of this paper. US education tends to be less individualistic and less steeped in the broad intellectual traditions of the liberal arts (see James, 2000). Individual subjects of study are also subject to changes in emphasis that may not be shared internationally (e.g. Hite and Hasseldine, 2001).

Education is largely formed by expectations. Students come to it, not as *tabula rasa*, but with strong ideas about what they want, and what they should receive. These expectations may temper the degree to which innovations of the sort described above can have influence. This article did not expressly consider these expectations despite their pervasive importance (Thelin, 2007). Attention should be given to these *a priori* conditions in future research. Here, the qualitative dimensions of learning are intertwined with the quantitative translation of effort into academic work (Wilson, 2004) for which students impose tight budgets for their time (Fogarty, 2009).

Some might reason that the changes advocated in this paper are motivated by a desire to render accountants into consultants. This would only be true if we accepted the false dichotomy whereby accountants, by virtue of a traditional fact-intensive accounting education, were personality-challenged masters of technical content, and consultants, benefitting from advanced skill-training were skilled salespeople, but short on substance. The desired output for education lies somewhere between these extremes. The wish to produce graduates who effectively command an important body of knowledge co-exists with the aspiration that they should also be able to communicate solutions effectively. One should not be put at odds with the other. We have the right to expect the best of both worlds.

A central consequence of this paper's limitation to the case of accounting education is the USA is that what is described is often no more than a consensus maintained by private sector organizations. In other words, unlike the UK, government has played a very minor role in specifying university curricula. Although this could change in the future, the US government, at either the state or federal levels, has not intervened sufficiently to merit notice. Government has been content to work through private sector regulators who have set up broad- brush guidelines that have had more influence. For example, accreditation groups (such as the AACSB) have specified that approximately 50% of course work for business students comprise non-business subjects. However, rules such as these do not guarantee much about the liberal arts and their realized value to students. Nonetheless, they do legislate against unlimited vocationalism by opening sufficient curricular space to air the dream of the liberal arts. Notwithstanding this largesse, accounting educators are better advised to decide what they want and to make it happen themselves.

This paper has argued that we should design what we want to make accounting education better and work assiduously to implement it. The job ahead is not assisted by the psychological leanings that underlie beliefs that the liberal arts disciplines, as they currently exist, offer ready-made solutions. The nostalgia for a mythical past and the tendency to believe that 'the grass is always greener' on the other side of the campus can be our enemies.

References

AASCB. (2009) Business School Data Trends and List of Accredited Schools. Available at http://www.aacsb.edu/publications/businesseducation/ (accessed 10 May 2010).

Accounting Education Change Commission (1990) *Objectives of Education for Accountants, Position Statement No. 1* (Torrence, CA: AECC).

Arendt, H. (1971) *The Life of the Mind* (New York: Harcourt Brace).

Argyris, C. and Schon, D. (1978) *Organizational Learning: A Theory of Action Perspective* (Reading, MA: Addison Wesley).

Arnold, J., Loan-Clarke, J., Harrington, A. and Hart, C. (1999) Students' Perceptions of Competence Development in Undergraduate Business Related Degrees, *Studies in Higher Education*, 24(1), pp. 43–59.

Arthur, Andersen, Co., Arthur Young, Coopers Lybrand, Deloitte Haskins Sells, Ernst Whinney, Peat Marwick Main Co., Price Waterhouse, and Touche Ross (1989) *Perspectives on Education: Capabilities for Success in the Accounting Profession* (New York).

Baldwin, R. and Baker, V. (2009) The Case of the Disappearing Liberal Arts College, *Inside Higher Education*, 9 July. Available at http://www.insidehighered.com/layout/set/print/views/2009/07/09/baldwin (accessed 10 May 2010).

Ballantine, J., Duff, A. and Lanes, P. (2008) Accounting and Business Students' Approaches to Learning: A Longitudinal Study, *Journal of Accounting Education*, 26(1), pp. 188–201.

Ballantine, J. and Larres, P. (2009) Accounting Undergraduates' Perceptions of Cooperative Learning as a Model for Enhancing their Interpersonal and Communication Skills to Interface Successfully with the Professional Accountancy Education and Training, *Accounting Education: an international journal*, 18(2), pp. 387–402.

Barsky, N. and Catanack, A. (2000) Some Thoughts on the Demise of the Accounting Major and Suggested Strategies for Survival. Paper presented at the annual meetings of the American Accounting Association, Philadelphia, 3–5 August 2000.

Bay, D. and McKeage, K. (2006) Emotional Intelligences in Undergraduate Accounting Students: Preliminary Assessment, *Accounting Education: an international journal*, 15(3), pp. 439–454.

Berry, K. and Ulstad, I. (2005) Participation in Introductory Analytic Classes. Paper presented at the meetings of the Midwestern Business Administration Association, Chicago, 27–29 March 2005.

Blanthorne, C., Bhamornsiri, S. and Guinn, R. (2005) Are Technical Skills Still Important? *CPA Journal*, 75(3), pp. 64–65.

Blumenstyk, G. (2010) Saving the Life of the Mind, *Chronicle of Higher Education*, 5 March, pp. 1, 22.

Bok, D. (2005) *Our Underachieving Colleges: A Candid Look at How Much Students Learn and Why They Should be Learning More* (Princeton, NJ, Princeton University Press).

Boyce, G., Williams, S., Kelly, A. and Yee, H. (2001) Fostering Deep and Elaborative Learning and Generic (soft) Skill Development: The Strategic Use of Case Studies in Accounting Education, *Accounting Education: an international journal*, 10(1), pp. 37–60.

Breton, G. (1999) Some Empirical Evidence on the Superiority of the Problem-Based Learning (PBL) Method, *Accounting Education: an international journal*, 8(1), pp. 1–12.

Brokaw, A. and Merz, T. (2000) The Effects of Student Behavior and Preferred Learning Style on Performance, *Journal of Business Education*, 76(Spring), pp. 44–53.

Byrne, M. and Flood, B. (2004) Exploring the Conceptions of Learning of Accounting Students, *Accounting Education: an international journal*, 13(1), pp. 25–37.

Catanack, A. (2006) Using Pricewaterhouse Coopers' Value Reporting Framework to Introduce Technical Financial Reporting Topics in the Classroom. Paper presented at the Colloquium on Accounting Educational Change, Long Beach. CA, 20–22 October 2006.

Cayton, M. (2007) The Commodification of Wisdom, *Chronicle of Higher Education*, 13 July, pp. B16.

Carr, S., Chua, F. and Perera, H. (2006) University Accounting Curricula: The Perceptions of an Alumni Group, *Accounting Education: an international journal*, 15(2), pp. 359–376.

Christensen, T., Fogarty, T. and Wallace, W. (2002) The Association between Directional Accuracy of Self-Efficacy and Accounting Course Performance, *Issues in Accounting Education*, 17(1), pp. 1–26.

Cohen, P. (2009) In Tough Times. The Humanities Must Justify their Worth, *New York Times*, 24 February, pp. B17–B18.

Cottell, P. and Millis, B. (1993) Cooperative Learning Structures in the Instruction of Accounting, *Issues in Accounting Education*, 8(1), pp. 40–59.

Crumbley, D. L. and Smith, L. M. (2000) Using Short Stories to Teach Critical Thinking and Communication Skills to Tax Students, *Accounting Education: an international journal*, 9(3), pp. 291–296.

Dallimore, E., Platt, M. and Hertenstein, J. (2009) Class Participation in Accounting Courses: Relationship among Preparation, Frequency, Comfort, and Learning. Paper presented at the annual meetings of the American Accounting Association, New York, 3–6 August 2009.

Dean, R., Ferris, K. and Konstans, C. (1988) Occupational Reality Shock and Organizational Commitment: Evidence from the Accounting Profession, *Accounting, Organizations and Society*, 13(2), pp. 251–262.

DeLa Harpe, D., Radloff, A. and Wyber, J. (2000) Quality and Generic Professional Skills, *Quality in Higher Education*, 6(2), pp. 231–243.

Demski, J. (2007) Is Accounting an Academic Discipline? *Accounting Horizons*, 21(1), pp. 153–157.

Dziuban, C., Moshal, P. and Hartmen, J. (2005) Higher Education, Blended Learning and the Generations: Knowledge is Power-No More, in: J. Bourne and J. Moore (Eds) *Elements of Quality Online Education* (Needham, MA: Sloan Center).

Ewell, P. (2004) *General Education and the Assessment Reform Agenda* (Washington, DC: Association of America Colleges and Universities).

Fogarty, T. (2008) Time Tight, Learning Unattainable, *Accounting Education: an international Journal*, 17(3), pp. 1–3.

Francisco, W., Noland, T. and Kelly, J. A. (2003) Why Don't Students Major in Accounting? *Southern Business Journal*, 29(1), pp. 37–40.

Frecka, T., Morris, M. and Ramanan, R. (2004) Back to the Future: Implementing a Broad Economic, Inquiry-Based Approach to Accounting Education, *Journal of Education for Business*, 80(1), pp. 69–75.

Fusfeld, A. (2009) Business: The New Liberal Art, *Business Week*, 22 October, p. 46.

Gardiner, L. (1995) Why We Must Change: The Research Evidence, *Thought and Action*, 11(1), pp. 71–88.

Gardner, C., Milne, M., Stringer, C. and Whiting, R. (2005) Oral and Written Communication Apprehension in Accounting Students: Curriculum Impacts and Impacts on Academic Performance, *Accounting Education: an international journal*, 14(3), pp. 313–336.

Gardner, H. (1993) *Multiple Intelligences: The Theory in Practice* (New York: Basic Books).

Giroux, H. (1996) Is There a Place for Cultural Studies in Colleges of Education? *Counternarratives*, pp. 42–58 (New York: Routledge).

Glenn, D. (2010) 2 Colleges in Vermont, 2 Paths that Defy Tradition, *Chronicle of Higher Education*, 5 March, pp. 26–27.

Graham, W. (1939) Accounting Education: Ethics and Training, *The Accounting Review*, 14(2), pp. 258–265.

Gray, R., Bebbington, J. and McPhail, K. (1994) Teaching Ethics in Accounting and the Ethics of Teaching Accounting: Educating for Immorality and a Possible Case for Social and Environmental Accounting Education, *Accounting Education: an international journal*, 3(1), pp. 51–75.

Hall, M., Ramsey, A. and Raven, J. (2004) Changing the Learning Environment to Promote Deep Learning Approaches in First-Year Accounting Students, *Accounting Education: an international journal*, 13(4), pp. 489–501.

Hite, P. and Hasseldine, J. (2001) A Primer on Tax Education in the United States of America, *Accounting Education: an international journal*, 10(1), pp. 3–13.

Holtfreter, R. (2005) People in the Accounting Classroom: An Empirical Study to Evaluate how they are Affected by Active and Passive Learning Styles. Paper presented at the North American Accounting Society meetings, Chicago, 18–21 March 2005.

Howe, N., Strauss, W. and Matson, R. (2000) *Millennials Rising: The Next Great Generation* (New York: Vintage Books).

Hwang, N. R., Lui, G. and Tong, M. (2008) Cooperative Learning in a Passive Learning Environment: A Replication and Extension, *Issues in Accounting Education*, 23(1), pp. 67–75.

Jackling, B. (2005) Perceptions of the Learning Context and Learning Approaches: Implications for Quality Learning Outcomes in Accounting, *Accounting Education: an international journal*, 14(2), pp. 271–288.

James, S. (2000) Teaching Tax Principles and Policy: Comparing the Single Textbook and Wider Reading Approaches, *Accounting Education: an international journal*, 9(2), pp. 281–289.

Jenkins, R. (2009) Our Students Need More Practice in Actual Thinking, *Chronicle of Higher Education*, 27 March, pp. B18–19.

Johnson, D., Johnson, R. and Smith, K. (1998) Cooperative Learning Returns to College: What Evidence is there that it Works? *Change*, 30(4), pp. 26–35.

Jones, D. (2010) Revival of the Liberal Arts? *Chronicle of Higher Education*, 5 March, pp. 22–24.

Kealey, B., Holland, J. and Watson, M. (2005) Preliminary Evidence on the Association between Critical Thinking and Performance in Principles of Accounting, *Issues in Accounting Education*, 20(1), pp. 33–50.

Kelly, M., Davey, H. and Haigh, N. (1999) Contemporary Accounting Education and Society, *Accounting Education:* an international journal, 8(3), pp. 321–340.

King, P. and Baxter-Magolda, M. (1991) A Developmental Perspective on Learning, *Journal of College Student Development*, 40(5), pp. 599–609.

Knechel, W. (1992) Using the Case Method in Accounting Instruction, *Issues in Accounting Education*, 5(2), pp. 205–217.

Krause, M. (2005) Bridging the Gap between Professors and Practitioners, *CPA Journal*, 75(11), p. 64.

Kronman, A. (2007) *Education's End: Why our Colleges and Universities Have Given up on the Meaning of Life* (New Haven: Yale University Press).

Lavoie, D. and Rosman, A. (2007) Using Active Student-Centered Learning-Based Instructional Design to Develop Faculty and Improve Course Design, Delivery and Evaluation, *Issues in Accounting Education*, 22(1), pp. 105–118.

Lucas, U. (1997) The Nature of Accounting as a Discipline: Views from Accounting Education. Paper presented at the Interdisciplinary Perspectives in Accounting Meeting, Manchester, UK, 10–12 July 1997.

Martin, E., Evans, P. and Foster, E. (1995) The Use of Videos in the Teaching of Accounting, *Accounting Education: an international journal*, 4(1), pp. 77–86.

McDermott, R. (2006) Using an Accounting-Based Novel to Teach Cost and Managerial Accounting Courses. Paper presented at the Colloquium on Change in Accounting Education, Long Beach, CA, 20–22 October 2006.

McKibben, W. (1992) *The Age of Missing Information* (New York: Random House).

Melancon, B. (2002) A New Accounting Culture, *Journal of Accountancy*, 194(4), pp. 27–32.

Miller, T. and Stone, D. (2009) Public Speaking Apprehension (PSA), Motivation and Affect among Accounting Majors: A Proof-of-Concept Intervention, *Issues in Accounting Education*, 24(2), pp. 265–298.

Murray, N. (1997) Welcome to the Future: The Millennial Generation, *Journal of Career Planning and Employment*, 57(3), pp. 36–40.

Musgrave, L. (2006) The Real Reasons Students Can't Write. *Inside Higher Education*. Available at http://www.insidehighereducation.com/layout/set/print/views/2006/04/28/musgrave (accessed 9 July 2010).

Nussbaum, M. (2010) The Liberal Arts are not Elitist, *Chronicle of Higher Education*, 5 March, p. 54.

Ornstein, S. and Sankowsky, D. (1997) Clarify Communication to Enhance Learning: Establish the Dual-Focus Classroom, *Journal of Management Education*, 21(3), pp. 395–408.

Paisey, C. and Paisey, N. (2005) Improving Accounting Education through the Use of Action Research, *Journal of Accounting Education*, 23(1), pp. 1–14.

Paul, R. (2009) The State of Critical Thinking Today: The Need for a Substantive Concept of Critical Thinking. Available at http://www.criticalthinking.org/resources/articles (accessed 6 June 2010).

Phillips, B. and Phillips, F. (2007) Sink or Swim: Textbook Reading Behaviors of Introductory Accounting Students, *Issues in Accounting Education*, 22(1), pp. 21–44.

Phillips, F. (2006) Using Real-World Fraud Cases to Introduce Fundamental Financial Accounting Concepts. Paper presented at Colloquium on Change in Accounting Education, Long Beach, CA, 20–22 October 2006.

Pinsker, S. (2009) We Need the Liberal Arts Now More than Ever, in: M. Shapiro (Ed.) *The Irascible Professor*, Available at http://www.irascibleprofessor.com/comments-03-06-09.htm (accessed 4 May 2010).

Previts, G., Coffman, E. and Tondkar, R. (1993) Integrating Accounting History into Financial Accounting Courses, *Issues in Accounting Education*, 8(1), pp. 18–39.

PricewaterhouseCoopers. (2002) *Educating in the Public Trust* (New York: PricewaterhouseCoopers).

Proctor, T. (2006) Enriching a Business Degree with More Liberal Arts Courses: One School's Experience. Paper presented at the Colloquium on Change in Accounting Education, Long Beach, CA, 20–22 October 2006.

Ramsay, A., Haulon, D. and Smith, D. (2000) The Association between Cognitive Style and Accounting Students' Preference for Cooperative Learning: An Empirical Investigation, *Journal of Accounting Education*, 18(2), pp. 215–228.

Ratliff, R. (2006) Integrating Professionalism, Ethics, and Communication Skills into a Single Master's Level Accounting Course. Paper presented at Colloquium on Change in Accounting Education, Long Beach, CA, 20–22 October, 2006.

Ravenscroft, S., Buckless, F. and Hassall, T. (1999) Cooperative Learning-A Literature Guide, *Accounting Education: an international journal*, 8(1), pp. 163–176.

Schleifer, L. and Dull, R. (2009) Metacognition and Performance in the Accounting Classroom, *Issues in Accounting Education*, 24(3), pp. 339–367.

Segal, C. (2010) Chiseling Away at the Humanities, *Chronicle of Higher Education*, 5(2) March, pp. B8–B9.

Skousen, K. (1977) Accounting Education: The New Professionalism, *Journal of Accountancy*, 144(2), pp. 54–57.

Stocks, K., Stoddard, T. and Waters, M. (1992) Writing in the Accounting Curriculum: Guidelines for Professors, *Issues in Accounting Education*, 7(2), pp. 193–204.

Strassburger, J. (2010) For the Liberal Arts, Rhetoric is not Enough, *Chronicle of Higher Education*, 28 February, p. 46.

Subotnik, D. (1987) What Accounting Can Learn from Legal Education, *Issues in Accounting Education*, 2(2), pp. 313–324.

Svetlik, D. (2007) When the Academic World and the Real World Meets, *Thought and Action*, 23(1), pp. 47–69.

Swain, M. and Stout, D. (2000) Survey Evidence of Teacher Development Based on AECC Recommendations, *Journal of Accounting Education*, 18(1), pp. 99–113.

Thelin, J. (2007) Expectations and Reality in American Higher Education, *Thought and Action*, 23(1), pp. 59–70.

Ungar, S. (2010) 7 Major Misconceptions about the Liberal Arts, *Chronicle of Higher Education*, 5 March, p. 25.

Violette, G. and Pryor, C. (2005) The Importance of Educators and Coursework in Choosing an Accounting Career, *The CPA Journal*, 75(3), pp. 66–67.

Weisbuch, R. (2007) What's Liberal? And Why Arts? *Chronicle of Higher Education*, 24 August, pp. B1–B2.

Willitts, S. (2009) Will More Liberal Arts Courses Fix the Accounting Curriculum? Presented at the Ohio Regional Meetings of the American Accounting Association, Geneva, 5–7 May 2009.

Wilson, M. (2004) Teaching, Learning and Millennial Students, *New Directions for Student Services*, 106(4), pp. 59–71.

Wyatt, A. (2004) Accounting Professionalism: They Just Don't Get It!, *Accounting Horizons*, 18(1), pp. 45–54.

APPENDIX

A Classification of Source Material

Educational Philosophers or Writers

Arendt, H. (1971)
Argyris, C. and Schon, D. (1978)
Bok (2005)
Ewell (2004)
Gardner (1993)
Kronman (2007)
McKibben (1992)

Academics Offering Empirical Evidence

Arnold *et al.* (1999)
Ballantine *et al.* (2008)
Ballantine and Larres (2009)
Bay and McKeage (2006)
Berry and Ulstad (2005)
Bok, D. (2005)
Boyce *et al.* (2001)
Breton (1999)
Brokaw and Merz (2000)
Byrne and Flood (2004)
Christensen *et al.* (2002)
Cottell and Millis (1993)
Dallimore *et al.* (2009)
Dean *et al.* (1988)
DeLa Harpe *et al.* (2000)
Gardiner (1995)
Gardner *et al.* (2005)
Holtfreter (2005)
Howe *et al.* (2000)
Hwang *et al.* (2008)

Jackling (2005)
James (2000)
Johnson *et al.* (1998)
Kealey *et al.* (2005)
Lavoie and Rosman (2007)
Miller and Stone (2009)
Phillips and Phillips (2007)
Ramsey, Haulon and Smith (2000)
Schleifer and Doll (2009)
Swain and Stout (2000)

Academics Taking Normative Positions or Relating their Personal Experiences

Baldwin and Baker (2009)
Barsky and Catanack (2000)
Blanthorne *et al.* (2005)
Blumenstyk (2010)
Catanack (2006)
Cayton (2007)
Carr *et al.* (2006)
Crumbley and Smith (2000)
Demski (2007)
Dziuban *et al.* (2005)
Fogarty (2008)
Francisco *et al.* (2003)
Frecka *et al.* (2004)
Giroux (1996)
Graham (1939)
Gray *et al.* (1994)
Hall *et al.* (2004)
Hite and Hasseldine (2001)
Jenkins (2009)
Kelly *et al.* (1999)
King and Baxter-Magolda (1991)
Knechel (1992)
Krause (2005)
Lucas (1997)
Martin *et al.* (1995)
McDermott (2006)
Murray (1997)
Nussbaum (2010)
Ornstein and Sankowsky (1997)
Paisey and Paisey (2005)
Pinsker (2009)
Previts *et al.* (1993)
Proctor (2006)
Ratliff (2006)
Ravenscroft *et al.* (1999)
Skousen (1977)
Stocks *et al.* (1992)
Strassburger (2010)

Subotnik (1987)
Svetlik (2007)
Thelin (2007)
Ungar (2010)
Violette and Pryor (2005)
Weisbuck (2007)
Willitts (2009)
Wilson (2004)

Journalists not Reporting Empirical Data
Cohen (2009)
Fusfeld (2009)
Glenn (2010)
Jones (2010)
Musgrave (2006)
Segal (2010)

Practitioners not Reporting Empirical Data
Melancon (2002)
Wyatt (2004)

Organizations Offering Empirical Evidence
AASCB (2009)

Organizations or Commissions Providing Normative Positions
Accounting Educational Change Commission (1990)
Arthur Andersen *et al.* (1989)
Pricewaterhouse Coopers (2002)

University Accounting Curricula: The Perceptions of an Alumni Group

SHIRLEY CARR, FRANCES CHUA & HECTOR PERERA

Massey University, New Zealand

ABSTRACT *Many of the problems associated with accounting education could be due to at least two reasons: inadequate attention given to the design of accounting programmes, and the narrow view of stakeholder approach adopted in examining education issues. The existing literature mainly focuses on students' perception about issues such as teaching quality, alumni experience in major accounting firms, and so on. This paper deals with the design of accounting programmes, and proposes to ascertain the views of an important stakeholder group (i.e. alumni) on this issue. The findings of this study give credence to some of the generally held views, e.g. that it is no longer appropriate for tertiary education providers to adopt a one-size-fits-all approach. However, in some other areas, the findings represent a stark contrast to the views on certain issues promulgated by the professional bodies in New Zealand and overseas including the USA, (for example, the issue of appropriate proportions of accounting, business and liberal studies in an accounting programme). Notably, the respondents in general placed a low importance on auditing as part of an education programme. Further, in terms of the emphases that should be placed in an accounting programme, contrary to the endorsement in the literature, 'work experience' was not considered as important as other areas of emphasis, (e.g. global perspective, local perspective, professionalism and social and environmental perspective).*

Introduction

Accounting education has been under scrutiny particularly since the 1980s, by policy makers, educators, researchers, practitioners, and the public. In the wake of the recent financial failures in many countries where accountants were implicated (for example, Enron and WorldCom in the USA, Parmalat in Italy), attention has been directed again to accounting education. Previously, for example, in the USA, there were reports highlighting the decline in the quantity and quality of accounting students and deficiencies in the curriculum and pedagogy of accounting programmes, factors underlying the repeated calls for competency-based accounting programmes (e.g. AAA, 1986; Arthur Andersen & Co. *et al.*, 1989; AECC, 1990; IMA, 1994; and Albrecht and Sack, 2000).

Accounting degree programmes may be influenced specifically by the accreditation requirements of professional associations, and others may be more broadly shaped by the vested interests of parties such as business, professional bodies, advisory groups, alumni, higher education groups (university administrators, staff, and/or students), and society at large (see Stout *et al.*, 2004). However, as McInnis (2002, pp. 38–39) points out, 'the policy significance of universities asserting their role in curriculum design is critical to the development of foundational knowledge', as the curriculum is 'the glue that holds knowledge and the broader student experience together and enables the knowledge to be used effectively by the student'.

With the escalating demand for public accountability in the past decades, there has been increased support for a stakeholder approach incorporating perspectives of multiple interest groups in accounting curriculum design in order to enhance the quality of student learning. For example, the Association to Advance Collegiate Schools of Business (AACSB) advises accredited institutions not to operate in an isolated fashion when setting the learning goals for their programmes as external constituencies can inject expertise and perspectives into the process that will be unavailable if they operate alone (AACSB, 2006, p. 62).

However, in the literature the so-called stakeholder view has often tended to take a rather narrow approach, focusing mainly on students' perceptions about various other issues, for example, teaching quality of accounting programmes (Byrne and Flood, 2003), the 150-hour rule (Bierstaker *et al.*, 2004), and an alumni account of their Big 6 experience (Marxen, 1996).

This paper recognises that the different views about the important characteristics of an accounting curriculum should be taken into account in designing an accounting degree programme (see also Perera *et al.*, 2002), and presents the results of an empirical study aimed at ascertaining the views of one stakeholder group (namely, university alumni) on this issue.

Competency-based Educational Programmes

Like a trail blazer, the concerns expressed and calls for change made by several interest groups have set off a trend of accounting education reform internationally, with professional associations (e.g. AICPA, 1999; IFAC, 1998, 2003; IMA, 1994, 1996, 1999; IIA, 1999), academia (e.g. AAA, 1986; AECC, 1990), practitioners and even employers in the corporate sector (e.g. Arthur Andersen & Co. *et al.*, 1989),[1] aiming at producing competent accounting graduates who are able to add value to their professional work. 'Competency', according to the International Federation of Accountants (IFAC) Education Committee (1998, p. 1), is 'the ability to perform the tasks and roles expected of a professional accountant, both newly- qualified and experienced, to the standard expected by employers and the general public.' Subsumed in this are the knowledge, skills, and abilities (KSAs) essential to a competent professional accountant. Explicit definitions of these KSAs are provided by the AICPA's *Core Competency Framework for Entry into the Accounting Profession* (1999), which is a comprehensive framework regarding the essential attributes needed by entry-level accountants. It encompasses most of the earlier recommendations on programme design in accounting (Bolt-Lee and Foster, 2003). The framework identifies three areas of competency, namely, functional, personal and broad business-perspective. Accordingly, *functional competencies* include decision modelling, risk analysis, measurement, reporting, research; *personal competencies* include professional demeanour, problem-solving and decision- making, interaction, leadership, communication, and project management; and *broad business-perspective competencies* include strategic/critical thinking, industry/sector perspective, international/global perspective, resource management, legal/regulatory perspective, and marketing/client focus. Leveraging technology is common to all three competencies. As part of the reform process, tertiary institutions were prompted to rethink the form and content of their academic programmes (Kress, 2000).

The IFAC (2003) has managed to integrate two competence-based approaches to accounting education: a functional approach emphasising performance outcomes of the education and training process favoured in the UK and Australia, and a process approach focusing on capabilities such as knowledge, skills and professional values favoured in the USA. In New Zealand, the decision to implement a competency-based approach for professional admission followed a trend started in the USA by the Bedford Committee Report and the AECC recommendations (see Lothian and Marrian, 1992).

In Pursuit of an 'Ideal' Accounting Curriculum

In the two decades since the Bedford Report (AAA, 1986) recommended a major reorientation in accounting education to fit in with the contemporary business environment, accounting departments within the USA and beyond have made some attempts to introduce competency-based educational programmes. However, such structural changes, according to Albrecht and Sack (2000), are not significant and far from the 'ideal'.

The Accounting, Business and Liberal Components

Suggestions have been made that the narrow technicist approach in accounting education be replaced with a more conceptually based analytical approach so that students can learn *to become* professional accountants, not *to be* professional accountants. Accordingly, an 'ideal' accounting programme should include skills (communicative skills, intellectual skills and interpersonal skills), knowledge (general knowledge, organisational and business knowledge, and accounting knowledge), and professional orientation (an appreciation of the obligation of a professional) (AECC, 1990). The challenge for educators then is to offer students a high quality, broad, general, liberal education 'that delivers the traditional specialist accounting core in a challenging and intellectually-stimulating way, while at the same time offering an expanded scope of business and management-related subjects that fit the expanding scope of work being taken up by the accounting profession' (Parker, 2001, p. 445). In short, the knowledge-oriented educational system must give way to a process-oriented approach (AECC, 1990) where the purpose is to *educate* students rather than to *train* them. The overriding objective of curriculum design is, therefore, to create a base upon which continuous improvement can be built.

Accounting Sub-disciplines

Ideally, accounting knowledge should reflect accounting as an information development and communication process (AECC, 1990). Historically, it has been offered in the general form, which covers broad themes such as financial statement preparation, information development, and management decision-making, and a more specialised form, which offers advanced study in a number of accounting sub-disciplines such as financial accounting, management accounting, auditing, taxation, information systems and the like. The structure and sequencing of these courses along the line of elementary, intermediate and advanced levels help to reinforce how accounting information is identified, measured, communicated, and used to enhance the decision-making process.

However, there have been suggestions to change the norm of such offering (for instance, to move subjects such as taxation and auditing from the undergraduate curriculum to postgraduate study to make room for more trendy courses such as process improvement and risk management - see the views of Warren Allen, former IFAC Education Committee chairman, cited in Parker, 2001). Another suggestion has been to reduce topic overlaps by rationalising related subjects, and to allow for a broader scope by combining them, for example, management accounting to be re-oriented towards strategic management, and auditing to be combined with information systems or others (Parker, 2001, p. 444).

Business Disciplines

Given the rapid pace of change in the business environment, accountants also need to understand the environments in which they work (for instance, the external underlying forces, the internal workings of organisations, and the intricate interpersonal and group dynamics). In the light of the impact of (information) technology on client organisations and accounting practice, it is necessary for professional accountants to understand the 'complex interdependence between the profession and society' (AECC, 1990). Hence, the curriculum should cover courses designed to develop knowledge in the functional areas of business, the types of organisations, the rules regulating business and so on. It should also be broad enough to cover a raft of business courses such as finance, marketing, management, human resource management, business law, information systems, and other areas.

Liberal Component and Expected Competencies

It is generally believed that, in a broad-based general education, the liberal component can contribute significantly to the acquisition of higher-level professional skills such as intellectual, interpersonal and communication skills (IFAC, 2003). For example, it can help to expand a student's intellectual horizons, leading to better comprehension and tolerance of diverse ideas and experiences, and most important of all, 'lifelong learning'. Apart from learning the skills to use accounting tools and techniques, this component of the curriculum should be designed to address not only the subject matter but also the integration of knowledge from various disciplines so as to develop the students' capacities for inquiry, abstract logical thinking, critical analysis, problem-solving, communication, synthesis, and working effectively in groups (Arthur Andersen & Co. *et al.*, 1989; AECC, 1990). Various survey reports have emphasised that future professional accountants are expected to be both generalists and specialists (e.g. IMA, 1994; CIMA, 1998; ICAA, 1998).

This expanding role has seen the increasing importance of a raft of competencies, the top five of which as derived by AICPA (1999) are: communications skills, strategic and critical thinking skills, client and market focus, interpretation of converging information, and technological adeptness.

Programme Emphasis

Professional accounting education must not only emphasise the needed skills and knowledge, but it must also instil the ethical standards and the commitment of a professional (AAA, 1986, p. 179). A good professional education must raise the students' awareness of the flow of events in history, the different cultures, and the economic, political and social forces in the world (Arthur Andersen & Co. *et al.*, 1989). In addition, it should instil some international and multicultural knowledge in students (AECC, 1990) and develop their professional orientation—the ability to identify with the profession, to understand the ethical obligations of a professional person, and to inculcate a concern for individual needs and for the public interest.

However, Albrecht and Sack (2000) found that there was a lack of programme emphasis to incorporate the changing environment in accounting programmes in the USA. This was supported by Parker (2001) who observed that the lack could also be found in accounting programmes outside of the USA where only minor credit was being given for the broader-based business and management studies. Further, he suggested that the accounting curriculum could be 'productively re-energised through the incorporation of multidisciplinary perspectives brought to bear on accounting issues, the exposure of students to critiques of conventional wisdom and current policy and practice, and the incorporation of emerging issues such as environmental responsibility, performance auditing, and electronic commerce into accounting courses' (Parker, 2001, pp. 443–444).

A Minor Specialisation

Accounting degree programmes have been criticized for a lack of sufficient structural flexibility to accommodate guided electives or double majors that permit students to undertake studies in some other areas (for example, marketing, strategic, human resource and international management; organisational behaviour and organisational change—Albrecht and Sack, 2000). According to Holstrum and Hunton (1998), such flexibility will lead to the benefit of an interdisciplinary approach to accounting and business education eminently suited to the broadening scope of the accounting profession, the greater attractiveness of accounting and business programmes to the best students (Albrecht and Sack, 2000), and the re-energization and enhancement of educators.

The Accounting Degree Programme at Massey University

There is only one professional accounting body in New Zealand, that is, the New Zealand Institute of Chartered Accountants (NZICA, hereafter, 'the Institute').[2] It grants accreditation to accounting degree programmes that meet its academic requirements. In 1994, the Institute adopted a policy whereby the academic entry requirements for the accounting profession from 1996 onward, would include four years' equivalent full-time study and the completion of an undergraduate degree. These broadly based academic entry criteria represent a major departure from the former narrowly focused, prescriptive approach based on its *The Body of Knowledge* (NZSA, 1986). The new requirements provide New Zealand tertiary institutions with considerable flexibility in developing their accounting degree programmes and an opportunity for differentiation. It also recognises that accounting graduates need to have a broad general education comprising not only business, accounting and liberal programmes, but also the attributes and skills suited for the marketplace.

In 1995, after a comprehensive review on the stakeholders' viewpoints regarding the existing programme, the Department offered a new four-year accounting degree programme (Porter and Carr, 1999), a somewhat modified version of the Department's 'ideal'. It was quite similar to the new admissions requirements of the Institute. In this programme, accounting graduates are expected to possess an in-depth knowledge of the 'basics' of accounting and business-related subjects, and to achieve the desired learning outcomes. It comprises 35–40% accounting-based subjects, 35–40% general business subjects, and 20–30% liberal education. Greater specialisation in accounting (and its sub-disciplines) is to be provided in the fourth (and subsequent) year(s) of the programme.

The 35–40% accounting courses are to include accounting fundamentals serving as introductory courses in financial accounting, management accounting, and accounting systems in organisations; principles of taxation and auditing; and specialisation in advanced accounting areas. The 35–40% business-related courses include subjects related to business organisation, management, business law, marketing, finance, economics, and business communications. The liberal studies component has been introduced with the aim to relax the prescriptive nature of previous accounting programmes and to provide accounting students with a broader knowledge base; hence, the 20–30% component can be made up from arts, humanities, natural sciences, applied sciences and social sciences. In addition to the knowledge-based components and the development of traditional technical skills, the programme aims to inculcate a set of 'higher level' or 'professional' skills in the graduates. This expanded set of competencies include the abilities to communicate both in writing and verbally; demonstrate ethical behaviour; research, analyse and synthesise information; work in a team and where necessary take a leadership role; organise themselves, peers and subordinates to achieve goals within deadlines; integrate their knowledge in various accounting sub-disciplines to arrive at informed accounting judgements in a range of business contexts; and understand and work with people from a range of other business disciplines within an organisational context (ICANZ, 2000).

In implementing a structured four-year programme, the three-year undergraduate degree allowed for 60 or more points (that is, four or five papers) as liberal electives. It was intended that, through course advice sessions, students would be encouraged to use these electives to complete a minor concentration in the social sciences or humanities (Carr and Mathews, 2004, p. 99).

Alumni as an Important Stakeholder Group

Researchers identify alumni as an important stakeholder group (e.g. Stout *et al.*, 2004; Stout and West, 2004)[3] who can provide valuable insights into strengths and weaknesses of their educational experience, which will benefit the design of the programmes. Indeed, the alumni of an educational institution are in a unique position to be able to provide valuable input into the design of the educational programmes, in terms of feedback on the current programmes and suggestions for improvement. On the one hand, they are fully aware of the content and delivery of the current degree programme, as they have successfully completed it. On the other hand, as they are presumably in employment, and they are experiencing the 'real world' accounting and related issues, they are able to assess the relevance of the educational programme to their professional work.

Alumni perceptions can act as filters by attaching meaning to the experiences they have had while at the same time emphasising a concern for the appropriateness of the programmes in the workplace. Perception is therefore 'both a product of the environment and a potential determinant of future interactions and outcomes' (Mayhew *et al.*, 2005, p. 392).

Environmental forces, both external and internal, led to significant changes in accounting degree programmes in New Zealand in the mid-1990s. With graduates completing these new degree programmes in the late-1990s onward, it is appropriate to assess the usefulness of the programmes from the perceptions of the alumni. In terms of curriculum design, alumni perception is an under-explored perspective that could add value to curriculum design. This, in turn, will help to provide some insights into whether the current CA-accredited degree provides accounting graduates with sufficient theoretical and practical education to function at the level the business world expects.

Research Design

A questionnaire[4] was used to determine whether there is alumni support for the current trends towards an increased focus on areas such as information technology, communication and ethics in accounting programmes and whether the alumni group's perceptions of accounting curricula align with the espoused views of the accounting education reformers.

Sample Selection

Participants for this study were selected on the basis that they had graduated with a Bachelor of Business Studies (BBS) degree majoring in Accountancy between the years 1995 and 2003. With the support and assistance of the University Office of Development and Alumni, copies of the questionnaire and a covering letter were sent to each of the identified graduates for whom the Office held a New Zealand address. For privacy reasons, rather than release the addresses of the selected alumni, the University Office took responsibility for both the original and follow-up mailings. The survey instrument contained no means by which individual respondents could be identified.

Copies of the survey instrument and postage-paid return envelopes were mailed to the entire population of 920 registered graduates who met the criteria and were contactable. A follow-up was conducted 35 days later.

Research Instrument

The survey instrument was adapted from one used to examine employers' expectations of university accounting programmes (Perera *et al.*, 2002). The instrument solicited respondents' demographic data and information regarding their perceptions of the importance of accounting programme characteristics. In particular, respondents' views on the proportions for the accounting, business and liberal components and their preferred weightings for the sub-disciplines/disciplines within these components were sought. Respondents were also asked on what perspective (for example, global, professional and so on) a programme should place emphasis and whether specialisations within a programme were desirable. Finally, the respondents' views on competencies expected of an accounting graduate were ascertained.

Response Rate

Twenty-two questionnaires were returned because of having incorrect addresses. A total of 237 responses were received, 236 of which were usable, giving a response rate of 26.4%. It has been reported that mail surveys are not the most effective response generators (Yu and Cooper, 1983).

The low response rate is a limitation of this study. Non-response bias can result from a low response rate and/or the missing responses affecting the conclusions about the variables being examined in the study. The anonymity of the survey responses combined with the limited data received initially about the sample population (due to privacy issues surrounding the database), made testing for non-response bias difficult.

Results

Respondents' Demographic Data and Employment Profiles

The age distribution of the survey respondents is shown in Table 1. As the graduating years 1995–2003 were used to identify the sample population, it is perhaps not surprising that only 3% of the respondents were in the older age bracket and that the majority (52.2%) of the respondents were under 34 years old. Of the 110 employed in accounting firms, 20.9%

Table 1. Demographics of respondents

	Total (n = 236) Frequency	Percentage
Gender		
Female	150	63.6
Male	86	36.4
Age		
Under 25	32	13.6
25–34	91	38.6
35–44	68	28.8
45–54	38	16.1
Over 54	7	3.0
Professional qualification		
ICANZ—CA	101	42.8
ICANZ—AT	19	8.1
ICANZ—ACA	3	1.3
ICANZ provisional member	28	11.9
Other[a]	4	1.7
None	84	35.6
Qualification		
BBS (Accountancy)	236	100.0
PG Diploma in Professional Accounting	42	17.8
Diploma in Business Studies	9	3.8
PG Diploma of Accountancy	1	0.4
BBS (Hons) in Accountancy	2	0.8
Other(s)	21	8.9
No response	1	0.4
Length current employment		
<2 years	57	24.2
2 to < 4 years	77	32.6
4 to < 6 years	35	14.8
6 to < 8 years	20	8.5
8 to < 10 years	10	4.2
10 to < 20 years	15	6.4
> 20 years	4	1.7
Self-employed	9	3.8
No response	9	3.8
Primary area of responsibility		
Business Advisory Services	52	22.0
Tax	37	15.7
A combination of areas	33	14.0
Auditing	14	5.9
Personnel and/or Administration	6	2.5
Other	86	36.4
No response	8	3.4

[a]Three of these respondents also had an ICANZ qualification

were 'under 25' years while only 5.9% of those employed in non-accounting firms were 'under 25' years. One explanation for this may be that full membership of the CA College of the Institute requires one year of general and two years of specified work experience in an Institute-Approved Training Organisation (ATO). The finding that a higher number of respondents employed in accounting firms were still at the provisional stage of their professional membership also supports this explanation. As perhaps expected, the majority of the respondents with the Accounting Technician (AT) designation were working for accounting firms as well. The finding that there were more CA-qualified respondents working in non-accounting firms (43.7%) than in accounting firms (42.7%) gives some support to the argument often promulgated by the professional bodies that the CA qualification has currency for careers in commerce, industry and the public sector as well as public practice. Seventy-five of the respondents (32%) had completed tertiary qualifications in addition to a BBS which probably reflects the introduction of a four-year tertiary education requirement for professional membership for those commencing their study in 1996 or later. Females had a higher representation (65.6%) in the survey sample population than they currently have in the Institute where their representation is increasing but is still only 34%.

The employment of the sample population was evenly distributed between accounting firms (47%) and non-accounting firms (50%). The seven respondents unemployed at the time the survey was conducted were female and their comments indicated that, for most of them, their current employment status was for family reasons and only temporary.

The cohort not employed in accounting firms was employed in a diverse range of firm types including education, public sector (including Inland Revenue Departments, health sector, local government, law enforcement and Government Audit Offices), construction, financial advising, media, manufacturing, banking, retailing, advertising, meat industry, forestry, wine, insurance, trust, consulting, information technology, travel, service section, and oil and gas. Since the survey participants were narrowed down to the graduating years 1995–2003, those who had been working for more than 10 years (there were 19 in total) had either been mature students and/or had studied part-time. The responses to the question 'what is your primary area of responsibility' were more diverse from those employed in the non-accounting firms.

The employment groupings of this survey's respondents provided an opportunity to examine whether work experience is likely to shape graduates' perceptions of their accounting education programme.

Programme Characteristics

The mean responses for the proportions of accounting, business and liberal papers that should be included in a four-year academic programme were approximately 54% accounting, 31% business, and 15% liberal (see Table 2). Notably, there was very little difference between the mean responses of the accounting firm and non-accounting firm cohorts.

Ranking the traditional accounting sub-disciplines based on the mean of the percentages assigned to them by the respondents, resulted in financial accounting and management accounting topping the list in that order. The 'not in accounting firm' group concurred with this order of ranking (with mean percentages of 23.6%, 20% and 14.5% for financial accounting, management accounting and taxation respectively). However, the respondents employed in accounting firms, ranked taxation marginally ahead of management accounting. The mean percentages for this cohort (21.4% for financial accounting, 18.7% for taxation and 17.2% for the management accounting component) were quite markedly different from those of the cohort not employed in accounting firms.

Table 2. Composition of accounting programmes: accounting, and business components

		Average percentage [a]		
Proportions	Total $n = 233$[b]	Not in accounting firm	In accounting firm	Unemployed
Within programme	($n = 233$)	($n = 117$)	($n = 109$)	($n = 7$)
Accounting papers	53.8	53.6	53.4	62.1
Business papers	31.3	31.6	31.4	27.1
Liberal papers	14.9	14.8	15.2	10.7
Within accounting component	($n = 233$)	($n = 118$)	($n = 108$)	($n = 7$)
Financial accounting	22.6	14.0	14.3	14.3
Management accounting	18.5	12.0	12.4	12.5
Taxation	16.5	14.2	14.1	15.7
Accounting information systems	14.2	23.6	21.4	25.0
Finance	14.2	20.0	17.2	12.1
Auditing	12.2	14.5	18.7	17.5
Other	1.8	1.7	1.9	2.9
Within business component	($n = 233$)	($n = 118$)	($n = 108$)	($n = 7$)
Business law	20.1	19.8	20.2	22.9
Information systems	18.9	15.1	17.0	13.0
Management	18.1	13.9	14.1	11.7
Economics	15.9	18.9	18.6	21.4
Human resource management	13.9	18.8	17.4	16.4
Marketing	11.8	11.8	11.7	11.7
Other	1.5	1.7	1.3	2.9

[a]Columns may not sum to 100% due to rounding.
[b]Due to no responses

Regarding the proportions for different disciplines within the business component of a programme, with the exception of economics, the average percentages for sub-disciplines were not very different between the two main employment groups. The respondents not employed in an accounting firm considered economics should be a smaller component of the programme. Ethics/governance; communication and business writing skills; business mathematics/statistics; and, strategic planning were variously identified in the 'other' category as additional subject areas to be included in the business component of an accounting degree programme.

Table 3 provides an overall summary of the respondents' preferences for the liberal component of an accounting programme, and for where emphasis should be placed in a programme. The respondents indicated their preferences by assigning '1' for their first preference, '2' for the second preference, and so on. They could indicate an equal preference for more than one item and have no preference for other items if they considered them relatively unimportant. For this reason, how frequently a liberal component was chosen has to be considered in conjunction with the averaged rankings.

In keeping with the perceived importance of systems papers generally, computer technology was chosen by most respondents (in both the accounting and non-accounting firm groups) and was the 'most preferred' subject for the liberal component. The frequencies and means for statistics and English suggest all respondents considered these to be important 'liberal' subjects as well. It is noteworthy that 15 respondents adopted a liberal attitude

Table 3. Composition of accounting programmes: liberal component

	Total (n = 236)		Not in accounting firm (n = 119)		In accounting firm (n = 110)		Unemployed (n = 7)	
	Freq.	Avg. ranking	Freq.	Avg. ranking	Freq.	Avg. ranking	Freq.	Avg. ranking
Preferences for liberal component								
Computer technology	216	1.9	111	2.0	100	1.9	5	1.6
Statistics	209	3.1	110	3.1	93	2.9	6	4.7
English	201	3.4	102	3.4	93	3.4	6	4.3
Psychology	194	3.9	104	3.9	84	4.0	6	3.5
Pure mathematics	184	4.7	98	4.9	81	4.3	5	7.8
Sociology	182	4.9	99	4.7	78	5.1	5	4.4
Philosophy	178	5.3	94	5.1	79	5.4	5	6.0
Modern languages (other than English)	177	5.7	93	5.6	78	6.0	6	4.2
History	173	6.0	92	5.8	76	6.3	5	6.2
Agriculture	168	5.1	83	5.7	80	4.6	5	4.2
Natural sciences	166	6.0	86	5.9	75	6.1	5	7.8
Other	15	4.8	8	5.5	6	2.7	1	12.0
No preference	9		2		7		0	
Preferences for emphasis								
Global perspective	227	2.8	114	2.4	106	3.2	7	2.9
Local perspective	231	1.8	115	1.8	109	1.9	7	2.1
Professionalism	230	2.0	116	2.1	107	2.0	7	2.0
Social and environmental perspectives	213	3.5	107	3.4	99	3.6	7	3.6
Work experience	219	2.8	109	3.0	103	2.6	7	2.0
Other	12	2.6	4	3.5	7	1.6	1	6.0
No preference	0		0		0		0	

to this part of the programme; they followed up with comments such as 'student's choice', 'any subject that challenges our thinking and isn't business' 'liberal means personal choice', 'creative arts' and 'classics/geography'. Clearly, these respondents considered this should be a more 'liberating' part of the programme rather than merely covering specific 'soft' skills.

As to what emphasis should be placed on a programme, 'local perspective', 'professionalism' and 'global perspective' were chosen by 98%, 97.5% and 96% of the respondents respectively. Interestingly, 'work experience' was ranked slightly ahead of 'global perspective' by those in accounting firms, whereas 'global perspective' was ranked third by those not in accounting firms. Although the 'social and environmental perspectives' option was selected by 90% of the respondents, it had the lowest frequency score which, combined with a preference mean of 3.5, made it clearly the least important area of emphasis.

With the exception of 'group interaction' and 'leadership', the various competencies expected of an accounting graduate were very similar for both employment groups. Even the differences in averaged rankings for 'group interaction' and 'leadership' were not large. Nonetheless, 'applying accounting techniques' was the most strongly supported of the competencies listed for an accounting graduate by the groups in the study; with 'Communication (oral, written and listening)' a very close second. The remaining listed competencies were ranked in the following order by the sample population in total: problem- solving (3.2); applying computer technology (3.4); critical thinking (3.4); time management (3.9); problem setting/identification (4.1); group interaction (4.2); and, leadership was last with a mean of 5.5 (Table 4).

Table 5 shows that 52% of the respondents (122) considered a minor specialisation within the accounting programme to be important, the majority of whom (57%) suggested it should be an information systems minor. The support for a specialisation, and for an information system one in particular, came mainly from the respondents who were not employed in accounting firms. 'A computer science minor' was ranked fourth behind the 'a non-business related minor' and 'a minor that is not business or computer-related' options. Although only 11.5% of the respondents chose these two latter options, their support suggests they were opting for a minor that gave more 'breadth' to an accounting programme.

Analysis and Discussion

Programme Composition

The findings of this study with regard to the accounting, business and liberal percentages for a four-year accounting programme contrast quite markedly with the percentages promulgated by professional bodies both in New Zealand and overseas. For academic accreditation purposes, the Institute requires the percentages 35–40% accounting, 35–40% business, and 20–30% liberal to be met in a four-year programme of study.[1] The AICPA (1988) proposed structure was for 17–27% accounting education, 23–33% business education and 40–53% general education. The alumni participating in this study placed greater emphasis on accounting education with the percentage ranging

Table 4. Competencies expected of accounting graduates

	Total ($n = 236$)		Not in accounting firm ($n = 119$)		In accounting firm ($n = 110$)		Unemployed ($n = 7$)	
	Freq.	Avg. ranking	Freq.	Avg. ranking	Freq.	Avg. ranking	Freq.	Avg. ranking
Communication (oral, written and listening)	233	2.3	117	2.2	109	2.5	7	2.3
Applying accounting techniques	231	1.9	116	2.0	108	1.9	7	2.1
Problem-solving	231	3.2	116	3.1	108	3.3	7	2.9
Critical thinking	227	3.4	116	3.4	105	3.3	6	3.8
Applying computer technology	225	3.4	113	3.3	105	3.6	7	3.4
Group interaction	223	4.2	113	3.9	104	4.5	6	4.7
Problem setting/identification	223	4.1	114	4.0	103	4.1	6	3.8
Time management	222	3.9	112	3.9	103	3.9	7	4.4
Leadership	213	5.5	108	5.2	99	5.9	6	6.2
Other	10	4.3	5	5.6	4	1.3	1	10.0
No preference	1		1		0		0	

Table 5. Importance and areas for minor specialisations

	Total	Not in accounting firm	In accounting firm	Unemployed
Are minor specialisations important?	Frequency	Frequency	Frequency	Frequency
Yes	122	68	50	4
No	110	49	58	3
No response	4	2	2	0
Total	236	119	110	7
A minor specialisation in				
Information systems	69	40	25	4
Non-business related	14	6	8	
Minor that is not business or computer-related	14	7	7	
Computer science	12	7	5	
Combination of above	9	5	4	
Other (business-related minor)	2	2		
No preference	2	1	1	
Total	122	68	50	4

from 20–80% (mean of 53.8%), less on business education with a range of 10–68% (mean of 31.3%) and less on liberal education with a range of 0–40% (mean of 14.9%). Furthermore, there was very little difference between the mean percentages of the two main employment groups. None the less, these findings support the literature in recognising that there is a need for all three components in an accounting programme.

Financial accounting has traditionally been considered the most important sub-discipline in the accounting component and this view was endorsed by the respondents in this study. Management accounting also received considerable support from the respondents overall but especially from those not employed in accounting firms. However, the importance the New Zealand professional body places on auditing in its four-year tertiary education requirements contrasts with this study's results and the literature (see for example, Andon and Free, 1999/2000; AICPA, 1988; Albrecht and Sack, 2000). The Institute's academic entry requirements stipulate that students must have completed, to an advanced level, at least two of the three areas of financial accounting, management accounting, and auditing and yet auditing was ranked the least important sub-discipline by the respondents in this study. The low importance placed on auditing by the respondents perhaps reflects the argument that is frequently raised in the literature (e.g. Allen, 1999/2000), namely, that auditing should be part of the professional/employment training programme rather than a component of tertiary education programmes. Furthermore, there was very little difference in the responses to the importance of auditing question between the accounting and non-accounting cohorts.

An accounting information system can be viewed as a specialised information system and indeed traditionally the 'financials' have been a (sub) system coming under the bigger umbrella of an enterprise-wide or management information system. If the information systems responses of this survey (which were split between the accounting and business components) are interpreted using this big umbrella approach, there is compelling evidence of its importance within an accounting programme. As a single disciplinary area, these findings suggest it should comprise the largest portion of the programme, a finding that is consistent with the emphasis placed on information systems by reports such as the White Paper (Arthur Andersen & Co. *et al.*, 1989), Bedford Committee Report (AAA, 1986), and Albrecht and Sack (2000). However, the academic entry requirements of the Institute do not reflect the same level of emphasis on information systems. Information systems are just one of six areas that a student can elect to take to a more advanced level: the only compulsion is to take 'Information Technology' to at least an intermediate level.[6]

The different responses of the accounting and non-accounting firm groups to the question of what weighting financial accounting, management accounting, taxation, and economics should be given in an accounting programme are perhaps not surprising given the recent changes in the market for accounting services. As Reckers (1995) points out, tertiary accounting educators no longer operate in a sellers' market with public accounting firms the one dominant consumer of their product; the market has changed, and is changing. There are ramifications for accounting educators in that not only are they facing new demands from old players but they are also facing new players who, with an expanding share of the market, demand attention. Thus our findings give some credence to the argument that it is no longer appropriate for tertiary education providers to adopt a one-size-fits all approach (Reckers, 1995; Albrecht and Sack, 2000). While the more traditional technical area of taxation is still of some importance to the alumni employed in accounting firms, and there is evidence that economics is also important, neither of these areas are of the same importance to the alumni in non-accounting firm employment. Management accounting is of particular importance to this latter alumni group.

The findings in this study regarding preferred liberal subjects suggest there is strong alumni support for having computer technology in the liberal component in an accounting programme. This is in accord with the literature (e.g. Marquardt and Berger, 2000; Parker, 2001). The subject computer technology was chosen by 92% of the respondents and was their 'most preferred' liberal subject with a mean preference of 1.9. Furthermore, the selection of statistics by 209 respondents (mean ranking 3.1) and English by 201 respondents (mean ranking 3.4) as preferred subjects for liberal study provides some support for the view that numeracy and literacy skills are important. Interestingly, psychology, chosen by 82% of the respondents and with a mean of 3.9, also had considerable support as the fourth highest ranked liberal subject. There was further evidence that the liberal component should be 'liberating' and not just an opportunity to enhance the 'softer' skills, in the respondents' comments such as 'student's choice', 'any subject that challenges our thinking and isn't business', 'liberal means personal choice', 'creative arts' and 'classics/geography'.

Emphasis

Contrary to the endorsement work experience receives in the literature (see, for example, Albrecht and Sack, 2000) it was not considered as important as other areas for emphasis (it was selected by 218 respondents with a mean ranking of 2.8). The findings indicate 'local perspective (e.g. professional standards and statutory requirements') and 'professionalism (e.g. professional judgement and ethical awareness') are the most important emphases for an accounting programme. No doubt, the recent adoption of International Financial Reporting Standards (IFRSs) in New Zealand (as well as in many other countries) will blur the distinction between a 'global' and 'local' perspective made in this study. It could also be assumed that recent accounting scandals have reflected badly on many of the respondents through their professional affiliations. Certainly, the responses appear to support the calls for reinforcement of professional judgment and ethical awareness in accounting education programmes.

Competencies

'Applying accounting techniques' and 'communication (oral, written and listening)' were the two competencies that almost all the respondents (231 and 233 respectively) expected an accounting graduate to have. The latter finding provides support for the generally held view that good communication skills are important. Problem solving was also selected by 231 respondents but the importance they placed on it (a mean of 3.2) was less than that placed on the former two competencies, which had means of 1.9 and 2.3 respectively. However, what was particularly noteworthy about the results in this part of the study was the greater importance the respondents who worked for local accounting firms placed on all the listed competencies compared to the importance the rest of the respondents placed on them. The responses to the competency question by this particular group of alumni may reflect a greater autonomy and empowerment in their employment because of the relatively small size of local accounting firms in New Zealand. If this is the case, the implications for accounting education are that students aiming for, or deciding on, this particular career path may require a higher level of achievement and a more comprehensive set of competencies than any other student group.

Specialisation

More than half the respondents (52%) supported the notion of being able to include minor specialisations in accounting degree programmes. However, their support was primarily for an information systems minor; not the range of business areas cited by Albrecht and Sack, 2000. Indeed, a business-related area outside of information systems was the least favoured area for a minor specialisation.

Conclusion

The need for accounting programmes to take a value-adding, stakeholder approach has been highlighted in most major reports that address the current problems of accounting education. Pressures from bodies such as IFAC and AACSB to have internationally recognised standards for accounting education programmes are affecting countries like New Zealand and have further reinforced the need to move away from a purely functional approach to a process approach focusing on designing a competency-based programme. However, the alumni's perspective on programmes has tended to receive less attention in the so-called stakeholders' approach than that given to some other interested parties. Taking a stakeholders' approach, this study proposed to ascertain the views of a university alumni group on the design of an accounting programme.

The findings of this study give credence to some of the generally held views, e.g. that it is no longer appropriate for tertiary education providers to adopt a one-size-fits-all approach. However, in some other areas, the findings represent a stark contrast to the views on certain issues promulgated by the professional bodies in New Zealand and overseas including the USA, for example, the issue of appropriate proportions of accounting, business and liberal studies in an accounting programme. Notably, the respondents in general placed a low importance on auditing as part of an education programme. Furthermore, in terms of the emphases that should be placed in an accounting programme, contrary to the endorsement in the literature, 'work experience' was not considered as important as other areas of emphasis, e.g. global perspective, local perspective, professionalism and social and environmental perspective.

The findings also indicate that, within a particular stakeholder group such as the alumni, the demands may differ. None the less, it is important that all 'voices' including that of the alumni are listened to and, where appropriate, responded to. The reflections of an alumni group provide particularly valuable feedback not only because they have successfully completed the programme being examined but also because they have the advantage of viewing it from a 'real world' perspective. It should be mentioned that, while recognising the importance of stakeholders in designing accounting programmes, it is clear that a programme's alumni cannot be the sole arbiter in this matter. Indeed, educators adopting a value-adding approach need to cast the net for a stakeholders' perspective as widely as possible to enhance the richness of the data they collect. Certainly, the paper draws attention to the fact that the issues involved are much more complicated than simply relying on the market or a particular group in the market for a solution.

The reality is that an accounting education programme and its curriculum will always be contested because of the complex interaction of all interested parties, its political nature, as well as educational matter. Questions need to be asked and possible alternatives explored. As Scott (1999, p. 193) points out: 'Good service provision does not necessarily mean "doing everything the customer wants"'.

Notes

[1]See Palmer (2004) for a history of competency studies in accounting.

[2]Prior to 1996, it was called the New Zealand Society of Accountants (NZSA). In 1996, it was renamed the Institute of Chartered Accountants of New Zealand (ICANZ). In August 2005, it underwent another name change and has since been known as the New Zealand Institute of Chartered Accountants (NZICA).

[3]Other stakeholder groups they have identified include Advisory Council, Business and AICPA, Staff, University and Society.

[4]The questionnaire used in this study is available on request from the corresponding author.

[5]The requirement for the four-year programme of study to meet the specified percentages is waived if the four-year programme includes an honours degree or a post-graduate qualification in accounting, or the student completes two or more bachelor's degrees.

[6]The Institute's Admissions Policy (2005) states that students must cover:

1. Four "advanced" elective topics from financial accounting, management accounting, auditing, taxation, business finance/treasury and accounting information systems, including at least two from financial accounting, management accounting and auditing.
2. Compulsory topics including:
   i. all the accounting sub-disciplines of financial accounting, management accounting, auditing, taxation and business finance/treasury, either as part of the four advanced electives or at a lower level, within their four year programmes; and
   ii. the five business-related topics economics (macro and micro), organisational management, quantitative methods/statistics at least at introductory level; and, information technology and commercial law (including the foundations of business law, contract law, and the law of entity structure) at least at intermediate level.

References

AACSB International (The Association to Advance Collegiate Schools of Business) (2006) *Eligibility Procedures and Accreditation Standards for Business Accreditation* (revised 1 January 2006) (Tampa, FL: AACSB). http://www.aacsb.edu

Accounting Education Change Commission (AECC) (1990) Objectives of education for accountants: position statement number one, *Issues in Accounting Education*, 5(2), pp. 307–312.

Albrecht, S. W. and Sack, R. J. (2000) *Accounting Educators: Charting the Course Through a Perilous Future*, Accounting Education Series Volume No. 16 (Sarasota, FL: American Accounting Association).

Allen, W. (1999/2000) The future of accounting education, *Pacific Accounting Review*, 11(2), pp. 1–7.

American Accounting Association (AAA) (1986) Committee on the Future Structure, Content and Scope of Accounting Education (The Bedford Committee) (1986) Future accounting education: preparing for the expanded profession, *Issues in Accounting Education*, 1(1), pp. 168–195.

American Institute of Certified Public Accountants (AICPA) Education Executive Committee (1988) *Education Requirements for Entry into the Accounting Profession* (Second Edition) (Reissueance and update of the 1977 Albers Report) (New York, NY: AICPA).

American Institute of Certified Public Accountants (AICPA) (1999) AICPA Core *Competency Framework for Entry into the Accounting Profession* (New York: AICPA). Available at http://www.aicpa.org/edu/corecomp.htm

Andon, P. and Free, C. (1999/2000) The Big-5 in new millennium: the transition to multidisciplinary service provision, *Pacific Accounting Review*, 11(2), pp. 9–21.

Arthur Andersen & Co., Arthur Young, Coopers & Lybrand, Deloitte Haskins & Sells, Ernst & Whinney, Peat Marwick Main & Co. Price Waterhouse, and Touche Ross (The Big-8) (1989) *Perspectives on Education: Capabilities for Success in the Accounting Profession* (The White Paper). New York.

Bierstaker, J. L. *et al.* (2004) Accounting majors' perceptions regarding the 150-hour rule, *Issues in Accounting Education*, 19(2), pp. 211–227.

Bolt-Lee, C. and Foster, S. D. (2003) The core competency framework: a new element in the continuing call for accounting change in the United States, *Accounting Education: an international journal*, 13(1), pp. 33–47.

Byrne, M. and Flood, B. (2003) Assessing the teaching quality of accounting programmes: an evaluation of the course experience questionnaire, *Assessment & Evaluation in Higher Education*, 28(2), pp. 135–145.

Carr, S. and Mathews, M. R. (2004) Accounting curriculum change and iterative programme development: a case study, *Accounting Education: an international journal*, 13(Supplement 1), pp. 91–116.

Chartered Institute of Management Accountants (CIMA) (1998) The changing role of the management accountant and its implications for qualification development, *Management Accounting*, 76(8), pp. 68–69.

Holstrum, G. L. and Hunton, J. E. (1998) New forms of assurance services for new forms of information: the global challenge for accounting educators, *The International Journal of Accounting*, 33(3), pp. 347–358.

Institute of Chartered Accountants in Australia (ICAA) (1998) *The Vision 2020 Taskforce Report: Chartered Accountancy in the Next Century—Radical Change or Diminished Influence?* (Sydney: ICAA).

Institute of Chartered Accountants of New Zealand (ICANZ) (2000) *Admissions Policy: Academic Component, CA College.* (Wellington, New Zealand: ICANZ).

Institute of Internal Auditors (IIA) (1999) *Competency Work for Internal Auditors* (Altamonte Springs, FL: IIA).

Institute of Management Accountants (IMA) (1994) *What Corporate America Wants in Entry-level Accountants: Executive Summary* (with the Financial Executives Institute) (Montvale, NJ: IMA).

Institute of Management Accountants (IMA) (1996) *The 1996 Practice Analysis of Management Accounting* (Montvale, NJ: IMA).

Institute of Management Accountants (IMA) (1999) *The 1999 Practice Analysis of Management Accounting* (Montvale, NJ: IMA).

International Federation of Accountants (IFAC) (1998) *Competence-Based Approaches to the Professional Preparation of Accountants* (New York: IFAC).

International Federation of Accountants (IFAC) (2003) *Towards Competent Professional Accountants* (New York: IFAC), available at http://www.ifac.org/store

Kress, G. (2000) A curriculum for the future, *Cambridge Journal of Education*, 30(1), pp. 133–145.

Lothian, N. and Marrian, I. (1992) *New Zealand Society of Accountants International Review of Admissions Policy* (Wellington: NZSA).

Marquardt, M. and Berger, N. O. (2000) *Global Leaders for the 21st Century* (New York: State University of New York Press).

Marxen, D. E. (1996) The big 6 experience: a retrospective account by alumni, *Accounting Horizons*, 10(2), pp. 73–87.

Mayhew, M. J. *et al.* (2005) Curriculum matters: creating a positive climate for diversity from the student perspective, *Research in Higher Education*, 46(4), pp. 389–412.

McInnis, C. (2002) The place of foundational knowledge in the Australian undergraduate curriculum, *Higher Education Policy*, 15(1), pp. 33–43.

New Zealand Institute of Chartered Accountants (NZICA) (2005) *Admissions Policy: Academic Component (CA College)* (Wellington: NZICA), available at www.nzica.com/staticcontent/Member/ATEI.cfm

New Zealand Society of Accountants (NZSA) (1986) *The Body of Knowledge*, updated and reissued in 1992 (Wellington: NZSA).

Palmer, K. N. *et al.* (2004) International knowledge, skills, and abilities of auditors/accountants: evidence from recent competency studies, *Managerial Auditing Journal*, 19(7), pp. 889–896.

Parker, L. D. (2001) Back to the future: the broadening accounting trajectory, *British Accounting Review*, 33(4), pp. 421–453.

Perera, M. H. *et al.* (2002) *Customer Focus as a Determinant in Designing Accounting Programmes: An Empirical Investigation into Employers' Perceptions* (Unpublished. paper presented at 14th Asian-Pacific Conference on International Accounting Issues, Los Angeles, November).

Porter B. A. and Carr, S. A. (1999) From strategic plan to practical realities: developing and implementing a zero-based accounting curriculum, *Issues in Accounting Education*, 14(4), pp. 565–588.

Reckers, P. M. J. (1995) Know thy customers, *Change in Accounting Education: A Research Blueprint* (Center for Research in Accounting Education. James Madison University).

Scott, S. (1999) The academic as service provider. Is the customer always right?, *Journal of Higher Education Policy and Management*, 21(2), pp. 193–202.

Stout, D. E. *et al.* (2004) A descriptive account of the development and implementation of an innovative graduate accounting program: an example of stakeholder-based decision-making, *Advances in Accounting Education: Teaching and Curriculum Innovations*, 6, pp. 249–272.

Stout, D. E. and West, R. N. (2004) Using a stakeholder-based process to develop and implement an innovative graduate-level course in management accounting, *Journal of Accounting Education*, 22(2), 95–118.

Yu, J. and Cooper, H. A. (1983) Quantitative review of research design effects on response rates to questionnaires, *Journal of Marketing Research*, 20(1), pp. 36–44.

Incorporating Sustainability into Accounting Curricula: Lessons Learnt From an Action Research Study

JAMES HAZELTON* & MATTHEW HAIGH**

*Macquarie University, Australia, **Groupe ESC Toulouse, France*

ABSTRACT *This paper chronicles the journey of two projects that sought to incorporate principles of sustainable development into predominantly technical postgraduate accounting curricula. The design and delivery of the projects were informed by Freirian principles of praxis and critical empowerment. The first author introduced sustainability-related material into a core technical accounting unit and created an elective unit. The second author participated with students to evaluate critically social reports of employers, current and potential. In terms of an objective of bringing reflexivity into the classroom, both projects were marked by some success, but efforts to create permanent curriculum change were hampered by the predominantly vocational orientation of student cohorts. In addition, the traditionally technical focus of the professional bodies and competing educational reform agendas (such as vocational skills) add to the difficulties for sustainability in penetrating already overcrowded curricula.*

1. Introduction

'Sustainability' has moved to occupy centre stage of global debates. Although there is a range of positions in regard to social and environmental justice (Hopwood *et al.*, 2005), it is evident that urgent action is required to address issues such as climate change, loss of biodiversity, deforestation, extreme poverty and the like. It is also evident that economic, environmental and social issues are intertwined. For example, the 2007 report of the Intergovernmental Panel on Climate Change predicts that between 75 million and 250 million Africans will be exposed to increased water stress due to climate change (IPCC, 2007, p. 13) with obvious health and economic implications, and that nearly all European regions are 'anticipated to be negatively affected by some future impacts of climate change, and these will pose challenges to many economic sectors' (IPCC, 2007, p. 14).

Accounting has long been implicated in perpetuating unsustainable practices. Far from being objective and neutral, accounting has been revealed as a highly partisan act (Tinker, 1991) accused of ignoring (or even concealing) the adverse social and environmental impacts of organisations (Gray *et al.*, 1996; Gray and Bebbington, 2001). Attempts to recast accounting as a positive force through such mechanisms as triple bottom line accounting or the Global Reporting Initiative have been controversial to say the least (Tinker *et al.*, 1991; Gray, 2001; Gray and Milne, 2002; Gray, 2006). Further, the lack of mandatory reporting regimes in most countries leaves social and environmental accounting open to be used for promoting corporate interests as opposed to genuine accountability (Deegan and Rankin, 1996; Deegan, 2002, Adams *et al.*, 2004).

Education has long been considered by some practitioners as central to achieving sustainable development. Agenda 21 (United Nations Division for Sustainable Development, 1992, p. 36.3) asserts that '[e]ducation is critical for promoting sustainable development and improving the capacity of the people to address environment and development issues'. However, education for sustainable development (ESD) received little attention in the period following the Rio Summit (Tilbury and Wortman, 2004). In an effort to refocus attention on the education sector, the United Nations has named 2005–2014 the Decade of Education for Sustainable Development. According to the UN's Draft International Implementation Scheme, the objective is 'to integrate the values inherent in sustainable development into all aspects of learning and to encourage changes in behaviour that allow for a more sustainable and just society for all' (UNESCO, 2005, p. 5).

The Australian National Strategy for Ecologically Sustainable Development recognises the importance of education to achieving its (albeit limited) view of sustainability. The Strategy documents an objective 'to incorporate ESD principles and approaches into the curriculum, assessment and teaching programs of schools and higher education' (Ecologically Sustainable Development Steering Committee, 1992: Objective 26.1). In 2000, the Commonwealth Department of the Environment and Heritage released a National Action Plan for Environmental Education (Environment Australia, 2000). One of the Plan's key initiatives was the 2004 launch of the Australian Research Institute in Education for Sustainability (within the Graduate School of the Environment at Macquarie University) in an effort to accelerate the implementation of sustainability principles across all levels of education.

The higher education sector is critical, but embedding sustainability has proved difficult. Segovia and Galang (2002, p. 294) consider that 'the university provides an environment that nurtures critical and independent critique of what government or business does. Academia has also the advantage of the social acceptability, technical credibility and the moral ascendancy to broker and realize SD linkaging at various levels.' In response to the groundswell of concern, universities around the world have signed various sustainability declarations (Johnston, 1995), beginning with the Tallories Declaration (AULSF, 1990) that called upon universities to embrace sustainability (however defined) in their research, teaching and administrative operations.

Implementation of these declarations, however, has proved difficult, particularly in the areas of research and curriculum change. Segovia and Galang (2002), Segreda (2002), and Verbitskaya *et al.* (2002) in the Philippines, Costa Rica and Russia respectively, report superficial outcomes, unaccompanied by substantial curriculum change. Verbitskaya *et al.* (2002) conclude that, before sustainability values and understanding can be embedded in the tertiary education sector, fundamental reform of the educational scheme is necessary. Successful Australian examples of ESD are scarce. Cosgrove and Thomas (1996) conclude that the then 300 or so environmental courses in Australian universities lacked coherence and direction. More recently, Howard *et al.* (2000) note the scarcity of published guidelines on introducing ecologically-sustainable development to Australian higher education. In terms of outcomes, Thomas (2004, p. 37) concludes a review of a number of recent studies by stating that 'the adoption of sustainability education that will empower all tertiary students in Australia is at a low level.'

What are the barriers to implementing ESD? Howard *et al.* (2000) suggest that traditional conservative university curricula in Australia tend to reinforce discipline-based learning with emphasis on theoretical abstract problems. Thomas (2004) finds a culture of indifference towards sustainability and insufficient support for teaching staff (especially in the area of training) results in a commitment to ESD that rarely transcends the superficial.

This limited implementation of ESD in tertiary education provided part of the impetus for The Action Research for Change towards Sustainability Project (ACTS), an interdisciplinary research project conducted in Australian universities. ACTS was a pilot project conducted over 2003–05, jointly funded by Macquarie University and the Australian Government Department of the Environment and Heritage. The objective of the project was to incorporate sustainability into postgraduate education by addressing three aspects of university teaching: research-based activities supporting curriculum change, teacher training and resource support, and cross-faculty involvement. Ten teaching academics from Macquarie University, the University of New South Wales and Griffith University were invited to participate in the project. Invitations came from the ACTS convenors, both of whom were based at Macquarie University's Graduate School of the Environment. Participants represented a diverse range of disciplines: accountancy (the authors), law, psychology, architecture, environmental studies, chiropractic studies, linguistics and language training. Apart from the authors (both male), all members of the participant group were female.[1] Participants met to receive instruction on the principles of project design and action research at Macquarie University on two occasions in 2003. The instructors were the ACTS convenors, who were located in the Graduate School of the Environment (see details in Tilbury *et al.*, 2004). Participants were briefed on the objectives of the ACTS project and on principles of action research.

This paper chronicles the authors' experiences as ACTS project participants from 2003 to 2004 and educators from 2004 to 2006. In accordance with two briefings supplied to the participant group in 2003, the authors designed and implemented action research projects that introduced ESD into the curriculum of postgraduate accounting classes. At the time of the projects (in the July–November 2004 teaching semester), the authors worked within the accounting and finance teaching departments of two large Australian public universities. Although the authors' projects were independent of each other and conducted at separate universities, the authors corresponded after conducting their respective projects and met to compare experiences on several occasions.

This paper seeks to make three main contributions to the extant literature. One, the authors utilised action research, a methodology which has received comparatively little attention in accounting education research (Paisey and Paisey, 2004, p. 88), but which the authors consider well-suited to projects of this type. Two, the focus of the paper is on postgraduate accounting education, an area which is also under-researched (Paisey and Paisey, 2004, p. 88). Three, and most importantly, the paper discusses specific interventions utilised by the authors, as well as the practical barriers which limited the authors' success. We hope this discussion enables the implementation of sustainability initiatives by others on their own accord with both less effort and greater impact.

This paper divides into three further sections. In Section 2, we discuss how Freire's theories of critical consciousness (2005, p. 37) resonate with the ideals of ESD efforts to incorporate sustainability into accounting education to date and action research methodology. Section 3 provides accounts of the design and delivery of the authors' projects. A final section reflects on experiences learnt by the educators in terms of an objective of orientation change in educators and students.

2. The ESD Action Research Project

Education for Sustainability

While the central aim of ACTS was to introduce ESD principles into tertiary curricula, the difficulty in defining 'sustainability' (Hopwood *et al.*, 2005) makes the term 'education for sustainability' similarly ambiguous. Bonnet (2006, p. 266) suggests there are two main schools of thought regarding how education might contribute to sustainable development. 'Environmentalism' presupposes a certain set of desirable principles a priori (such as low resource consumption and egalitarianism) and seeks to instil these principles into students. By contrast, 'action competence' encourages development of a rational critical perspective on environmental issues with the intention that this perspective can be utilised to solve whatever sustainability issues later confront the student. This latter approach resonates with the work of Freire, discussed below. Bonnet argues that sustainability requires a metaphysical transformation, because sustainability is conceived as a 'frame of mind' (p. 268), comprising the set of 'the most fundamental ethical, epistemological and metaphysical considerations which describe human being' (p. 270). Bonnet suggests that this can be achieved by engaging students 'in the kinds of enquiry which reveal the underlying dominant motives that are in play in society; motives which are inherent in our most fundamental ways of thinking about ourselves and the world' (p. 275). Reflecting similar concerns, UNESCO (2005) urges ESD designed according to interdisciplinary, holistic, values-driven, critical, multi-method, participatory, applicable and locally relevant principles. Similarly, Tilbury and Wortman (2004) identify five central themes to ESD: futures thinking (consideration of long-term social welfare), critical thinking, participation in decision-making, engaging in partnerships, and systemic thinking.

In addition to ESD theory, the authors surveyed some of the broader educational literature and they were particularly drawn to the work of Paulo Freire. In *Education for Critical Consciousness* (2005), Freire argues that effective education of adults (in his case, in basic literacy in his native Brazil), requires the design of educational programs in such a way that they will develop learners' critical faculties. For Freire, 'simply passing on to the people prescriptions formulated in the teacher's office' (Freire, 2005, p. 37) was to be condemned as a tool of subjugation:

> Instead of communicating, the teacher issues communiqués and makes deposits which the students patiently receive, memorize, and repeat. This is the 'banking' concept of education ... [which is] a characteristic of the ideology of oppression. (Freire, 1996, p. 53).

Providing a contrast to such a 'banking' style of education endemic to university accounting and other business vocational education (Boyce, 2002; Carr *et al.*, 2006), Freire seeks to further the empowering and invigorating potential of education. Freire abandons the conventional style of education he views as anti-democratic, colonialising and enfeebling in preference to an explicitly transformative approach, in the sense of bringing transformative, cathartic meaning to people's lives. In the concept of *conscientização* (as translated from the Portuguese, the term refers to the process of achieving a critical consciousness: Freire, 2005, p. 17), adults learn to write and read (and, by extension, to account), and to adopt responsibilities as citizens active in society.

The underlying objective of Freire's approach is a radical one which seeks to avoid unreflective activism as much as theorising without action (Goulet, 2005, p. vii). The objective is consonant with redressing the social responsibilities of accounting academics (Tinker *et al.*, 1991; Parker, 2005), the liberating aspect of accounting for sustainability (Everett and Neu, 2000; Coulson and Thompson, 2006; Bebbington *et al.*, 2007) and the reflexivity demanded of action research in the social sciences (Woolgar and Ashmore, 1998, p. 2). So informed, the authors recognised teaching approaches that seek to empower accounting students as particularly relevant in ESD curricula. Their shared recognition formed the guiding principle in designing the action research/teaching projects. In addition, the principles of praxis and critical reflection are central to action research methodology.

An Action Research Paradigm

Various practitioners have successfully utilised action research to change higher education curricula (Krockover *et al.*, 2002; Burchell, 2000) and it is particularly appropriate for ESD-driven curriculum reform for two reasons. One, the core objective of action research is to create change. Success is measured by 'catalytic validity', the degree to which change as desired by the educator eventuates (Tilbury *et al.*, 2004) and which is consistent with the calls for systemic change appearing in the SD literature (Birkin *et al.*, 2005). However, in terms of Freirian objectives of instilling critical consciousness, the validity of the projects must also be assessed from the perspective of change desired by students. As we discuss below, this is problematic given that students with a predominately vocational orientation may not welcome sustainability-related education.

Two, action research operates from a critical perspective that includes the researcher as a specific research subject. It should be emphasised that it is the educator, not the student, who is actually engaged in action research. The objective of the educator is to improve the experience of the students via the research. As Kemmis (1990, p. 82) explains:

> In critical research, the researcher aims to develop or improve people's actions, understandings and situations through collaborative action. Behind this mode of viewing the people being researched is an interest in emancipating people from constraints of irrationality, injustice, oppression and suffering which disfigure their lives.

The objective of action research was considered by the ACTS convenors as cohering with the core principles of education for sustainability as outlined above. In the context of the project's objective of curriculum change, research methods considered as appropriate for action research include empirical-analytical, interpretive, critical and poststructural approaches (Fein, 2002, p. 243). Guided by the sensitivities of Freire and of action research methods, the teaching projects of the authors (described in detail in the next section) were primarily critical and designed to dismantle the conventional relation between teachers and students in tertiary accounting education. In particular, the projects required the design of significant elements of the tasks by design, the process contributing to their assessment. The guiding objective of the authors' projects can be expressed by Freire: 'In a humanizing pedagogy the method ceases to be an instrument by which the teachers can manipulate the students because it expresses the consciousness of the students themselves.' (1996, p. 50). As such, the appropriate design of the projects required the use of methods that 'would be the instrument of the learner as well as of the educator, [and] would identify learning *content* with the learning *process*.' (Freire, 2005, p. 43, emphasis in original.)

3. Applying the Principles of ESD to Accounting Education

As noted above, attempts to recast accounting as a positive force have been controversial (Tinker *et al.*, 1991; Gray, 2001; Gray and Milne, 2002; Gray, 2006) and the lack of mandatory reporting regimes in most countries leaves social and environmental accounting open to be used for promotion of corporate interests (Deegan and Rankin, 1996; Deegan, 2002; Adams *et al.*, 2004).

Given the above, as well as the significant percentage of university student cohorts represented by accounting students, changes to accounting curricula have the potential to influence sustainability outcomes significantly. Researchers and practitioners have repeatedly called for advances in accounting curricula beyond their traditional technical focus to topics that provide broader social skills and encompass issues such as globalisation, environmental reporting and sustainability (Holland, 2004; Gray and Collison, 2002; Heffes, 2001; Bebbington, 1997; Gray *et al.*, 1994). The collapse of Enron also highlighted the amoral nature of accounting education and brought renewed calls for both a wider and deeper perspective in higher education (Diamond, 2005; Humphrey 2005; Parker 2005).

The technical focus of accounting curricula is manifest in materials such as accounting texts (Sikka *et al.*, 2007), but as Parker (2007, p. 44) points out, accounting academics also perpetuate this paradigm:

> [A]ccounting academics, as their economics lecturer forebears did in the 1960s and 1970s, have largely tried to preserve the number of compulsory accounting subjects and their technicist number-crunching focus: defending their market share of the business degree and minimizing the course preparation, revision and change required of them as teachers.

Part of the reluctance to change stems from the increasing pressure on academics to lift their research output. Mathews (2007) notes that accounting academics are expected to publish far more articles than could ever appear within the limited space of reputable accounting journals. In addition, the increasingly commercial orientation of universities themselves places ideological and logistical constraints on innovation (Parker, 2002; 2005). A contrary finding was a survey by Mangion (2006, p. 347), showing that social and environmental accounting 'has been implemented to a much greater extent in Australian universities than indicated in the literature, or anticipated by the researcher', though the study did not identify whether implementation was a matter of substance or merely of form.

Students also seem unenthusiastic about a broader accounting education. For example, Carr *et al.* (2006, p. 369) report that 236 surveyed New Zealand accounting alumni considered 'social and environmental perspectives' as the least important area for curriculum emphasis (compared to 'global perspective' 'local perspective,' 'professionalism' and 'work experience').

In this project, in light of the above and adopting Freirian principles, the authors sought to avoid the use of 'slogans, communiqués, monologues, and instructions' (Freire, 1996, p. 48), and instead consider such tools as multi-media, practical projects outside of classroom settings, and the dialogue of students (Freire, 1996, p. 61). Key principles included an 'active, dialogical, critical and criticism-stimulating method', changes to course content and the use of appropriate techniques like thematic breakdown (Freire, 2005, p. 40). Such an approach endeavours to move students towards the deep learning advocated by English *et al.* (2004) and is broadly consistent with the framework adopted by Coulson and Thompson (2006). The remainder of this section details the specific interventions of each author, respectively.

Design of Project One

Project One involved two postgraduate teaching units. The first was represented by a 'core' technical accounting course, mandatory for students wishing to major in accounting.

The second was an interdisciplinary business ethics course offered to students as an elective enrolled in business and accounting programs.

Core technical unit. The first step was an evaluation of the unit using core ESD principles of critical and reflective thinking, values clarification and analysis, active and experiential learning, participation and communication, action orientation, flexibility, equity and holism. The unit fared poorly in all these aspects, primarily as it was a technical unit designed to enable the accounting by students of a specific range of transactions in accordance with statutory accounting standards. As such, critical thinking and values clarification were constrained to noting whether accounting treatments conformed to accounting standards. The mode of delivery of pedagogical material (in common with most accounting courses) was passive, in which accounting principles were explicated and then applied to textbook problems. Active student participation was limited to marking their own and each other's assignments and putting questions to the instructor.

The second step was conducting a traditional unit evaluation in which students were asked a standard set of questions relating to their perceptions of the unit. Interestingly, students' assessments were very positive. The unit was concerned primarily with consolidation accounting, a skill fundamental for financial accountants in the preparation, review or evaluation of financial statements, and many students remarked on how 'practical' and 'relevant' the course was to their jobs. The student evaluation serves to illustrate a crucial issue in teaching sustainability within technical disciplines: the extent to which students will consider it appropriate for the instructor to 'deviate' from technical skills and canvas wider issues (discussed further below).

In the light of these two evaluations, two changes were made to the content of this unit:

(i) The mid-semester assignment became team-based and included a role-play as well as a written element. The change to a team structure followed the ESD evaluation that had revealed students' concerns regarding the extent of interaction between students. The role-play was of an accountant reporting the implications of changed accounting standards to his/her finance director. The role-play was included to make the unit more collegial, mimic accounting workplaces, and to encourage an executive perspective in students by forcing their consideration of likely questions which might be put by the finance directors to their more junior colleagues.

(ii) A teaching week that had previously related to a technical topic (joint ventures) was replaced by a new topic of triple-bottom-line accounting (an introduction to accounting for social and environmental impacts). The joint ventures material was selected for replacement as the topic has limited relevance in the workplace and its deletion did not compromise the main technical skills of consolidation accounting imparted by the unit. The new topic was taught in an informal, discursive style as considered appropriate for the nature of the material. Apart from imparting some understanding of the issues, an important objective was to enable informed decisions by students relating to the choice of pursuing this area in more depth. At the conclusion of the lecture, students were given an overview of the material covered by the elective unit which formed the second element of Project One.

Elective unit. The foundation for the elective unit *Business and Professional Ethics* was an existing undergraduate unit of the same name which the author had jointly developed with the Philosophy Department. This undergraduate unit was reviewed in three ways. One, written unit evaluations were obtained and analysed. Two, the 32 students who had taken the unit in the previous semester were invited to participate in a roundtable meeting. Three students accepted and discussed the unit alongside the four academics who had been involved in teaching the unit.[2] Four, the unit content and methodology was reviewed against the five ESD principles noted above. Drawing from these three approaches, the researcher implemented certain changes into the curriculum, as described below.

The review process revealed that many ESD elements were already in place, with many topics implicitly and explicitly considering sustainability. However, the unit was predominantly 'about' sustainability, and students noted that there was an emphasis of theory over real-world application. While the assessment tasks enabled some choice of topics, they were mostly evaluated on the basis of students' analytical abilities relating to the theoretical arguments presented in the course. While in some sense this might be considered critical reflection, as the subject matter was largely predetermined it also had an element of what Freire might consider the 'banking' paradigm. In particular, there was no effort to motivate students toward action; as Marx might have concluded the course helped students understand the world, but not to change it.

In an attempt to encourage a more 'activist' orientation, the two undergraduate essay assignments were replaced by a single assignment with three components. First, each student was required to select a company of his/her choice, with the only restriction being that no two students could select the same company (a list of topical companies was provided but students could (and did) choose from outside the list). Students were required to evaluate the ethical quality of the company's performance in relation to each key stakeholder (shareholders, government, employees, customers, the community and the environment) and select one key ethical issue for more detailed discussion. Second, students gave a five minutes presentation to the class outlining their findings. Third, students wrote a one-page letter identifying a specific change they wished to see occur, addressed to a party who had the ability to make the change (company executive, legislator, regulator, etc.). In addition, students were asked to find one media article each week that related to a business ethics issue and analyse the issue from the perspective of the three major ethical theories previously discussed (utilitarian, Kantian and virtue ethics).

Conclusions from Project One

In the context of professional education, measurement of desired change in the curriculum from teaching and learning perspectives can be problematic. With respect to the technical course, the curriculum changes were successful to some extent. There was little feedback on the role-play innovation and the co-convenor of the unit, who took sole responsibility for the unit in 2005, reverted to a more traditional assignment structure. The main reason for this was logistical as the co-convenor was not campus-based and, as such, would have been inconvenienced by the additional campus attendance required to evaluate role-plays. The response to the triple-bottom-line seminar was more positive. Informal discussions held with students afterwards by both the researcher and co-convenor revealed many found the new topic interesting and the change in style to be refreshing. The co-convenor retained the ESD topic, despite having the option of reverting to the original structure, and the author continues to teach this week of the unit as a guest lecturer. However, one of the desired short-term outcomes was that students would be interested enough to choose an elective business ethics unit. While five students took the two units simultaneously, none of the 138 students who took the technical unit during second semester 2004, first and second semester 2005 and first semester 2006, subsequently chose the elective unit.

In order to investigate the reasons for this outcome, the 63 students from two classes who participated in the triple bottom line seminar in Semester 2, 2006, were asked to complete a short survey at the end of the seminar. The students were asked whether they expected to have graduated before the elective was next offered (Semester 2, 2007), if not whether they would choose the elective and the reasons for their decision. Only seven students did not expect to have graduated before the elective was next offered, due to most students being enrolled in a one-year Master's program. Of these seven students, four indicated that they would choose the elective while three would not. A total of 23 students provided comments. Nine students discussed the logistical difficulties of choosing the course, and offered suggestions such as running the unit over the summer break. Eight students reported that the unit was interesting, and of these three considered it topical. Many students, however, expressed reservations about the practicality of the unit. For example, Student 16 stated 'It is not my interest. This course seems to provide some general knowledge. It is not practical.'

Even two of the four students who indicated they intended to take the unit in 2007 shared these reservations: 'Business ethics is very interesting and heated discussion now. But it is not very technical.' (Student 33); and 'Maybe that will be a yes. Since that really have a good ideas about ethical issues. But the most problem is the word "ethics" => boring. More writing and theories question' (Student 32).

In addition, as indicated by the grammatical quality of these quotes, a further issue is low English skills of many international students. Student 30 summed up these concerns:

> The subject sounds very interesting. However, I think (as an international student) most overseas students will be scared of such subjects since it seems to involve a lot of "high level" English. Most of post-grad are currently international students who may be more interested in "technical" or "practical" subjects with more relevant use for the future (especially those will return to countries).

Overall, the responses suggest that three issues need to be addressed in order to boost enrolment in the elective. One, the logistical barriers need to be overcome by offering the elective more frequently. Two, the utility of the unit has to be established compared to more technical courses. Three, the English requirements of the unit need to be managed so that the unit is accessible to non-native English speakers whilst maintaining its integrity.

The response to the elective unit has also been somewhat encouraging. The enrolment numbers have been small (15 in 2005 and 25 in 2006) but they should be considered in the context of typical technical unit cohorts of around 100. By contrast, the accounting students taking the undergraduate elective (17 in 2004; 37 in 2005 and 33 in 2006) form a much lower percentage of students given technical unit cohorts of approximately 1,000. Interestingly, in 2005, approximately 30 students enrolled in the unit but half subsequently dropped out after attending the first lecture. Discussions with some of these students indicated that the primary concern was the standard of English required, which resonates with the comments made by Student 30 above. In an effort to address this problem in 2006, the volume of readings was condensed and students were reassured in the first lecture that non-native English speakers could successfully pass the unit. While this had the desired effect of reducing the dropout rate (to seven students), it also resulted in some lower quality students taking the unit.

Formal student evaluations for 2005 rated the unit substantially higher than the Accounting Department and Economic and Financial Studies Division averages in six out of seven categories—most notably organisation, learning support and intellectual challenge where the unit was at least 0.75 points above average on a five point scale.

The category where the unit was similar to the averages was 'appropriate assessment'. The primary problem here was that a few students misunderstood the requirements for the mid-semester assignment and provided a descriptive versus moral analysis of their company and faired poorly in terms of marks. The explanation of what is required was strengthened and resulted in an improved survey result in 2006.

The assignment was successful in encouraging students to evaluate critically business-driven sustainability issues. As hoped, the open-ended approach resulted in a diverse range of businesses and issues; from Nike's recent performance in China to a local bakery where the student's daughter was employed as an apprentice. Students were generally able to apply different ethical theories to the performance of their selected companies in relation to key stakeholders and the better students clearly articulated points of consistency and tension. In the final lecture, students were asked whether this part of the unit had been useful and responded enthusiastically (though the 2005 cohort also raised the assessment issue noted above).

While these aspects have been encouraging, some areas remain problematic. The quality of the letters asking for change was poor, in that few students were able to mount an argument that might drive change or even clearly articulate the specific change they desired. It was not a requirement that the letters were actually sent, and to the author's knowledge none were, which also suggests that the assignment remained an intellectual exercise rather than praxis. In subsequent offerings, the author intends to make this a point of discussion in the final lecture.

More generally, the perspective of this unit (and that of its undergraduate cousin) is often that of the business executive, making decisions about whether to invest in a particular country, to manufacture particular products and so forth. Many postgraduate students, however, are working in junior positions and it may be many years before they face these types of ethical dilemmas. The aspects of the discussions which have most resonance are issues such as exploitation of employees, to which (sadly) virtually all students can relate, and unethical advertising. A challenge going forward is to better relate issues around sustainability to the concrete experiences and immanent decisions being made by students, especially given the vocational orientation of students discussed in the final section of the paper.

Design of Project Two

The project designed by the second author followed two stages. The first stage was a lecture on sustainability which outlined responses of the accounting profession towards 'environmentalist' agendas, including 'triple bottom line' reporting and 'ethical' investing. The second stage was an assignment in which students were asked to conduct 'employer audits', being comparative assessments of prospective and current employers on a range of student-nominated 'sustainability factors'.

Stage one. A financial auditing course was chosen for the project, with a student cohort comprising both postgraduate and undergraduate students. (Although the ACTS research grant was designed for postgraduate teaching, Project Two was designed for postgraduate and undergraduate students as the series of lectures and tutorial classes were shared.) The postgraduate students were enrolled in a Master of Professional Accounting program and they had not taken university accounting subjects previously. The undergraduate students were accounting majors. The title of the relevant lecture in the auditing course was given as 'Sustainability and Employer Choice'. Its scheduling towards the end of the 13-week course followed by a professional ethics lecture and a presentation on 'job skills' made by a visiting chartered accountant.

The ESD lecture was designed to guide students and educator to challenge the typical design of accounting courses aimed at professional accreditation (Tinker and Koutsamadi, 1997). As Freire (1996, p. 54) outlines the limiting assumptions of traditional teaching: 'the teacher teaches and the students are taught; the teacher knows everything and the students know nothing; the teacher chooses the program content, and the students (who were not consulted) adapt to it'. Taking heed of this criticism, the educator invited students to reflect on graduate recruitment as an expression of their values and life plans.

In keeping with the appropriate emancipatory role of vocational/professional education (Prasad and Caproni, 1997), the project was designed to promote three outcomes:

1. The terms of the research grant required the researcher to introduce material on ESD, corporate social responsibilities, environmental awareness and social activism, as considered appropriate in the context of the teaching course. The material was designed in such a way as to relate to students' career choices.
2. The project was designed to promote critical reflection on values clarification and futures thinking (Tilbury and Wortman, 2004).
3. The project was designed to promote a desire in students to 'unravel false consciousness' and systems of manipulative behaviour in society (Freire, 2005, p. 10).

For many students, the auditing lecture represented the final subject in their degree program. Graduate employment was an important consideration for many in the student cohort and the subject matter of ESD, which includes labour conditions among other social and environmental considerations, would have been particularly relevant to many.

In an exploratory attempt to meet these design criteria, the ESD lecture was structured in four sequential parts. Students were informed that they would be given an assessable assignment in which they would compare two organisations against a range of sustainability factors. The lecture began by introducing some of the business and accounting literature on socially sustainable economic development. The topic's relevance to the professional auditing course was emphasised in terms of social-economic sustainability risks that might be present in audit clients. An example given was the exposure of industrial sectors such as mining and agriculture to government environmental regulations. As an example, social reporting emanating from two Australian property developers was compared (one mentioned social issues only in terms of its charity contributions; the other had issued standalone sustainability reports for some years). British Petroleum, Royal Dutch Shell and BHP Billiton were given as examples of prominent social reporters.

The second part of the lecture, informed by the objective to use methods that 'would identify learning *content* with the learning *process*' (Freire, 2005, p. 43), described the critical use of research methods such as content analysis, discursive analysis and theme analysis. Relevant examples were shown from published scholarly accounting papers, all of which examined environmental and social accounting issues. (The academic papers were subsequently posted to the student intranet). Students were invited to consider these methods when conducting their 'employer audit' assignment.

Next, an extract of 30 minutes from the popular film *The Corporation* was shown in the lecture theatre. The extract consisted of an episode which examined the extent to which Western (mostly North American) industrial corporations had escaped liability for manifestly destructive effects wrought on urban and non-urban environments. The decision to use popular film as an educational tool for critical consciousness was informed by Freire (2005, p. 49). The appropriateness of using the film extract had been discussed previously with the ACTS participant group at the time of the ACTS briefings. While they watched the film, students were asked to consider if their current or intended employers recognised the types of social and environmental sustainability principles addressed.

After the film showing, students were invited to suggest 'sustainability factors' which they would use when evaluating employers and their own employment prospects. 'Sustainability,' therefore, was left to students to define for themselves. Suggestions were noted on an overhead projector by the instructor. The resulting list was transcribed and posted to the student intranet. In individual projects conducted outside class, students used the list to conduct 'employer audits', in which current and/or prospective employers were assessed. Bearing some relevance to the auditing curriculum, students were asked to investigate how organisations verified reports that claimed they addressed environmental and social matters. Students were also asked to attempt to verify such claims themselves. No format or other requirement was imposed on the project, other than the students made an effort to identify and talk with an appropriate person in the assessed organisation. Students were also encouraged to examine and compare two organisations in the same industry sector. The assignment formed one of 10 assignments completed by students in the course.

Stage two. The second part of the project was conducted in tutorial classes two weeks after the ESD lecture. As each student orally presented his/her project to the class, tutors transcribed on the blackboard the criteria used, the industrial sector and the names of organisations assessed. Immediately after each presentation, tutors and students ranked and re-ranked the criteria in terms of perceived importance. After all presentations and rankings had been made, multiple-choice questionnaires were administered to students (the last three questions in the Appendix). The questions were designed to encourage students to consider if the project had changed their career expectations. This aspect of the project is a practical reflection of Freire's philosophy of 'a form of education enabling the people to reflect on themselves, their responsibilities, and [...] their very *power* of reflection' (Freire, 2005, p. 13, emphasis in original).

Conclusions from Project Two

One immediate outcome from Project Two is that the teaching of sustainability, social accounting and critical thinking had been successfully integrated and inserted into a vocational accounting degree, marking a return after a lapse of some years in the teaching department. Judging from the quality of students' oral presentations and the depth of written responses, the pedagogical methods used were effective in terms of promoting the primary learning objectives: to challenge students to critically assess that which is not conventionally criticised, and to provide some evidence of the success of ESD in accounting education.

Most students had engaged with the spirit of the project, making incisive assessments of organisations' information disclosures that intimated a willingness to embrace a critical consciousness. This can only be considered a short-term result. The reception of students to the showing of the film extract was generally positive. No students left the classroom in the showing and the level of enthusiasm shown for suggesting relevant 'sustainability assessment factors' after the showing was animated and interactive. Several students expressed an opinion to the author that the film extract had contributed to the lecture on corporate social responsiveness and that they had begun to reflect on values that they sought in employers.

The learning experience considered most interesting by the second author was the comparisons of organisations. That project (see the Appendix) had facilitated values clarification and particularly so when the students ranked organisations in the classroom setting. Providing for an objective of values clarification is important in terms of the particular objective of using action research in ESD to empower students and teachers with critical faculties. Introducing interactive dialogue as a substantive part of the ESD lecture proved a rewarding experience and the author was encouraged to apply the method to other topics in the same teaching unit. In terms of personal objectives, Project Two aimed to expose assumptions underlying the author's teaching approach; namely, if his teaching approach was patronising of students in terms of their vocational choices and if so, how his teaching approach could be modified to empower students and encourage teacher learning. The teaching approach with regard to sustainability changed, as intended, from one based on a passive expectation of historical student 'performance' to a richer understanding of the subjective nature of sustainability issues. Such an understanding was formed (and could only be formed) by the educator engaging collaboratively with students to rank organisations on matters of relevance to students' lives. For example, the inventories of 'sustainability factors' constructed in classes required the educator to discard, at least temporarily, the conventional relation of dominating teacher and passive student. This successful instance of reflexive practice, although an 'essentially local accomplishment' (Woolgar and Ashmore 1988, p. 10), can be considered significant in and of itself.

Indifference towards ESD in collegial contexts (Thomas, 2004) was noted by both authors. Such indifference proved a continual source of frustration in terms of providing space for reflective thought and achieving the ostensible objective of ACTS. As Woolgar and Ashmore (1988, p. 4) find, '[. . .] the conventions of realism constrain our exploration of knowledge practices and inhibit the development of reflexive practice' Departmental administrators showed little enthusiasm for the new pedagogical material, one explaining that 'it had all been tried before' and that the then-lecturer had since left. Perhaps unsurprisingly, such indifference is reflected in the student cohort. The initial take-up of the elective unit (Project One) was disappointing. Approximately two in five students in the second author's classes chose to forgo available marks for presenting their assignment and did not attend class in that week. Several students also queried the relevance of sustainability issues in a vocational business course, echoing the sentiments of students in the technical unit in Project One. The use of multiple research and teaching approaches and multi-media for effective teaching breakthroughs, if measured by teacher and student enthusiasm for the project, appears insufficient to achieve long-term learning outcomes.

4. Reflections on Educating for Sustainability

Given the nature of the projects, long-term outcomes on students' thinking resulting from the projects could not be readily gauged. In terms of the research objectives of the ACTS project, introduction of the material into the curriculum was considered sufficient. Evaluation of 'success,' therefore, is highly subjective, but the authors feel justified at least in outlining some of the particular challenges they faced (and only partly overcame) in implementing ESD within an accounting context.

The most immediate, and perhaps obvious, challenge is to find space within the accounting curriculum. In Australia, the professional accounting bodies (the Institute of Chartered Accountants in Australia (ICAA) and the Australian Society of Certified Practising Accountants (CPA)) dictate accounting curricula. The two bodies jointly specify the minimum number of subjects and content within those subjects that must be covered in undergraduate and postgraduate accounting degree courses, and the predominantly technical focus of these bodies means the curriculum of professional accounting degree programs is overwhelmingly comprised of technical subjects. Although Mathews (2004) found some diversity in accounting courses operating within this framework, this technical focus gives rise to strong competition for the few (often only one) elective slots available. In such a crowded teaching environment, consideration of sustainability is at great danger of being superficial. Therefore, while the reports of increased adoption of sustainability education within accounting are encouraging, until the bodies give the area explicit support it is unlikely that such education can operate with sufficient breadth and depth, and substantive changes are restricted to pedagogical approach. Mathews (2004, p. 81) makes a similar point in relation to communication and ethics:

> Despite documented concerns about both communication skills and business ethics, there are very few instances of required subjects in these areas within the accredited degree programmes ... it may be argued that these are areas where the accreditation process could benefit academic programmes by directing greater attention towards enhanced communication skills and the study of professional ethics.

While the professional bodies have considered sustainability issues—for example, the ICAA established a Triple Bottom Line Special Interest Group (now disbanded) and sponsored research papers such as Deegan (2003), Environmental Accounting Task Force (1998) and Rankin (1996)—perhaps the greatest current opportunity is in the related area of ethics. The International Federation of Accountants (IFAC) recently released an Information Paper and Exposure Draft investigating ‘Approaches to Developing and Maintaining Professional Values, Ethics and Attitudes’ (IFAC, 2006a; b), based on a broad international survey and semi-structured interviews. Three of the consensus views of practising accountants are particularly pertinent to the ESD implementation issues raised above. One, that ethics should be learned as part of the pre-qualifying programs and should be taught in dedicated units as well as integrated within technical units. Two, professional accounting bodies have a significant role in ethics education and should prescribe the nature of ethics education. Three, that ethics education should be introduced as part of a broader program to develop accountants’ professional values, ethics and attitudes (IFAC, 2006a, p. 5). Such conclusions suggest that the professional bodies’ attitude towards ethics education (and overlapping sustainability issues) should shift from relative indifference to strong support or even prescription, but it remains unknown if they would be willing to jettison the cherished cargo of technical content.

More broadly, the various efforts made to disseminate topics of sustainability, social accounting and environmental cost systems in accounting education appear sporadic and uncoordinated, underlining their marginal place in the profession. The spaces in which such initiatives are promulgated in professional education remain, unfortunately, disparate and unconnected. To wit, the funding partner of the ACTS project (the Department of the Environment and Heritage) did not seek the involvement of the private sector, nor did it consult the professional accounting bodies. Admittedly, this brief was outside the scope of the interdisciplinary ACTS project (Tilbury *et al.*, 2004). A corollary, however, is the distance that the Triple Bottom Line Special Interest Group of the ICAA sought to place between itself and the government.

Pragmatically, student numbers and cohort characteristics, especially at the undergraduate level, can be considered to restrict pedagogical innovation. Cohorts ranging from 600 to 1,000 per teaching unit, in which the teaching is shared among 10–15 staff, are routine. Any curriculum change involves not only the unit convenor but also the entire teaching panel, members of which must be educated to deliver a different approach. Limitations of a more personal nature arise from the effort and time necessary for the development of the projects relative to a realisation that academic promotional paths are rewarded by publications ahead of teaching innovation.

Perhaps the greatest challenge to effective deployment of sustainability teaching, however, is the vocational orientation of students themselves. In concordance with Boyce (2002, p. 597), the authors consider that 'educational change is only possible in conjunction with wider social and political change'. ESD is both a cause and an outcome of a wide range of sustainability initiatives promoted by various governmental and non-governmental bodies, but is also embedded within the wider *zeitgeist*. Efforts to evaluate critically business and accounting must contend with a pervasive consumer culture. This culture is reflected in tertiary education choices. The majority of Australian tertiary students select vocational degrees: in 2004, of the approximately 950,000 students, less than a third (290,000 or 30%) chose the less vocational areas of Society and Culture, Creative Arts or Non-Award courses. Of the remaining areas (Science, Information Technology, Health, Engineering, Architecture, Education and Commerce), Commerce was by far the largest, accounting for 28% of all students (Commonwealth of Australia, 2005). The primary objective of Australian accounting students is to secure a 'good' job, permanent residency or both; the authors are yet to encounter a student studying accounting solely for the intrinsic joy of mastering the discipline. Such sentiment was clearly expressed by the accounting students surveyed by researcher one, many of whom had dismissed non-technical education as irrelevant and a waste of time, and the non-participation of students in Project Two.[3]

Yet the commodifying pressure on accounting education to produce graduates 'suitable' for employment are manifestly contrary to the emancipatory objective of critical thinking (Tinker and Koutsamadi, 1997). Faithfulness to Freire's desire to 'generate critical consciousness and empower [students] to alter their relations with nature and social forces [in a] reflective group exercise' (Goulet, 2005, p. ix) therefore requires the teacher/researcher to adopt imaginative approaches to dealing with institutional structures and the embedded short-term expectations of students. Moreover, while both authors enjoy the 'luxury of experimenting, the freedom to fail' (Goulet, 2005, p. xiii) in their ESD projects, vocational students, in particular, are unlikely to view academic experimentation so favourably. While this reality may be sobering, we do not wish to suggest that attempting to engage students in sustainability discourse is futile. Indeed, the experience of both researchers from the ACTS project is that some students will respond very positively to such opportunities. Effective learning outcomes (in terms of the principles of ESD outlined above) can be gained from presenting pedagogical material that frames sustainability issues as relevant extensions to 'core' course curricula, and a relatively enthusiastic reception can also be expected if sustainability material is framed in terms of employment-related skills. This conclusion echoes the findings of Tinker and Gray (2003, p. 751), discussing an attempt at a critical perspective to accounting student curricula at The City University of New York (CUNY):

> The emerging self-consciousness of students in CUNY is, in some respects, a more obvious instance of the praxis-as-consciousness-raising. However, this case also has its surprises. The course teacher was schooled in a traditional scholarly disdain for crass student concerns with "career" and "money". However, experience at CUNY quickly shows that these are the basic necessities for many students. They have little margin to indulge themselves beyond this. It was a slow and humbling lesson (for which the professor earned, at best, a "C"), to not only begin to acknowledge this, but then to incorporate the realization into the course design, making work, career, and wages vital motivational components.

At an ideological level, the very notion of sustainability is a term contested in a variety of theatres. It is vital for accounting students (and their teachers) that the classroom is one of those theatres, as the neutrality of the classroom can provide a clearing space for reflection and debate to an extent difficult to emulate in more partisan environments. At the same time, it must be acknowledged that engaged students are the exception. Given this scenario, accounting academics have to walk a tightrope between meeting the expectations of students, many of whom (together with their families) have made considerable sacrifices to afford university studies, and meeting the societal imperative of comprehensive ESD. It is hoped that by providing some insights into how we approached this challenge, this paper has added another strand to our collective safety net and encourages other academics to embark on this difficult, yet vital, journey.

Acknowledgements

The authors acknowledge the financial assistance and pedagogical material provided by Macquarie University's Graduate School of the Environment and the Australian Government Department of the Environment and Heritage. The comments of Jan Bebbington, Barbara Flood and participants at the 2005 Environmental Justice and Global Citizenship conference at the University of Oxford are acknowledged. The authors appreciate the encouraging comments and support of the two anonymous referees and the Associate Editor.

Notes

[1]Descriptions of the project objectives and bases of participant selection can be found in Tilbury *et al.* (2004).

[2]Owing to the success of the roundtable meeting for the business ethics unit, the researcher attempted to replicate the process in a large undergraduate unit with approximately 750 students. Approximately 100 invitations were sent but only seven students volunteered to participate so the planned sessions were not held. It was noted by support staff involved in this process that some incentive (such as movie tickets) might result in an acceptably high response rate.

[3]The choice of some students not to participate in the assignment for Project Two might be attributed to its insignificance in terms of course assessment. The assignment was one of 10 weekly assignments to which 15% of the course assessment was allocated. Several participating students complained that the effort required for the assignment and presentation warranted more marks.

References

Adams, C., *et al.* (2004) Triple bottom line: a review of the literature, in: A. Henriques and J. Richardson (Eds) *The Triple Bottom Line: Does it All Add Up*? pp. 17–25 (London, Earthscan).

Association of University Leaders for a Sustainable Future (AULSF) (1990) The Talloires Declaration: University Presidents for a Sustainable Future (Winnipeg, International Institute for Sustainable Development). Available at http://www.iisd.org/educate/declarat/talloire.htm (accessed 17 May 2005).

Bebbington, J., *et al.* (2007) Theorizing engagement: the potential of a critical dialogic approach, *Accounting Auditing & Accountability Journal*, 20(3), pp. 356–388.

Bebbington, J. (1997) Engagement, education and sustainability: a review essay on environmental accounting, *Accounting, Auditing & Accountability Journal*, 10(3), pp. 365–381.

Birkin, F., Edwards, P. and Woodward, D. (2005) Accounting's contribution to a conscious cultural evolution: an end to sustainable development, *Critical Perspectives on Accounting*, 16(3), pp. 185–208.

Bonnett, M. (2006) Education for sustainability as a frame of mind, *Environmental Education Research*, 12(3–4), pp. 265–276.

Boyce, G. (2002) Now and then: revolutions in higher learning, *Critical Perspectives on Accounting*, 13(5–6), pp. 575–601.

Burchell, H. (2000) Facilitating action research for curriculum development in higher education, *Innovations in Education and Training International*, 37(3), pp. 263–269.

Carr, S., Chua, F. and Perera, H. (2006) University accounting curricula: the perceptions of an alumni group, *Accounting Education: an international journal*, 15(4), pp. 359–376.

Commonwealth of Australia (2005) Higher Education Report 2004–05 (Canberra, Commonwealth of Australia). Available at http://www.dest.gov.au/NR/rdonlyres/136CDC4E-9770-464D-BDCF-72E56B031C6A/8092/highered_report_fullversion11.pdf (accessed 14 October 2006).

Cosgrove, L. and Thomas, I. (1996) Categorising tertiary environmental education in Australia, *Australian Journal of Environmental Education*, 12(1996), pp. 27–34.

Coulson, A. and Thompson, I. (2006) Accounting and sustainability, encouraging a dialogical approach; integrating learning activities, delivery mechanisms and assessment strategies, *Accounting Education: An International Journal*, 15(3), pp. 261–273.

Deegan, C. (2002) The legitimising effect of social and environmental disclosures: a theoretical foundation, *Accounting, Auditing and Accountability Journal*, 15(3), pp. 282–311.

Deegan, C. (2003) Environmental Management Accounting: An Introduction and Case Studies (Sydney, Institute of Chartered Accountants in Australia). Available at http://www.icaa.org.au/upload/download/Emap_print.pdf (accessed 26 May 2005).

Deegan, C. and Rankin, M. (1996) Do Australian companies report environmental news objectively? an analysis of environmental disclosures by firms prosecuted sucessfully by the environmental protection agency, *Accounting, Auditing and Accountability Journal*, 9(2), pp. 50–67.

Diamond, M. (2005) Accounting education, research and practice: after enron, where do we go? *European Accounting Review*, 14(2), pp. 353–362.

English, L., *et al.* (2004) Encouraging a deep approach to learning through curriculum design, *Accounting Education: An International Journal*, 13(4), pp. 461–488.

Ecologically Sustainable Development Steering Committee (1992) Report of the National Strategy for Ecologically Sustainable Development (Canberra, Commonwealth of Australia). Available at http://www.deh.gov.au/esd/national/nsesd/strategy/index.html (accessed 21 May 2005).

Environment Australia (2000) Environmental Education for a Sustainable Future—National Action Plan (Canberra, Commonwealth of Australia). Available at http://www.deh.gov.au/education/publications/nap/pubs/nap.pdf (accessed 21 May 2005).

Environmental Accounting Task Force (1998) Impact of Environmental Matters on the Accountancy Profession (Sydney, Institute of Chartered Accountants in Australia). Available at http://www.icaa.org.au/upload/download/tblpaper4.htm (accessed 26 May 2005).

Everett, J. and Neu, D. (2000) Ecological modernization and the limits of environmental accounting?, *Accounting Forum*, 24(1), pp. 5–29.

Fein, J. (2002) Advancing sustainability in higher education: issues and opportunities for research, *International Journal in Higher Education*, 3(3), pp. 243–255.

Freire, P. (1996) *Pedagogy of the Oppressed* Trans. M. B. Ramos (London: Penguin Books).

Freire, P. (2005) *Education for Critical Consciousness* Trans. M. B. Ramos (New York: Continuum).

Goulet, D. (2005) Introduction, in + P. Freire, *Education for Critical Consciousness* Trans. M. B. Ramos, pp. vii–xiv (New York: Continuum).

Gray, R. (2001) Thirty years of social accounting, reporting and auditing: what (if anything) have we learnt?, *Business Ethics: A European Review*, 10(1), pp. 9–15.

Gray, R. (2006) Social, environmental and sustainability reporting and organisational value creation? whose value? whose creation?, *Accounting, Auditing and Accountability Journal*, 19(6), pp. 793–819.

Gray, R. and Bebbington, J. (2001) *Accounting for the environment* (London, Sage publications).

Gray, R., *et al.* (1994) Teaching ethics in accounting and the ethics of accounting teaching: educating for immorality and a possible case for social and environmental accounting education, *Accounting Education: An International Journal*, 3(1), pp. 51–75.

Gray, R. and Collison, D. (2002) Can't see the wood for the trees, can't see the trees for the numbers? accounting education, sustainability and the public interest, *Critical Perspectives on Accounting*, 13(5–6), pp. 797–836.

Gray, R. and Milne, M. (2002) Sustainability reporting: who's kidding whom?, *Chartered Accountants' Journal of New Zealand*, 81(6), pp. 66–70.

Gray, R., *et al.* (1996) *Accounting and Accountability* (Hemel Hempstead, Prentice Hall).

Heffes, E. M. (2001) Making accounting relevant and attractive, *Financial Executive*, 17(3), 49–52.

Holland, L. (2004) Experiences from a student programme designed to examine the role of the accountant in corporate social responsibility (CSR), *International Journal of Sustainability in Higher Education*, 5(4), pp. 404–416.

Hopwood, B., *et al.* (2005) Sustainable development: mapping different approaches, *Sustainable Development*, 13(1), pp. 38–52.

Howard, J., *et al.* (2000) Is today shaping tomorrow for tertiary education in australia? a comparison of policy and practice, *International Journal of Sustainability in Higher Education*, 1(1), pp. 83–96.

Humphrey, C. (2005) 'In the aftermath of crisis: reflections on the principles, values and significance of academic inquiry in accounting': introduction, *European Accounting Review*, 14(2), pp. 341–351.

Intergovernmental Panel on Climate Change (IPCC) (2007) Summary for policymakers, in: M. L. Parry C *et al.* (Eds) *Climate Change 2007: Impacts, Adaptation and Vulnerability. Contribution of Working Group II to the Fourth Assessment Report of the Intergovernmental Panel on Climate Change*, pp. 7–22 (Cambridge, Cambridge University Press).

International Federation of Accountants (IFAC) (2006a) Approaches to Development and Maintenance of Professional Values, Ethics and Attitudes in Accounting Education Programs: Information Paper (New York, IFAC). Available at http://www.ifac.org/Store/ (accessed 23 August 2006).

International Federation of Accountants (IFAC) (2006b) Approaches to Developing and Maintaining Professional Values, Ethics and Attitudes; Exposure Draft (New York, IFAC). Available at http://www.ifac.org/Guidance/ (accessed 21 September 2006).

Johnston, D. (1995) Declarations for Sustainable Development: The Response of Universities (Winnipeg, International Institute for Sustainable Development). Available at http://www.iisd.org/educate/declare.htm#dec (accessed 17 May 2005).

Kemmis, S. (1990) Improving education through action research, in: O. Zuber-Skerritt (Ed.) *Action Research for Change and Development*, pp. 79–100 (Nathan, Queensland: Centre for the Advancement of Learning and Teaching, Griffith University).

Krockover, G. H., *et al.* (2002) Reforming and assessing undergraduate science instruction using collaborative action-based research teams, *School Science and Mathematics*, 102(6), pp. 226–284.

Mangion, D. (2006) Undergraduate education in social and environmental accounting in australian universities, *Accounting Education: An International Journal*, 15(3), pp. 335–348.

Mathews, M. R. (2004) Accounting curricula: does professional accreditation lead to uniformity within Australian bachelor's degree programmes?, *Accounting Education: an international journal*, 13(Supplement 1), pp. 71–89.

Mathews, M. R. (2007) Publish or perish: is this really a viable set of options?, *Accounting Education: An International Journal*, 16(3), pp. 225–240.

Paisey, C. and Paisey, N. (2004) An analysis of accounting education research in *Accounting Education: An International Journal*—1992–2001, *Accounting Education: An International Journal*, 13(1), pp. 69–99.

Parker, L. D. (2002) It's been a pleasure doing business with you: a strategic analysis and critique of university change management, *Critical Perspectives in Accounting*, 13(5–6), pp. 603–619.

Parker, L. D. (2005) Corporate governance crisis down under: post-enron accounting education and research inertia, *European Accounting Review*, 14(2), pp. 383–394.

Parker, L. D. (2007) Professionalisation and UK accounting education: academic and professional complicity—a commentary on professionalizing claims and the state of UK professional accounting education: some evidence, *Accounting Education: An International Journal*, 16(1), pp. 43–46.

Prasad, P. and Caproni, P. J. (1997) Critical theory in the management classroom: engaging power, ideology, and praxis, *Journal of Management Education*, 21(3), pp. 284–291.

Rankin, M. (1996) *Corporate Reporting—The Green Gap* (Sydney, Institute of Chartered Accountants in Australia). Available at http://www.icaa.org.au/tech/index.cfm?id=A103528612 (accessed 26 May 2005).

Segovia, V. M, and Galang, A .P. (2002) Sustainable development in higher education in the Philippines: The case of Miriam College, *International Journal of Sustainability in Higher Education*, 3(3), pp. 288–296.

Segreda, A. M. (2002) Sustainability and peace in Costa Rica: the case of the University of Costa Rica, *International Journal of Sustainability in Higher Education*, 3(3), pp. 271–278.

Sikka, P., *et al.* (2007) Professionalizing claims and the state of UK professional accounting education: some evidence, *Accounting Education: An International Journal*, 16(1), pp. 3–21.

Thomas, I. (2004) Sustainability in tertiary curricula: what is stopping it happening? *International Journal of Sustainability in Higher Education*, 5(1), pp. 33–47.

Tilbury, D., *et al.* (2004) Action Research for Change towards Sustainability: Change in Curricula and Graduate Skills towards Sustainability, (Sydney, Australian Commonwealth Department of the Environment and Heritage and Macquarie University). Available at http://www.aries.mq.edu.au/pdf/ACTS_Report_Final.pdf (accessed 21 May 2005).

Tilbury, D. and Wortman, D. (2004) Engaging People in Sustainability (Cambridge, IUCN Publications Unit). Available at http://www.aries.mq.edu.au/pdf/EngagingPeopleV5.pdf (accessed 21 May 2005).

Tinker, T. (1991) The accountant as partisan, *Accounting, Organisations and Society*, 16(3), pp. 297–310.

Tinker, T. and Gray, R. (2003) Beyond a critique of pure reason: from policy to politics to praxis in environmental and social research, *Accounting, Auditing & Accountability Journal*, 16(5), pp. 727–761.

Tinker, T. and Koutsamadi, A. (1997) A mind is a wonderful thing to waste: think like a commodity, become a CPA, *Accounting, Auditing & Accountability Journal*, 10(3), pp. 454–467.

Tinker, T., *et al.* (1991) Falling down the hole in the middle of the road: political quietism in corporate social reporting, *Accounting, Auditing and Accountability Journal*, 4(2), pp. 28–54.

United Nations Educational Scientific and Cultural Organization (UNESCO) (2005) United Nations Decade of Education for Sustainable Development 2005–2014, International Implementation Scheme (Draft) (Paris, UNESCO). Available at http://www.portal.unesco.org/education (accessed 21 May 2005).

United Nations Division for Sustainable Development (1992) Agenda 21 (New York, United Nations). Available at http://www.sidsnet.org/docshare/other/Agenda21_UNCED.pdf (accessed 21 May 2005).

Verbitskaya, L. A., *et al.* (2002) Sustainable development in higher education in russia: the case of St Petersburg State University, *International Journal of Sustainability in Higher Education*, 3(3), pp. 279–287.

Woolgar, S. and Ashmore, M. (1988) Introduction to the reflexive project, in: S. Woolgar (Ed.) *Knowledge and Reflexivity: New Frontiers in the Sociology of Knowledge*, pp. 1–11 (London, Sage Publications).

Appendix

Student Project: Researcher Two

Use any of the following factors as guidelines to compare two organisations that you imagine might be suitable places to work. (Note: factors are as tabulated in lecture.) You may already be employed in one.

1. **Career prospects**
   - Recruits graduate employees from a wide range of disciplines.
   - Range of available career paths and training opportunities after initial hiring.
   - Range of available locations for work, options for split or shared positions, parental leave conditions.
   - Starting salary and social prestige.

2. **Corporate governance reporting**
   - Composition of boards of directors: what directors do, remuneration, nationality, genders.
   - Number of personal investor meetings, communications on sustainability issues, stakeholder engagement, philanthropic activities. How such policies are monitored and reported.
   - Management consulting fees paid to external auditors.

3. **Social indicators**
   - Code of conduct followed by employees and suppliers. How compliance is monitored and reported.
   - Organisational impacts on employees and communities. Examples: equal employment policies, employee access to medical officers, responses to bribery and corruption, use of recognised labour standards, labour conflicts. How such policies are monitored and reported.

4. **Environmental indicators**
   - Environmental management systems used.
   - Policies developed on matters such as biodiversity, climate change and ozone-depleting chemicals, energy, mining and quarrying, nuclear power, pesticides, resource productivity, transport, waste and toxic chemical management? (The relevance of such matters will depend on the organisation's industrial sector.) How such policies are monitored and reported.

5. **Ethical indicators**
   - Involvement of services and products with matters such as alcohol and tobacco abuse, animal testing, gambling, genetic engineering, human rights, involvement with the military or repressive regimes or nuclear power. How such practices are identified, monitored and reported.

What would you do in the following scenarios?

1. Imagine you had a choice between an interesting job in an organisation whose practices or products you don't agree with. For example, you might consider its products, such as tobacco products, not very helpful for society. If you do not choose this job, you might end up with a boring job or no job at all, and regret your decision.
2. Imagine you already have an interesting job. However, you have become aware that your employer is involved in morally questionable practices. If you leave the job and are forced to disclose that the reason you left was that you did not agree with the employer's activities, you would be liable for defamation.
3. What questions would you pose to yourself when evaluating an employer?

Impact of an Ethics Presentation Used in the USA and Adapted for Italy

GHEULA CANARUTTO*, KATHERINE T. SMITH** & L. MURPHY SMITH**

*Bocconi University, Italy, **Texas A&M University, USA

ABSTRACT *The purpose of this study is twofold: (1) to determine if an ethics presentation at an Italian university can change students' perceptions of ethics; and (2) to compare the results of this study with previously published results from US students. The ethics presentation, previously developed by Smith, Smith and Mulig (2005)* Journal of Business Ethics, *61(2), pp. 153–164, for accounting and business classes, made available on the Internet, was adapted and used in classes in Italy. As in the USA, Italy has faced significant financial scandals and corporate failures in recent years. Both Italian and US penal laws have been changed to prevent future financial frauds, but there are limits to what laws can accomplish. The ethics presentation described in this Teaching Note was an effort to encourage students to consider the importance of ethics. The impact of the presentation on Italian students' perspectives is described. In addition, a comparison is made of the impact of the presentation in Italy and in the USA, which shows that students in both countries regard ethics as a very important topic.*

Introduction

Corporate financial scandals have occurred around the world in some of the most famous companies. Consequently, ethical reasoning is a contemporary and relevant issue, both to accounting practice and thereby to accounting education. Ethics has become a *conditio sine qua non* ('without which it could not be') for the economic environment. Ethical reasoning is required in business for many reasons. One is that legal systems are often unable to cover all the areas in which an ethical dilemma can occur. Laws are limited by their inflexibility, as well as implementation costs. Laws cannot translate every ethical requirement into an objective legal principle nor regulate all the ethical aspects that can arise in the business and social framework (Weiss, 1994).

Free-market and regulated market mechanisms do not always offer information and instruments that can be used to implement decisions in a way that incorporates their moral impact. When the free market is corrupted with unethical behaviour, negative consequences can arise for society. Legal requirements or voluntary ethical interventions are thus necessary in order to achieve the best result for society overall. The law is limited in what it can achieve, but people acting according to ethical principles can achieve the best for society. Company policies are limited in covering human aspects of dealing with a company's stakeholders. Codes of ethics, formal policies and ethical programs may not be sufficient in certain situations, nor do they always offer a clear direction on behaviour when people must choose between alternatives (Rockness and Rockness, 2005; Coates, 2004).

Ethics plays a vital role in business because laws are often absent or insufficient to guide morally complex decisions. As a result, educators must find a way to inculcate ethical values into future business leaders. In this way, educators can provide a means for students to face moral dilemmas and make right choices (Smith, 2003). The purpose of this study is twofold: (1) to determine if an ethics presentation at an Italian university can change students' perceptions of ethics; and (2) to compare the results of this study with previously published results from US students.

Motivation to Teach Ethics

Recent scandals have shown that hoping for ethical behaviour in managers and business leaders is not always reasonable. In society today, there is uncertainty about what is right and what is wrong. Society cannot afford to face business scandals as frequently as they have occurred in the last several years. We must strive to prevent future unethical behaviour and to pave the way for a better business environment for the next generations. 'Homo homini lupus,' meaning 'man is a wolf to man,' is an ancient Roman proverb by Plautus. If people do not have any rule, any moral code, any moral background, they will really be '*lupus*' to each other.

]Research has shown that ethics education has an impact on students' ethical perceptions and subsequent behaviour (Keller, Smith and Smith, 2007; Williams and Dewett, 2005). If those who do not behave in a correct and fair way did not go through any ethical preparation and study, how can we blame them for their lack of ethics? Graduate and post-graduate courses generally offer a very technical curriculum to the students. This means that students will finish their studies equipped with many technical skills but often deficient in moral judgment skills (Keller *et al.*, 2007). This situation is unwarranted. Educators can and should take steps to address the lack of ethical understanding in students (Smith, 2003). This study describes an ethics presentation aimed at the university level.

In his book on corporate governance and business ethics, Rezaee provides several plausible motivations for integrating business ethics education into the business curriculum. Among these motivations are the following: (a) financial scandals and regulatory responses underscore the importance of effective corporate governance and ethical behaviour and conduct by corporations and, thus, business schools in training future corporate leaders; (b) in past years, corporate governance and business ethics have not been properly integrated into business education; and (c) teaching and research in corporate governance and business ethics have been strongly recommended and encouraged (Rezaee, 2009).

Prior Research

Starting about two decades ago, a number of academic researchers began to examine the status of business ethics education. Examples of that literature include, among others,

Davis and Welton (1991), Piper, Gentile and Parks (1993), Donaldson and Freeman (1994), Trevino and McCabe (1994), and Ameen, Guffey and McMillan (1996). Davis and Welton (1991) studied business students' perceptions of professional ethics. Piper *et al.* (1993) examined teaching approaches at the Harvard Business School. Donaldson and Freeman (1994) presented business from a humanities approach. Trevino and McCabe (1994) made recommendations about how to create honourable business school communities. Ameen *et al.* (1996) examined ethical sensitivity in accounting students.

More recent literature advances the business ethics research stream, including Hartmann (2006), McCabe, Butterfield and Trevino (2006), McPhail (2006), Kolb *et al.* (2005), Williams and Dewett (2005), Goshal (2005), Brinkmann (2001), and Greenwood (2000). Hartmann (2006) derived an Aristotelian approach to ethics education. McCabe *et al.* (2006) looked at the extent and causes of academic dishonesty in graduate business programs. They propose corrective actions. McPhail (2006) offered observations regarding civilising accounting ethics education. Kolb, LeClair, Pelton, Swanson and Windsor (2005) took a panel approach to evaluate the role of ethics in the business curricula. Williams and Dewett (2005) provided a review and research agenda for teaching business ethics.

Goshal (2005) argued in one of his last works that many of the worst excesses of recent management practices have their roots in a set of ideas that developed out of business school academics over the last 30 years. Students are not given a sense of moral responsibility and hence these morally deficient business school graduates may have facilitated some of the worst financial scandals. Brinkmann (2001) offered insights on business ethics and morals. Greenwood (2000) took a unique look at teaching business ethics. Her study provided an example of how narrative literature, such as Dr Seuss, can be used to teach ethics within management education.

Ethics research has often examined various business disciplines and specific teaching techniques. Keller *et al.* (2007), Cowton and Bampton (2002), Schweiker (1993), and Flory, Phillips, Reidenbach and Robin (1992) focused on ethics models applied to the accounting field. Brinkmann (2000) studied real estate students. Marnburg (2003) described the use of short courses in ethics and philosophy. Moore (2006) reviewed empirical evidence in relation to ethics codes and suggested how ethical issues in higher education might be managed. Cunningham (1998) proposed use of the 'Golden Rule' in teaching ethics. Trezise (1994) examined difficulties of teaching business ethics to undergraduates. His study disclosed difficulties for both students and teacher. Higginson and Moore (1994) developed a computerized game to be used as a teaching aid for business people and management students, with a goal of teaching ethics while playing the game.

The Humanities Approach to Teaching Ethics

In their book, Donaldson and Freeman (1994) indicate that the competitive advantage that corporations will have in the future lies 'in the hearts and minds of the people who are employees.' Donaldson and Freeman argue that the scope of typical business education is too narrow and does not enable business managers to grasp the systematic and profound changes affecting modern business. These authors believe that adding '*humanities*' in business curricula is essential. Humanities in business education programs will enable future managers and employees to see the whole picture, enabling them to face and resolve deeper and more complex problems, including ethical dilemmas.

In the humanities tradition, books of literature often emphasize the consequences of good and bad moral choices. An example of a book that involves moral choices for accounting and business people is *The Bottom Line is Betrayal* (Smith, Smith and Crumbley, 2008). The business people in this fictional novel travel the globe using business skills and teamwork in order to solve the problems of a multinational corporation, which include ethical dilemmas. Aristotle taught that education requires much more than technical training. Education should include moral reasoning, which must encompass history, philosophy, literature, theology, and logic.

Traditionally, business education provides technical skills enabling future managers to seek long-term value maximization, to follow accounting rules, and to achieve production efficiency. Business education should also include 'soft skills,' that include the moral and ethical implications of business decisions on people, society, and the world at large. Decision makers should understand that any decision they make affects third parties. Decisions will likely have consequences that go beyond the financial considerations.

Bennis and O'Toole (2005) write that they are impressed with the University of Dallas's recognition that an overly narrow approach to business education may have been a factor in the Tyco, Arthur Andersen, WorldCom, and Enron scandals. In the same article, Thomas Lindsday (the former provost at the University of Dallas) points out that business education in the USA has become too devoted to technical training alone. He says that even before Enron, research showed that executives who fail financially, as well as morally, rarely do so from a lack of expertise. He says that executives fail because they lack interpersonal skills and practical wisdom; what Aristotle called prudence.

Some suggest that the importance of teaching ethics cannot be overemphasized, such as Donaldson and Freeman (1994), who cite John Stuart Mill: 'People are people before they are lawyers, or physicians, or merchants, or manufacturers; if you make them capable and sensible people, they will make themselves capable and sensible lawyers, physicians, or merchants.' However, scholars are not in agreement that business ethics can be taught. Whether ethics can be taught is actually a very ancient question. According to Carroll (2005), Socrates, in ancient Greece, believed that the faculty of discerning between what is right and what is wrong could and should be taught. If ethics should be taught, the next question is how ethics should be taught.

Carroll (2005), surveyed students to assess their perceptions on ethics education and the ways in which they prefer ethics lessons to be presented. The students ranked the different ways of teaching, assigning the first choice to lectures and presentations by the instructor; the second choice was assigned to student case presentations and instructor-led discussion.

Adapting the Presentation to the Italian Environment

The ethics presentation described in this study was implemented in class sessions at a major Italian university. This session on ethics was the first and only ethics-related presentation the Italian students received during their business studies. The ethics session was inserted in the curriculum as an extra activity.

The ethics presentation was given individually to three classes containing upper level and graduate accounting and business students. Before and after each class, students provided anonymous feedback on a survey questionnaire. Each class could dedicate one complete session (one-and-a-half hours) to the presentation. Seventy students participated in the survey at the Bocconi Business School in Italy.

The curriculum in Italian business schools is very technical-skills oriented. The ethics session was a change of pace and generated much discussion among students. The ethics session was started with a handout indicating that ethics is now a top agenda item in international corporate boardrooms. The students were told that a business firm's ethical reputation and corporate social responsibility affect the firm's customer loyalty, the firm's capacity to raise capital, the firm's relationship with suppliers, and the firm's ability to attract and retain employees. The handout was intended to start the ethics session with a pragmatic perspective, to show students the practical benefits of positive ethical behaviour.

An ethics presentation previously developed for US accounting and business classes (Smith, Smith and Mulig, 2005) was adapted for use in Italian classes. The US version included music clips in the presentation; the Italian version did not. The slide files and descriptions used in the ethics presentation for Italian students are shown in Table 1. The impact on perceptions of Italian business students will be compared to the American results previously obtained by Smith *et al.* (2005). The usefulness of comparing responses from students in different countries is to determine if the ethics presentation affected both of the diverse groups.

For the Italian case, the US presentation was adapted to the Italian environment by expanding on topics and themes with which Italian students are more familiar. In Italy, many famous managers and entrepreneurs have expressed themselves on ethical matters, especially after major financial scandals in Italy. Diego Della Valle, one of the most famous Italian entrepreneurs asserted: It is much easier attaining riches and success if you determine to have it at any price. If you want to excel without stepping on your fellow man, it may be a bit harder, but you will have much more satisfaction (see Table 1, slide 10).

Wealth creation is not a final goal achievable at any cost. Managers generally understand that, in order to create a long-term value, they must first respect their colleagues and the environment. On the website of Unilever, one of the biggest multinational corporations, there is a statement that explains operating views of the company. Recently the company changed its logo: the current logo uses the sun, birds, and sea to symbolize the company goal of respecting the environment. Having valuable products is not, by itself, a sufficient condition anymore. Anna Maria Artoni, the President of Giovani Confindustria, the association of young Italian entrepreneurs, said that markets today require more and more quality, brand identity, transparency of production processes, and a social image (see Table 1, slide 11).

For companies to survive in the long-term, it is necessary to be aware of the new requirements of the market and of the stakeholders. Einstein, many years ago, expressed a similar concept: 'The value of a man resides in what he gives and not in what he is capable of receiving' (see Table 1, slide 15). The idea can be easily transferred to the economic environment where all transactions are based on what the company takes and gives. At one time, a company was valuable if it was able to create value and wealth for itself. Many people now believe that a company should try its best to give externally as well. It is also important to try to help shape individual values and goals. People make up the society, the economic environment, and the global scenario. If greed and over-reaching ambition are the engines that move the world, then scandals and bankruptcies will be ordinary events. Desire for approval and recognition is a healthy motive, but the desire to be acknowledged as better, stronger or more intelligent than a fellow being or fellow scholar can lead to an excessively egoistic psychological adjustment, which may become injurious for the individual and for the community (see Table 1, slide 17).

When success is achieved, people must remember that they have to pay a price in order to maintain success in the long-term. Winston Churchill expressed this concept saying that the price of greatness is responsibility. Once a person has achieved success and power, there starts the trial. To be genuinely successful requires one to acknowledge

Table 1. Slides for the ethics presentation for Italian business students

Slide	Description
Part 1. WHY?	
1	Title: Ethics presentation, with current date. Background: World from space.
2	Ethics: What's the fuss?
3	When evaluating one's goals and objectives, a vital question must be asked: What is your highest aspiration?
4	'If integrity is second to any of the alternatives, then it is subject to sacrifice in situations where a choice must be made. Be on guard: Such situations inevitably occur in everyone's life' (Smith *et al.*, 2005).
5	Why talk about ethics? Eva Joly, Special counsellor to the Norwegian Government, Integrity Awards winner 2001, said that 'Corruption can destroy the strongest democracy if it is not dealt with. So fight it. Don't participate in it; don't allow it to take root. Show your support for policies that deal with these kinds of social issues, and you will touch the lives of all the people in your region'.[a]
6	Students who are dedicating most of their time to studying should keep in mind that knowledge has its limitations. Samuel Johnson said that integrity without knowledge is weak and useless, and that knowledge without integrity is dangerous and dreadful.[b]
7	But can ethics be taught? Teddy Roosevelt[c] said 'To educate a person in mind and not in morals is to educate a menace to society.' Albert Einstein[d] said: 'Education is what remains after one has forgotten everything he learned in school.'
8	What do educators think? In a survey of college faculty, 187 educators responded to several statements about teaching ethics, such as 'The importance of ethics and personal integrity should be stressed in the courses I teach.' Average rating was 4.75 on a scale from 1 = Strongly Disagree to 5 = Strongly Agree. (Smith, 1993, p. 18).
9	If students lack ethics in high school and college, then no one should be surprised that they lack ethics in their careers. Greed and over-reaching ambition often end in disastrous personal consequences. Convicted inside trader, Dennis Levine, in *Fortune* magazine wrote: 'I have painful memories of Sarah learning to walk in a prison visiting room, and of Adam pleading with a guard who wouldn't let him bring in a Mickey Mouse colouring book.' (Levine, cited in Smith, *et al.*, 2005).
Part 2. Managers' and companies' points of view	
Slide	Description
10	Diego Della Valle, one of the most famous Italian entrepreneurs, said that it is much easier accumulating riches or having success if you determine to have it at any price, but that if you want to do it trying not to step on your fellow it will be a little bit harder but it will give you much more satisfaction. (Della Valle, 2004, p. 27).
11	Anna Maria Artoni, President of Giovani Confindustria, said that ethics for companies is not a luxury but an economic necessity; that markets require more and more quality, brand identity, transparency of production processes, a social image; this requires that companies become more aware of their relationship with society. (Artoni, 2003).
12	On the Unilever website there is written this statement that reminds us that companies nowadays must consider being ethical. The world we operate in is changing. Consumers are demanding more and more from the companies behind the brands, increasingly bringing their views as citizens into their buying decisions. They want brands they can trust. Unilever has always had high standards of corporate governance, product quality, and has a long history of working with communities and the environment. Standing visibly as Unilever behind our products will enable us to take the next step in transparency and accountability.[e]

(Table continued)

Table 1 *Continued*

Slide	Description
13	A business may operate according to minimum legal standards but ethics requires standards of propriety. (Jennings and Entine, 1998).
Part 3. Learning from those who changed our world. . ..	
Slide	Description
15	Albert Einstein[f] said 'Only a life lived for others is a life worthwhile.' 'Try not to become a man of success, but rather try to become a man of value.' 'The value of a man resides in what he gives and not in what he is capable of receiving.'
16	Albert Einstein quotations continued: 'Strange is our situation here upon earth. Each of us comes for a short visit, not knowing why, yet sometimes seeming to a divine purpose. From the standpoint of daily life, however, there is one thing we do know: That we are here for the sake of others . . . for the countless unknown souls with whose fate we are connected by a bond of sympathy. Many times a day, I realize how much my outer and inner life is built upon the labours of people, both living and dead, and how earnestly I must exert myself in order to give in return as much as I have received.'
17	Albert Einstein quotations continued: 'We act as though comfort and luxury were the chief requirements of life, when all that we need to make us happy is something to be enthusiastic about.' 'When I was still a rather precocious young man, I already realized most vividly the futility of the hopes and aspirations that most men pursue throughout their lives.' 'Desire for approval and recognition is a healthy motive, but the desire to be acknowledged as better, stronger or more intelligent than a fellow being or fellow scholar easily leads to an excessively egoistic psychological adjustment, which may become injurious for the individual and for the community .'
18	Winston Churchill said 'The price of greatness is responsibility.' 'Success is not final; failure is not fatal; it is the courage to continue that counts.'[g]
19	John Quincy Adams (6th US president) said: 'If your actions inspire others to dream more, learn more, do more and become more, you are a leader.'[h]
Part 4. What are the advantages in being ethical? (slide 20)	
Slide	Description
21	Between those companies that are ethics-oriented (through training, ethics programs and incentives), 3 out of 4 perform better than companies which are not ethics-oriented. These companies get financial results that on average are 18% higher than the market.[i]
22	A 10-year study shows that companies which try their best to balance the interests of all their stakeholders, have a grow rate which is four times higher than the market. Employees' rate of growth is eight times higher than those companies which try to satisfy only the shareholders' expectations.[i]
23	Many experts argue that a company's commitment to social responsibility improves its financial performance by attracting more investment. For examples, 9 of the 15 largest social funds are in the top quartile of investment categories based on a three-year performance.[i]
24	In a survey of business employees, 78% of interviewed employees say that they would prefer working for an ethical company, which has a good reputation, instead of receiving a higher salary.[i]
25	A recent survey by McKinsey & Company, focusing mostly on developed countries, confirms that institutional investors are prepared to pay a premium of more than 20% for shares of companies that demonstrate good corporate governance.[i]
26	CSR and ethics can have a big effect on attracting and retaining good employees. Employees want good remuneration, good prospects—but increasingly people also want to feel proud of the company for which they work. Motivation is often based on values rather than cash.[i]

(*Table continued*)

Table 1 *Continued*

Slide	Description
27	Interbrand estimated that 96% of Coca Cola's value are intangibles—reputation, knowledge and brand; for Kelloggs, 97% and for American Express, 84%.[i]
28	A Fleishman Hillard study showed that 86% of European consumers would be more likely to buy a product from a company 'engaged in activities to help improve society'. About 1 in 6 shoppers say that they frequently buy or boycott products because of the manufacturer's reputation (Cowe and Williams, 'Who are the ethical investors?').[i]
Part 5. Where Do We Start? Upon What Can We Agree?	
Slide	Description
29	Whether we derive a code of ethics from religious beliefs, a study of history and literature, or personal experience and observation: We can all agree upon some basic values.
30	In an issue of *Management Accounting*, James Brackner stated 'The universities are responding with an increased emphasis on ethical training for decision-making. For the most part, however, they ignore the teaching of values. For moral or ethical education to have meaning there must be agreement on the values that are considered "right."' (Brackner, 1992, p. 22).
31	'Be sure you are right, then go ahead' (Davy Crockett, 1786–1836). (Crockett, D., cited in Smith *et al.*, 2005).
32	'Until about 50 years ago, it was commonly accepted that universities were to provide students not only with knowledge and skills, but also moral guidance based on the essentials of the Western tradition' (Business Professor Geoffrey Lantos). (Lantos. 1989, pp. 4, 6).
33	Can you make a difference?
34	'To sin by silence when they should protest makes cowards of men' (Abraham Lincoln). [j] 'Great spirits have often encountered violent opposition from weak minds' (Albert Einstein).[f]
35	The reputation of a thousand years may be determined by the conduct of one hour (Japanese proverb).[k]
36	At the US Congressional Hearing on Accounting and Business Ethics in July 2002, Truett Cathy, the Founder of Chick-Fil-A quoted Proverbs 22:1—'A good name is more desirable than great riches; to be esteemed is better than silver or gold.'[l] The truth is that fame and fortune are nothing compared to personal honour.
37	As a conclusion, now we can understand that 'A moral attitude is the choice that a rational mind would make after having made all its calculations' (Bauman, 1989).

Source: This presentation was adapted from the presentation described in Smith *et al.* (2005). This presentation is available on the Internet. http://acct.tamu.edu/smith/ethics/EthicsPowerPoint.htm

[a]Transparency. Available at http://www.transparency.org (accessed 1 September 2006).

[b]Wikiquotes. 2008. Samuel Johnson. Wikiquotes. Available at http://en.wikiquote.org/wiki/Samuel_Johnson (accessed 24 April 2008).

[c]Roosevelt, T., Famous Quotations. Available at http://www.quotes.telemanage.ca/quotes.nsf (accessed 1 August 2006).

[d]Einstein, A., Famous Quotations. Available at http://www.famousquotes.com (accessed 1 July 2006).

[e]Unilever. Web site: www.unilever.com, 1 February 2006.

[f]Einstein, A., Heart Quotes. Available at http://www.heartquotes.net/Einstein.html (accessed 1 February 2006).

[g]Churchill, W., quotations page. Available at: www.quotationspage.com/quotes/Sir_Winston Churchill/ (accessed 1 February 2006).

[h]Adams, John Q., thinkexist.com. Available at http://en.thinkexist.com/quotation/if_your_actions_inspire_others_to_dream_more/339093.html (accessed 1 February 2006).

[i]CSR Europe. Available at http://www.CSREurope.org (accessed 15 January 2006).

[j]Lincoln, A., quotes db. Available at http://www.quotedb.com/quotes/3682 (accessed 28 April 2008).

[k]Japanese proverb, quoteful.com. Available at http://quoteful.com/tag/Japanese (accessed 28 April 2008).

[l]Cathy, T., Testimony to the US House of Representatives Subcommittee on Commerce, Trade, and Consumer Protection: Hearing on Oath Taking, Truth Telling, and Remedies in the Business World, 26 July 2002.

that every step one takes affects not only the player but also many other parties (see Table 1, slide 18).

Former US President, John Quincy Adams, said that if your actions inspire others to dream more, learn more, do more and become more, then you are a leader. Who can be a better teacher about the essence of a true success than those who reached the highest positions during their lives? (See Table 1, slide 19).

In the Italian presentation, a section was dedicated to the practical advantages of being ethical. In one author's experience, the pragmatic approach demonstrating how ethics relates to specific business practices was preferred to a philosophical one that omits practical guidance. In a previous discussion held with MBA students on ethics (during a meeting of the Ethica Club), it was clear that students expected the ethics session to give them indicators showing that ethics is necessary and beneficial to the economic environment. Students liked the 'philosophical' approach, but they wanted to be reassured that, once an individual or company undertakes an ethical path, there will be a reward for the effort. Acting ethically is inherently the right thing to do, and therefore should be sufficient motivation for being ethical. Acting ethically is also better for business in the long-term. A business cannot survive if it loses customers' trust, which will eventually happen if the business is engaged in unethical practices.

The ethics presentation provides two critical perspectives: The first perspective, which is shown in Parts 1 to 3 of Table 1, includes the philosophical and social aspects of ethics. The second perspective, which is shown in Part 4 of Table 1, examines the advantages of adopting an ethical approach and the resulting long-term value-creation of this approach.

The last part of the presentation challenges students to ask: 'Where Do We Start? Upon What Can We Agree?' When students have reasoned on the philosophical and on the pragmatic aspects of ethics, they can deduce (as did Zygmunt Bauman) that a moral attitude is the choice that a rational mind would make after having made all its calculations (see Table 1, slide 37).

Impact of the Italian Ethics Presentation

This section presents the impact of the ethics presentation on the Italian students. Later in the paper, the US students' reactions will be used as a comparison. Some of the pre-presentation comments indicated that students had thought about ethics, but not as part of their educational programme. In their comments, many of the students asserted that ethics is a major issue, but none of them mentioned adding ethics education to the business curriculum. Many students perceived a trade-off between profit and doing what is ethically right. Following are some of the pre-presentation comments made by students:

- 'It is very important to educate on values, but when a manager faces a trade-off between revenue objectives and ethical behaviour, a big issue arises. So sometimes it is too late to educate managers and business men and education on ethics should start much earlier.'
- 'Examples given by politicians, managers and public authorities are very poor under an ethical profile. It is difficult to believe in ethical values with such examples.'
- 'Trust is the key. Educators must communicate it. Students should realize that a fair behaviour is one of the key success factors.'
- 'Ethics seems to constantly be in conflict with the goals of business people. Enforcement could help if properly applied and moral suasion and education can play a vital role for the future.'
- 'Teach people that it is possible to make business without necessarily hurting others.'

- 'It is very important that managers always keep in mind the interest of society and not simply the interest of the individual or of the firm.'
- 'There is a link between long-term profitability and ethics.'
- 'I think it is hard to change people's beliefs on ethical issues. Education should start much earlier.'
- 'There is the lack of ethical education in the university.'

On the pre- and post-presentation survey, students responded to several statements on a Likert scale from 1 (strongly disagree) to 5 (strongly agree). The same method used by Smith *et al.* (2005) comparing pre- and post-presentation results was used with the Italian students. Average responses are shown in Table 2.

The pre- and post-presentation survey responses of the Italian students were tested to determine if significant changes occurred in students' perceptions on ethics. For this analysis, a two-sample *t*-test was used. The *t*-values and level of significance are provided in Table 2. Specific observations regarding the Italian students' perception change for each survey statement are provided below.

Statement 1, shown in Table 2, indicates: 'Ethics is a major issue in business and accounting.' Results showed there was not a significant increase in the average score between the pre and post-presentation.

For Statement 2, 'Professionals must abide by a high ethical standard because of their responsibility to honour the public trust,' the scores were almost at the same level before and after the presentation, (pre-presentation score was 4.30 and post was 4.32). This can be explained by the fact that the recent scandals occurring in the financial world make it clear that

Table 2. Pre- and post-presentation Italian and US students' perceptions toward ethics

	Italy Pre-	Post-	*t*-value	Sig.	USA Pre-	Post-	*t*-value	Sig.
1. Ethics is a major issue in business and accounting	3.81	3.97	−0.831		4.85	4.96	−1.754	b
2. Professionals (e.g. attorneys, CPAs, engineers) must abide by a high ethical standard because of their responsibility to honour the public trust.	4.30	4.32	−0.150		4.80	4.94	−1.411	a
3. When individuals lack ethics, that hurts society at large.	4.43	4.60	−1.668	b	4.55	4.80	−1.955	b
4. Some students need ethical and moral direction.	4.07	4.27	−1.428	a	4.45	4.72	−2.357	b
5. Some business people need ethical and moral direction.	4.33	4.22	0.720		4.51	4.71	−1.768	b
6. Some students would benefit from presentations on ethics and morality.	3.93	4.25	−2.172	b	4.02	4.64	−5.196	c
7. Some business people would benefit from presentations on ethics and morality.	4.07	4.27	−1.367	a	4.06	4.60	−4.412	c

Note: Rating scale was from 1 = strongly disagree to 5 = strongly agree. The survey included 70 Italian and 276 US business students.
For significance: [a]0.10, [b] 0.05, [c]0.01.

professionals must abide by ethical standards. The perspective also emerged in class during discussion. Almost all students agreed that ethical behaviour by professionals is an essential condition, but for many students it was not clear how ethical behaviour could be guaranteed.

Statement 3 asserts 'When individuals lack ethics, that hurts society at large.' Students more heartedly agreed with this statement after the ethics presentation. The change in perspective was significant ($P < 0.05$). This change in perspective was also apparent in the class discussion. For Statement 4, 'Some students need ethical and moral direction,' there was a significant increase in agreement ($P < 0.01$).

While students generally agreed with Statement 5, 'Some business people need ethical and moral direction,' there was not a significant change in the average score between pre and post-presentation. During the discussion, many students said that it is very hard to change managers' view on ethical issues; education should start much earlier in order to have a pragmatic impact on society. Yet, students felt that the ethics presentation could help business people to stop and think about ethics. This is also shown by the significant increase in the scores regarding Statement 7, as described below.

The highest difference between the pre and post-presentation scores is found for Statement 6, which asserts 'some students would benefit from presentations on ethics and morality.' It was very encouraging to note that students significantly increased their agreement with this statement after experiencing the ethics presentation ($P < 0.05$). Students expressed their appreciation for the ethics session in the post-presentation comments and felt that the ethics presentation was useful and stimulating. Indeed, some students said that they never thought ethics could be taught, until they took part in the ethics session. After the presentation, students expressed thanks for having opened a discussion on ethics for the first time in their academic studies.

For Statement 7, 'Some business people would benefit from presentations on ethics and morality,' students significantly increased their level of agreement ($P < 0.10$). Students thought that exposing business managers to an ethics presentation would help them think a bit more about ethics. In the presentation itself, a positive link is described between ethical behaviour and positive financial performance, thus demonstrating that ethics is not only a philosophical issue but also one that can lead to pragmatic business advantages.

Post-presentation comments strongly indicated that students came to realize the importance of ethics education. The following post-presentation comments indicate that the ethics presentation had a profound impact on students' perspectives regarding ethics.

- 'Business ethics should be presented as a new business opportunity.'
- 'Business ethics sessions should be integrated into curricular courses and not as an extra session.'
- 'This is a subject that should be COMPULSORY and treated as an entire course; here we had only one session presentation.'
- 'The topic is far too important to be presented in an extra-curricular session.'
- 'No comments. Just more sessions.'
- 'More practical suggestions on which actions should be taken in order to be ethical.'
- 'More discussion time.'
- 'More ideas on how to improve ethics in companies.'
- 'I appreciated the purpose but there was not enough time .... It created discussions and thinking.'

Most students asked for more time for discussion on ethics, even though the topic was initially perceived as not generally teachable. After the presentation, many students indicated some change in their perspectives. Students considered ethics to be a very important topic and therefore should be included in the curriculum. Overall, the students took a positive view of the presentation. Responding to the question 'How would you rate this presentation?' students' responses averaged 3.8 on a scale from 1 to 5.

Comparing the US and Italian Results

The second purpose of this study was to determine if the ethics presentation produced changes in ethical perceptions of Italian students similar to those of US students, as reported by Smith *et al.* (2005). This was determined by comparing the pre and post-presentation scores of the two countries. The earlier results for US students are shown in the last four columns of Table 2. The purpose of Table 2 is not to compare the individual scores of specific survey statements of US students and Italian students. Differences in presenters, cultures, and settings would make such a comparison problematic. While a US-to-Italy comparison of scores on individual survey statements is inappropriate, it is appropriate to compare general changes in scores of US students with those of Italian students. The findings in each country showed how the ethics presentation led to changes in ethical perceptions of students.

In both settings, the USA and Italy, the highest increase in scores was obtained for Statement 6, 'Some students would benefit from presentations on ethics and morality.' This is a notable finding, as it shows that the ethics presentation was favourably received by both groups and succeeded in being helpful to Italian students and US students alike.

After the ethics presentation, students from both countries had significant increases in their scores for statements 3, 4, 6, and 7. After learning about the consequences of unethical practices, it was not too surprising that both groups more strongly agreed that individuals who lack ethics hurt society. Both groups more readily agreed that students and business people need ethical direction.

There were three statements in which the change in perceptions differed for the US and Italian students. The US students had significant changes from pre to post-presentation scores on statements 1, 2, and 5. However, the change in Italian students' scores was not significant for those statements. Statement 1 declared that ethics is a major issue in business. Perhaps Italian students were already in agreement with the statement and the presentation did not add to their perception. Another possible explanation is that the US students were more predisposed to significantly increasing their ethical perception scores on this statement because the US financial scandals were more prominent than those in Italy were. This may have caused US students to be more aware of unethical business practices. The US students also agreed more firmly with the necessity of professionals abiding by high ethical standards (Statement 2). Last, US students significantly increased their agreement that business people need ethical direction (Statement 5).

Conclusions

For accounting and business, ethics is widely recognized as an important topic, especially after recent financial scandals in corporations around the world. Many accounting and business students have little knowledge about the causes of ethical dilemmas and their possible solutions, and finish their studies with many technical skills but little appreciation for ethical matters. Research suggests that ethics should be taught to future business managers.

An ethics presentation, previously used in US universities, was adapted and used in an Italian university. Some changes were made to the presentation in order to adapt it to the Italian context. The results suggested that ethics could be effectively presented in this way to both contexts. Students showed appreciation for the ethics presentation and even asked for more sessions. The ethics presentation was favourably received by both groups and succeeded in being helpful to Italian students and US students alike. Post-presentation comments strongly indicated that Italian students heightened their perceptions of the importance of ethics education.

The presentation used in this study, along with the pre and post-presentation surveys, can be adapted for use in most accounting and business classes as a method of presenting ethics to students and of assessing the presentation's impact on student perspectives. Ethics is an internationally relevant topic and ethical responsibility is essential for doing business anywhere in the world.

References

Ameen, E. C., Guffey, D. M. and McMillan, J. J. (1996) Gender differences in determining ethical sensitivity of future accounting professionals, *Journal of Business Ethics*, 15(5), pp. 591–597.

Artoni, A. M. (2003) Innovative ideas and entrepreneurial courage, *Outlook*, 1. Available at http://www.Accenture.com/Outlook (accessed 7 December 2007).

Bauman, Z. (1989) *Modernity and The Holocaust* (Ithaca, NY: Cornell University Press).

Bennis, W. G. and O'Toole, J. (2005) How business schools lost their way, *Harvard Business Review*, 5(1), pp. 96–104.

Brackner, J. (1992) History of moral and ethical education, *Management Accounting*, 74, p. 22.

Brinkmann, J. (2000) Real estate agent ethics: selected findings from two Norwegian studies, *Business Ethics: A European Review*, 9(3), pp. 163–173.

Brinkmann, J. (2001) On business ethics and moralism, *Business Ethics: A European Review*, 10(4), 311–319.

Carroll A. (2005) An Ethical Education, Biz-ed, January-February, pp. 36–40.

Coates, B. E. (2004) Corporate culture, corporate mischief, and legislated ethics: the Sarbanes-Oxley Act, *Journal of Public Affairs*, 7(1), pp. 39–58.

Cowton, C. J. and Bampton, R. (2002) The teaching of ethics in management accounting: progress and prospects, *Business Ethics: A European Review*, 11(1), pp. 52–61.

Cunningham, W. P. (1998) The golden rule as universal ethical norm, *Journal of Business Ethics*, 17(1), pp. 105–109.

Davis, J. R. and Welton, R. E. (1991) Professional ethics: business students' perceptions, *Journal of Business Ethics*, 10(6), pp. 451–463.

Della Valle, D. (2004) Interview, *Class*, p. 27.

Donaldson, T. J. and Freeman, R. E. (1994) *Business as a Humanity* (Oxford: Oxford University Press).

Flory, S. M., Phillips, T. J., Reidenbach, R. E. and Robin, D. P. (1992) A multidimensional analysis of selected ethical issues in accounting, *The Accounting Review*, 67(2), pp. 284–302.

Goshal, S. (2005) Bad management theories are destroying good management practices, *The Academy of Management Learning and Education*, 4(2), pp. 75–91.

Greenwood, M. (2000) The study of business ethics: a case for Dr Seuss, *Business Ethics: A European Review*, 9(3), pp. 155–162.

Hartman, E. M. (2006) Can we teach character? An Aristotelian answer, *Academy of Management Learning & Education*, 5(1), pp. 68–81.

Higginson, R. and Moore, G. (1994) Using a computerised game in teaching business. Ethics, *Business Ethics: A European Review*, 3(3), pp. 160–164.

Jennings, M. and Entine, J. (1998) Business with a soul: a reexamination of what counts in business ethics, *Hamline Journal of Public Law and Policy*, 20(1), Available at http://www.jonentine.com/articles/business_with_soul.htm (accessed 8 December 2007).

Keller, A. C., Smith, K. T. and Smith, L. M. (2007) Do gender, educational level, religiosity, and work experience affect the ethical decision-making of US accountants?, *Critical Perspectives on Accounting*, 18(3), pp. 299–314.

Kolb, R., LeClair, D., Pelton, L., Swanson, D. L. and Windsor, D. (2005) Panel: the role of ethics in business curricula, *Journal of Business Ethics Education*, 2(1), pp. 5–12.

Lantos, G. (1989) Relative vs. fixed values, choice is absolutely clear, *Marketing Educator*, 8(1), pp. 4–6.

Marnburg, E. (2003) Educational impacts on academic business practitioner's moral reasoning and behavior: effects of short courses in ethics or philosophy, *Business Ethics: A European Review*, 12(4), pp. 403–413.

McCabe, D. L., Butterfield, K. D. and Trevino, L. K. (2006) Academic dishonesty in graduate business programs: prevalence, causes, and proposed action, *Academy of Management Learning & Education*, 5(3), pp. 294–305.

McPhail, K. (2006) Going public: a brief note on civilising accounting ethics education, *Business Ethics: A European Review*, 15(3), pp. 306–309.

Moore, G. (2006) Managing ethics in higher education: implementing a code or embedding virtue?, *Business Ethics: A European Review*, 15(4), pp. 407–418.

Piper, T. R., Gentile, M. C. and Parks, S. D. (1993) *Can Ethics be Taught? Perspectives, Challenges, and Approaches at Harvard Business School* (Boston: Harvard Business School).

Rezaee, Z. (2009) *Corporate Governance and Business Ethics* (Hoboken, New Jersey: John Wiley and Sons, Inc.).

Rockness, H. and Rockness, J. (2005) Legislated ethics: from Enron to Sarbanes–Oxley, the impact on corporate America, *Journal of Business Ethics*, 57(1), pp. 31–54.

Schweiker, W. (1993) Accounting for ourselves: accounting practice and the discourse of ethics, *Accounting, Organizations and Society*, 18(2–3), pp. 231–252.

Smith, K., Smith, L. M. and Crumbley, D. L. (2008) *The Bottom Line is Betrayal* (New York: Cengage Publishers).

Smith, L. M. (1993) Teaching ethics: an update, part two, *Management Accounting*, April, p. 18.

Smith, L. M. (2003) A fresh look at accounting ethics, *Accounting Horizons*, 17(1), pp. 47–49.

Smith, L. M., Smith, K. and Mulig, E. V. (2005) Application and assessment of an ethics presentation for accounting and business classes, *Journal of Business Ethics*, 61(2), pp. 153–164.

Trevino, L. K. and McCabe, D. (1994) Meta-learning about business ethics: building honourable business school communities, *Journal of Business Ethics*, 13(6), 405–416.

Trezise, E. K. (1994) Practical reflections on teaching business ethics to undergraduates, *Business Ethics: A European Review*, 3(3), pp. 180–185.

Weiss J. (1994) *Business Ethics. A Managerial, Stakeholder Approach* (New York: International Thomson Publishing).

Williams, S. D. and Dewett, T. (2005) Yes, you can teach business ethics: a review and research agenda. *Journal of Leadership and Organizational Studies*, 12(2), pp. 109–120.

Contextualizing the Intermediate Financial Accounting Courses in the Global Financial Crisis

ROBERT BLOOM and MARIAH WEBINGER

Department of Accountancy, Boler School of Business, John Carroll University, Ohio, USA

ABSTRACT *This paper represents an attempt to incorporate concepts and issues stemming from the global financial crisis (GFC) into the typical Intermediate Accounting, two-course sequence as taught in North American colleges and universities. The teaching approach which the authors advocate embeds the GFC throughout these courses. The main expected outcome from this project is a greater appreciation on the part of the accounting and finance majors that other business disciplines 'matter.' Put differently, those disciplines, including economics, banking, and management, interface with accounting and finance. Therefore, to understand accounting, students must be conversant with the other disciplines. The principal interrelating concepts we cover in this approach are as follows: capital maintenance, liquidity, solvency, financial leverage, efficient market hypothesis, transparency in disclosure, derivatives, fair valuation, moral hazard, and ethics.*

EDITOR'S NOTE: The continuing repercussions of the GFC were felt on the day when the final version of this paper was submitted (8 August 2011) due to Standard & Poor's downgrading the credit rating of the USA for the first time ever (from AAA to AA+) and this, coupled with problems relating to financial stability across the Eurozone, triggered huge falls on stock markets throughout the world.

Introduction

The global financial crisis (GFC) has significant implications for the way we teach our business courses, including accounting, finance, and economics. Students cannot learn about accounting in a vacuum, separate and apart from the other business disciplines.

In particular, accounting relates closely to finance and banking, so the course material should be delivered in an interdisciplinary fashion. The question is how business school programs can incorporate the lessons learned from this crisis and also serve as a catalyst to prevent future crises of this magnitude. One approach, albeit long-run and time-consuming, is to break down the disciplinary silos that currently exist in most business schools and to develop team-taught, cross-disciplinary courses, including the GFC. A second approach, more amenable to short-term results and considerably less ambitious in nature, is to infuse concepts and techniques inherent in the GFC throughout the curriculum in each department.

This paper outlines the proposed teaching pattern that was tested at John Carroll University (USA) following the second approach in the undergraduate financial accounting program—i.e. embedding the crisis in the curriculum. Intermediate Accounting, taught to both accounting and finance majors, was examined in the context of the GFC. The specific aim of this project is to improve the financial literacy of accounting majors. The issues underlying the financial crisis are inextricably linked to financial accounting and reporting, representing the intersection of banking, economics, and accounting. While accounting students also undertake courses in these other disciplines, they seem unable to integrate the concepts and techniques acquired in those courses into accounting. Therefore, incorporating material throughout these courses about the crisis can assist in making the Intermediate course sequence pertinent to current developments and to integrate the disciplines. Accordingly, this paper consists of a proposed approach to bring the GFC into the Intermediate Accounting course sequence as a key part, not as peripheral material, with a particular emphasis on the placing of events under specific topics in these courses and the use of clear-cut definitions of new terms.

Teaching Approach to Integrating the Financial Crisis

Intermediate Accounting represents the main requirement in financial accounting within the typical North-American undergraduate accounting curriculum. Generally consisting of two sequential, three-hour per week courses, each of which is 14 weeks long; Intermediate Accounting follows the Introductory Financial Accounting and Introductory Managerial Accounting course sequence. (See Appendix A for a typical North-American undergraduate accounting program.)

The GFC material serves various purposes. While it acquaints students with the multi-dimensional aspects of the GFC, it also enriches and enlivens the Intermediate Accounting courses by providing a context of fresh examples of accounting applications covered in this sequence. In so doing, this material can spark students' interest, questions, and research projects for those who wish to pursue the subject further as part of their course grade or as a senior honors thesis.

In our experience, the material promotes class discussion and students' participation in view of the current nature of this crisis, encouraging students to keep abreast of its latest developments. In fact, the subject matter has been evolving bit-by-bit for three years, allowing the students and faculty alike to learn about its ever-tantalizing twists and turns in communal fashion, sharing their newly-acquired knowledge in the classroom and beyond. Consequently, students (who seldom see faculty outside of the class setting) have been flocking to faculty offices, individually and in groups, to further analyze the GFC in its many dimensions, to raise questions, and to offer their own perspectives and judgments and, in the process, enhancing student-faculty rapport. Other faculty (in economics, finance and management) may become interested, if not also involved, in this endeavor as well, in terms of offering teaching tips, collaborative teaching ideas, and joint research endeavors with their accounting colleagues. Alumni working in financial institutions can be invited to the campus as guest speakers, offering their views on the role of accounting in the GFC. The subject matter also affords students an opportunity to recognize the importance of, and hence to examine, corporate regulatory bodies. The GFC affords a context in which to examine the legal and accounting manner in which governments actually acquired majority interests in private business firms.

This material conveys to the students a greater appreciation of the role of accounting in finance, economics, and management, helping them to overcome the 'tunnel vision' inherent in considering accounting as a discipline unto itself. Specifically, as examples, the students can achieve an enhanced understanding of such concepts as the efficient market hypothesis, representing the foundation of capital market deregulation; moral hazard, incentivizing bad behavior; and financial reporting transparency, calling for increased disclosure. Regarding the last concept, accounting and financial regulators accentuate the need for disclosure in contrast to banking regulators who emphasize the importance of maintaining financial and economic stability in financial institutions, ever concerned about disclosure overload precipitating bank runs. Moreover, given the current nature of the subject, the students are more inclined to voice their opinions, enhancing their communication skills through active learning in the Intermediate Accounting courses.

As the GFC presents an opportunity to reform existing practices (especially in accounting, finance, and banking) and to upgrade existing regulations, students are motivated to develop and debate their own ideas for reform, arguing for and against specific proposals as contained in the Dodd-Frank Act (2010) in the USA and current discussions about such regulations for the European Union (Schlamp, 2010). In this manner, students can be proactively engaged in the learning process and can enhance their critical thinking skills.

Implementation

The implementation of this material into the courses is effectuated by introducing facets of the GFC throughout the two-course Intermediate Accounting sequence on an anecdotal basis, bringing in, wherever germane, the following resources: mini-cases, vignettes, accounting journal entries, financial statements, disclosures, regulatory reports, and using news articles and videos in the instructional process. Nevertheless, the material used is based on a specific set of topics and content, which in turn can be used by other faculty at other universities. Additionally, guest speakers come to the campus to furnish their perspectives and insights on the GFC, with a particular emphasis on its accounting and auditing angles. The material can be delivered by faculty using a variety of teaching styles—whether sole lecture, lecture-discussion, or Socratic by individual instructors or instructional teams representing faculty from more than one discipline. Handouts, postings, and e-mails can enhance the teaching/learning process. As introducing a new material into a traditional course sequence involves experimentation to observe what works and what does not, what follows are our suggestions based on our experiences.

- First, an instructor must give students general background information about the GFC. The instructor may provide the students early in the course, if not on the first day of classes, with an overview of the GFC in terms of a timeline (see Appendix E) in order to facilitate subsequent class discussions (Coy and Reed, 2008; El-Erian, 2009). Based on our experience, college students, for the most part, do not read the newspapers, nor watch news programs on television or the Internet; therefore, they have only a vague sense of what happened during this crisis and even less for its international aspects.

- Another way to convey the background information is to require students to read the online editions of *The Financial Times*, *The Economist, New York Times*, and *The Wall Street Journal*, for material to incorporate into a 'scrapbook' on the GFC, to which they can contribute on a weekly basis.
- A third option to the integration is to use a comprehensive case covering the major events, organizations, and individual people involved.
- A fourth option is to use vignettes about the GFC to emphasize concepts and their applications.

However, none of the options is mutually exclusive or collectively exhaustive. In any event, the instructor ought to encourage the students to analyze the accounting implications of the GFC, what went wrong with accounting standards and accounting regulation, and what specific improvements could be made. The instructor should attempt to be nonjudgmental in this process, serving as a facilitator to allow students to form their own viewpoints and to make up their own minds. Wherever possible, the instructor should use journal entries and financial statements to explain transactions and to raise provocative questions about specific issues throughout the courses as well as to discuss how financial reporting could be improved.

A byproduct of this teaching material is that students, by the end of the two courses, generally perceive the necessity for as well as the complexity of global financial accounting standards, which cannot flourish in the absence of global financial auditing standards along with audit independence requirements, uniform interpretations, and enforcement of all those standards.

First Intermediate Financial Accounting Course

The following are common Intermediate Accounting topics taught in North-American universities. They are organized in the order in which they are generally taught in these courses, although the order is not necessary for adequate integration of the GFC in this course sequence. Within these topics, we reflect on how we incorporate the crisis.

Environment of Financial Reporting

The fundamental events in the GFC can be sketched out during the first week of this course using the timeline (see Appendix E), touching on the accounting aspects of the crisis. Some of the issues to be covered include:

- What role did the Bank of England play in this crisis? The IASB and FASB have been blamed for creating the crisis on fair valuation.
- What role did they play?

The first topic on the *Environment of Financial Reporting* should cover the Conceptual Framework, including the objectives of financial reporting and the definitions of the elements in the financial statements. The importance of full disclosure and transparency in financial reporting can also be emphasized to avoid misleading investors and creditors. However, bankers are concerned about full disclosure as they contend that bad news could cause a run on banks.

The GFC also affords an opportunity to consider the efficient market hypothesis (EMH), based on the premise of full disclosure, which is used to justify deregulation of the capital markets—i.e. that the markets police themselves. In fact, the breakdown of the bond market, which was not self-policed, was a principal event in the GFC. While EMH does not imply that the markets are omniscient or that securities are necessarily priced correctly, EMH does assert that security prices are based on all publicly-available information.

Also in the context of EMH, off-the-balance-sheet financing may be covered, including special purpose entities (SPE) or structured investment vehicles (now called 'variable interest entities' or 'VIE' in the USA), used by many enterprises, including banks and other financial institutions on both sides of the Atlantic. These entities are owned essentially by other parties. SPE securitized loans and mortgages, without consolidation of entities if external parties did not control these entities in substance, based on whether the sponsoring company bore most of the benefits and risks associated with the SPE—Amendment to FRS 2, 2009, 'Accounting for Subsidiary Undertakings 'Legal Changes' (Accounting Standards Board, 2009) 'and IASB SIC 12', 1998, 'Consolidation—Special Purpose Entities' (IFRIC, 1999). In US accounting, consolidation of SPE is required if such parties own at least 10% of the capital at risk under FIN 46(R) (FASB, 2003), which was in effect prior to the current standard, FAS 167, ASU 810, 'Consolidation', (FASB, 2009).

A key issue stemming from the GFC is the lack of disclosure by securitizing firms of the SPE they used in this process along with any actual or implicit guarantees made to the SPE. Under FRS 2, SIC 12, IAS 27, and FAS 167, the ASB, IASB, and FASB, respectively, now call for the primary beneficiary company to consolidate its SPE based on qualitative factors pertaining to who actually owns them. On accounting for SPEs, the instructor should ask:

- How would banks react to such consolidation?
- How would this practice improve financial reporting for financial institutions, in particular?
- If a bank consolidates its SPEs, how would it raise capital to support the SPE risky assets, considering current economic conditions?
- Is there compatibility between the financial accounting goal of transparency and the bank regulation goal of stability?

Statement of Financial Position

Coverage would include unrealized losses on long-term securities. There has been a dearth of disclosures by banks and other financial institutions on the fair values of toxic financial assets (bad loans and mortgages) which they held. The instructor should ask the students how disclosures could be improved in specific terms relative to the following standards:

FRS 26 (2004)	Financial Instruments: Recognition and Measurement;
FRS 29 (2005)	Financial Instruments: Disclosure;
IAS 39 (2009)	Financial Instruments: Recognition and Measurement;
IAS ED (2010)	Measurement Uncertainty Analysis: Disclosure for Fair Value Measurements; and
FAS 157 (ASU 820, 2006)	Fair Value Measurements, and its amendments on fair valuation approaches.

Income Statement and Statement of Cash flows

Coverage would include an overview of impairments and fair valuation of trading securities, to be expanded upon later in this course. The instructor would briefly contrast impairments under FRS 11 (Accounting Standards Board, 1998), 'Impairment of Fixed Assets and Goodwill' versus FAS 142, ASU 350–20–35, (FASB, 2001a) 'Goodwill and Other Intangible Assets' and FAS 144, ASU 360–10–35 (FASB, 2001b)'Accounting for the Impairment or Disposal of Long-Lived Assets' versus IAS 36 (IAS, 2009b) 'Impairment of Assets.' Impairments are more likely to occur under UK and IASB principles rather than FASB standards since the former compare the higher of present value and net realizable value to carrying value in a single step whereas the latter compares undiscounted cash flows to carrying value to first observe whether an impairment is necessary.

The subject of impairments will be reinforced later in this course under the topics of property, plant, and equipment and intangible assets. On the fair valuation of trading securities, the instructor should emphasize that, since these are current assets, holding gains and losses on these securities are reflected in the income statement. In introducing the statement of cash flows, the instructor may wish to touch on the topic of margin calls, to be covered later in the course under Investments. Most students consider buying and selling as being the only investment activities with cash flow effects. However, investments may produce significant cash flow effects through margin calls, which will be covered in greater depth in the Investments topic later in the course. (Also see Appendix D.)

Income Measurement and Profitability Analysis

The instructor would distinguish among the following terms: comprehensive income, net income, and other comprehensive income. In addition, the instructor would discuss the basis for measuring executive bonuses, asking the students for alternative bases and the pros and cons of each. For example, should net income or comprehensive income be used? Many executives at banks and financial institutions received bonuses for undertaking short-term, risky ventures, which have subsequently resulted in huge long-term losses for those enterprises; yet 'clawbacks' of these bonuses after such enterprises have been bailed out by the US government and governments in other countries have occurred only minimally. The instructor should ask the students to explain the concept of 'moral hazard' implicit in such bailouts. European member countries in the G-20 have been especially concerned about bonuses, claiming that this was the root of the GFC, largely occurring in the USA and the UK. In particular, the G-20 Summit in Pittsburgh in September 2009 has called for clawbacks. The UK imposed a one-time tax on these bonuses in 2009, adding £1.9 billion to the government's coffers, but that has not stopped banks from issuing lavish bonuses (Murphy and Parker, 2010). In the USA, Kenneth Lewis, CEO of Bank of America, resigned under fire for having promoted a takeover of Merrill Lynch by this bank, apparently without advising the stockholders of Bank of America of Merrill's huge pending losses and contractual bonus payments to its executives. Instead of paying such bonuses, banks could be retaining their income to sustain capital after all the losses they have suffered. In fact, many of these banks received extensive government bailouts, but they have not been lending to any significant extent and therefore not stimulating the economy. Additionally, in the UK and the USA, in particular, the central banks had been engaged in 'quantitative easing,' or effectively printing money by buying government bonds and corporate commercial paper from banks and other financial firms at a higher than going market price to lower interest rates and to expand the money supply in order to move out of recession.

Time Value of Money

Details should be covered on the mechanics of present valuation, which is a method of fair valuation. The instructor would ask the students why we have traditionally used present valuation sparingly in financial accounting and reporting and for which particular assets and liabilities. Present valuation is needed with or without inflation, but inflation would impact interest rates and forecasts of future cash flows. While inflation has not been a concern either in the UK or in the USA in the recent past, there are concerns about inflation and volatile interest rates in view of the large cash reserves which banks are holding. The instructor should ask the students: 'How would inflation affect accounting measures?' As some economists are worried about deflation, the instructor should ask the students: 'What are its characteristics?' Deflation is characterized by slow growth, significant unemployment, and falling prices, which hurts investors and debtors in particular. 'How could deflation affect accounting figures?'

Cash and Receivables

These are among the most liquid assets. The GFC revealed a distinct lack of liquidity among financial firms. Emphasis in this topic would be placed on fair valuation of current assets, showing accounts receivable at net realizable value after deducting the uncollectible allowance; bank loans at net realizable value, reflecting loan loss reserves analogous to the uncollectible allowance pertaining to accounts receivable; trading securities at fair market value using the following standards: FRS 26, FRS 29, IAS ED 2010/7, and FAS 157, including their different levels of fair value measurement (Accounting Standard Board, 2004; 2005; IASB, 2010b; FASB 2006).

Inventories

The instructor would cover the difference between the lower of cost or market in the UK and IASB versus US SSAP 9 (1975) and IAS 2 (2003), 'Inventories' use net realizable value for market, requiring reversals of write-downs, in the lower of cost or market. In the USA, 'market' is current replacement cost with net realizable value as a ceiling and net realizable value less a normal profit margin as a floor. The USA does not allow reversals of any write-downs or impairments.

Other Inventory Issues

The instructor would cover the process of factoring and use as a comparative illustration the securitization of mortgage loans, serving as collateral for issuance of investment securities.

Investments

Coverage would include accounting for Available-for-Sale and Held-to-Maturity securities as well as the nature of derivatives and subprime mortgages. Application of fair valuation of securities also belongs under this topic. The consequences of fair value (Curtis, 2009) would also be considered, especially downside risk, in the income statement and on the balance sheet. The losses that have been occurring on financial assets, including a brief overview of the accompanying capital maintenance issues, would be discussed under stockholders' equity in the second Intermediate Accounting course.

Some investments to focus on include collateralized debt obligations (CDO), which are pools of mortgage 'backed' securities (the top slice or 'tranche' being the safest, the other tranches less so) that were often overrated by the rating agencies and later proved to be toxic (*Report*, 2009). CDO belongs under the topic of investments, as they were assets to such financial institutions as Lehman Brothers and Bear Stearns, although actually issued by the SPE of these financial institutions. The rating agencies, including Fitch, Moody's and Standard & Poor's, advised banks on how to structure the SPE, so the new securitized investments could be rated. The CDO then had to be marked to market, but could not be directly valued in inactive markets; instead, they were marked to model. In many cases, the fair value write-downs led to 'margin calls' from creditors. The instructor should go over the examples of margin calls in Appendix D at this point in the course.

Another investment to consider is credit default swaps (CDS). AIG, the insurance giant, issued CDS to offset the risk of CDO default. CDS are quasi-insurance contracts in which an insurable interest in the underlying property or security is not required; that is analogous to taking out insurance on the home of your neighbor. CDS were also assets to many financial institutions, including Goldman Sachs. Among other financial institutions, Goldman Sachs sold its own CDO to other firms and then acquired CDS, betting that defaults would occur on the securities they created, which were significantly overvalued by the credit rating agencies based on outdated models (indicating non-significant losses from underlying subprime mortgage collateral).

In fact, Wall Street firms pay those agencies to rate their securities, and therefore have an incentive to shop around for the best ratings. The Securities and Exchange Commission (SEC), which regulates the sale of securities in the USA within interstate commerce, alleges that in one case Goldman Sachs facilitated the creation of a synthetic CDO portfolio with John Paulson, a prominent hedge fund manager, which consisted of CDS on junk, subprime collateral CDO, that was, nevertheless, highly rated by S&P and Moody's (Philips, 2010). Goldman sold this CDO package to institutional investors, including pension funds, without advising them of Paulson's significant role in selecting the portfolio. In turn, Paulson bet against the portfolio while the other investors bet for it. When the CDO tanked, Paulson received £745 million from the CDS, which the other investors including Goldman lost. The instructor should ask the students: Did Goldman have a duty to disclose Paulson as the selector of the portfolio and as the counterparty even to highly sophisticated institutional investors under SEC disclosure Rule 10B-5, which prohibits any act or omission resulting in fraud or deceit in connection with the purchase or sale of any security?'[1] In the UK, the Fraud Act of 2006 defines fraud in terms of false representation, failure to disclose information, or abuse of position.

Derivatives

The instructor should emphasize that CDS were unregulated (under the US Commodity Futures Modernization Act of 2000 and unregulated in the UK as well), as over-the-counter derivatives that did not involve capital maintenance reserves as with real insurance contracts, but were priced by actuaries like insurance contracts (Paletta, 2010).[2] AIG had to be bailed out by the US Federal Reserve when it could not meet the margin calls on CDS it sold based on bets pertaining to the viability of CDO, nor pay counterparties on very significant declines in the market price of the CDO relative to their notional amounts. In fact, AIG as the issuer of those CDS lacked the capital reserve for such payments.[3] In rescuing AIG, the US government acquired nonvoting preferred stock and warrants from its cash infusion, securities which can be discussed under the stockholders' equity or investments topics in the first and second Intermediate Accounting courses, respectively.

Fair Value of Securities

While some have accused the accounting community of precipitating the GFC through fair valuation of securities and the unrealized holding losses and capital deficiencies stemming from such valuation (FRS 29, IAS ED 2010/7, FAS 157), the Financial Crisis Advisory Group (2009) observed that most financial institutions worldwide do not fair value their securities, and hence have delayed reflection of losses on these investments (*Report*, 2009). The instructor should ask the students about the pros and cons of alternatives that financial institutions could pursue with their remaining toxic assets at this juncture, which would include the following courses of action:

- doing 'nothing';
- hoping that they will regain value at a later date;
- marking them to market and showing unrealized losses, or attempting to counteract their toxicity by issuing new shares of stock for cash.

In fact, the FASB modified its fair value standard, FAS 157, as did the IASB to allow significant judgment in fair valuation of such financial assets within inactive markets.

Operational Assets

The instructor would cover IAS 39 on optional fair valuation of categories of fixed assets in this domain.

Utilization and Impairment

The instructor would contrast US impairments of fixed assets, intangibles other than goodwill versus FRS 11. The US approach is more complex; involving two steps and is less likely to show impairments (as previously indicated). Both FRS 11 and IAS 36 compare book value to fair value (higher of present value or net realizable value). For goodwill, FAS 142 compares the fair value and book value of the reporting unit to see whether an impairment is needed and then compares the book value with the implied fair value (from offsetting the fair value of the reporting unit with the fair value of its net assets excluding goodwill) to arrive at goodwill. Additionally, the ASB and IASB require a comparison of book value and fair value of the cash generating unit, which is often a lower level than the reporting unit, to measure goodwill. The ASB, IASB, and FASB do not allow reversal of goodwill impairments.

Second Intermediate Financial Accounting Course

Current Liabilities

The instructor would re-emphasize the importance of short-term liquidity as the GFC has revealed, indicated by various key ratios such the current ratio, acid-test ratio, and working capital. The instructor would also include in this topic area a discussion of commercial paper (see Appendix B)—defining it, indicating how it is used with journal entries, and pointing out the intervention role by the Bank of England and Federal Reserve to shore up this source of funding during the GFC. That intervention involved the guaranteeing of commercial paper issued by corporations for unsecured short-term loans. Without such guarantees, those corporations would not have been able to meet their vendor payments and payrolls, among other operating cash requirements.

In the context of current liabilities, the instructor can also return to the subject of how bonuses are measured, revisiting this matter from the first Intermediate Accounting course. The typical European view, as opposed to that of the UK and the USA, on the GFC focusing on capital maintenance emphasizes contractual bonuses to banking executives, creating misplaced incentives or moral hazards for them. In particular, the 2009 G-20 Summit in Pittsburgh (USA) stressed the importance of linking bonuses to long-run risk management of the enterprise.

Also, the subject of current liabilities typically includes loss contingencies (Accounting Standards Board, 1998; IASB, 1998; FASB, 1975). In contrast to the US standard, contingencies are more likely to be booked under the British and IASB standards since the threshold for probability is lower under these standards—more likely than not, meaning greater than 50%, as opposed to the US notion of highly probable, meaning a considerably higher percentage such as 70%. Under the UK, IASB, and FASB standards, remote contingencies are not required to be disclosed. However, under the FASB standard even remote contingent losses are required disclosures should they pertain to off-the-balance-sheet financing. It is evident that banks and other financial institutions, among many other companies, have not disclosed guarantees, both explicit and implicit, of the debt issued by SPE set up for various purposes including the securitization of assets, which were kept off-the-balance-sheet by those financial institutions.

Additionally, on the topic of current liabilities, Lehman Brothers used 'Repo 105' to temporarily exchange multiples of securities as collateral for cash at the end of financial-reporting quarters, using the cash received to reduce its financial leverage, and then borrowing to repay the repo and reacquire the securities just days afterwards. Lehman reflected these transactions as sales rather than loans, thus representing off-balance-sheet financing. (No Accounting for Deception, 2010) There was no disclosure by Lehman of such transactions, which lacked legitimate economic substance (Rapoport, 2010a).

Specifically, Lehman sold securities to another financial firm to obtain a cash infusion and thereafter repurchased those securities a day or so later at a set price higher than the previous sales price. This is typically accounted for as a loan under US GAAP FAS 140, ASU 405–20 (FASB, 2000b), 'Extinguishments of Liabilities' and IFRS 9 (IFRS, 2009c), 'Financial Instruments'. However, Lehman, with the assistance of its auditor Ernst & Young and a British law firm, structured the transaction as a sale. They were able to remove the securities from its balance sheet by repurchasing the securities for 105% or in some cases 108% (Repo 108) of the previous sales price rather than 98 to 102%, which were the requirements for reflecting a loan under FAS 140 (FASB, 2000b). (See Appendix C for more detail.) A principles-based standard, FAS 166 (FASB, 2000a), in effect in 2010, supersedes FAS 140, and contains no bright-line percentages. Accordingly, FAS 166, IFRS 9, and IFRS 7 (IASB, 2009c; 2007), 'Financial Instruments: Disclosure' assert that if there is a transfer of the risks and rewards of ownership, there is a sale; otherwise, the transaction is a loan.

Long term liabilities

The instructor would emphasize the importance of the firm's ability to pay its debts in the long-term, as indicated by key solvency ratios such as debt-to-assets and debt-to-equity. In addition, the instructor would include in this topic area troubled debt restructuring, using journal entries to clarify the different approaches to such accounting, whether involving assets or changes in the terms of the debt amount, life, or interest rates. (See Appendix B.) The downfall of Lehman Brothers and Bear Stearns (the latter taken over by JP Morgan Chase) can be attributed to their issuance of CDO and the contingent liabilities stemming from margin calls on the underlying securities. In covering long-term liabilities, the instructor should also discuss restrictive covenants between creditor and debtor; for example, in its General Motors takeover, there was a detailed covenant underlying the loans which the US government made. The instructor would request students to examine recent government filings from major financial companies to determine the mechanism the government used in 'nationalizing' such companies (Valukas, 2010).

Leases

In discussing this topic, the instructor would emphasize the attractiveness of leasing in terms of off-balance-sheet financing (revisiting the application of SPE from the first Intermediate Accounting course as used by Enron and, more recently, by banks and other financial institutions as another example of off-balance-sheet financing). The current UK, IASB, and FASB standards on leasing are 'broken,' to the point of allowing too many companies to reflect what should be financing or capital leases as operating leases. The UK standard, in particular, is SSAP 21 (1984), 'Accounting for Leases and Hire Purchase Contracts,' (ICA, 1984) which asserts that a finance lease transfers most of the risks and rewards of ownership from the lessor to the lessee, typically based on the present value of minimum lease payments constituting most of the fair value of the leased asset these standards are expected to be superseded by a new standard once the IASB and FASB finish the joint standard which they are developing, which will prohibit all but short-term operating leases and thus eliminate most off-balance-sheet financing with leases.

Accounting for Income Taxes

This topic would include differences in accounting and tax treatment of assets such as fair value of AFS and Trading Securities and their deferred tax consequences and differences between accounting and tax reporting on amortization of most intangibles and impairments of goodwill.

Compensation, Pensions and Other Postretirement Employee Benefits

The instructor would reinforce the concept of Other Comprehensive Income for defined benefit plan adjustments, including amendments for past service cost and gains and losses on plan assets and plan liabilities.

In the UK, Sir Fred Goodwin, arguably the most vilified individual in the GFC, was ousted as head of the Royal Bank of Scotland, which was taken over by the government in a 70% bailout when the bank became technically insolvent due to huge asset write-downs and inadequate capital maintenance. Yet Goodwin received a hefty retirement pension annuity of £700,000, of which he finally agreed to take half after considerable public outcry. Also in the UK, Mervyn King, governor of the Bank of England, lashed out at the outrageous bonuses paid to key executives, whose banks have received government bailout funds. In December 2009, the UK government announced a 50% tax on bonuses exceeding £25,000. In the USA, the Obama Administration ordered the largest companies receiving government bailouts to reduce the compensation packages of their key executives by more than one-half (Grunwald, 2010).

Shareholders' Equity

The instructor would emphasize capital maintenance from accounting and bank perspectives in terms of the ability to sustain the existence of the enterprise. In accounting, financial capital maintenance sustains the money invested capital; physical capital maintenance sustains the operating capability of the enterprise. While the subject of capital maintenance is sorely neglected in US accounting programs (though typically covered from a banking perspective in a money and financial institutions course), the GFC provides an opportunity to examine the importance of capital maintenance requirements for banks. A key question for the instructor to raise in class is: 'What impact did the financial crisis have on capital maintenance?' The instructor should point out that bank regulators may or may not stipulate capital reserve ratios for banks in order to protect their soundness. Moreover, lax regulators are not inclined to require banks to adhere to specific debt-equity ratios. Accounting regulators may be satisfied with accounting that fits the regulatory laws rather than considering debt-equity and debt-asset ratios for balance sheet stability.

The Basel Committee on Banking Supervision has been working on new international guidelines for bank capital maintenance with more emphasis on portfolio risk management – most recently, Basel III. An organization created by the central banking regulators of G-10 nations, consisting of eleven industrial nations—Belgium, Canada, France, Germany, Italy, Japan, The Netherlands, Sweden, Switzerland, the UK and the USA, the Committee issued Basel I in 1988 and set minimum capital requirements for banks based on a ratio of equity to risk-weighted assets. Under Basel I, cash received a 0% risk rating while very risky assets such as unsecured debentures were given a 100% weighting. Basel I set two minimum requirements. Tier 1 capital was put at 4%, and only core capital would count as equity. Core capital consists of paid-in-equity including common stock and perpetual preferred stock along with retained earnings, which are amounts that cannot be removed from the bank by any customer or investor. Tier 2 capital was generally set at 8%, including all items in Tier 1 capital as well as undisclosed reserves, hybrid equity instruments, and unrecognized gains/losses not in net income.

Basel II was published in 2004, retaining the regulatory focus of Basel I, but updated for the modern conglomerates that have dominated the financial industry. Specifically, Basel II outlined two pillars. The first pillar set capital maintenance regulations for three separate risk components: credit risk, operational risk, and market risk. The second pillar dealt with enforcement mechanisms for the capital maintenance requirements set in the first pillar. Following the financial crisis, these capital maintenance regulations were considered insufficient.

In 2010, Basel III was released, a set of regulations to be phased in over the next 10 years, to increase the capital ratios and to require banks to hold capital against derivatives and other off-balance-sheet items (Ewing, 2010; Onaran, 2010). Banks are now required to hold 4.5% of Tier 1 capital plus a 2.5% cushion. Banks operating above the minimum but within the cushion will face restrictions on dividends and bonuses (Basel III, 2010). It is important for the instructor to point out the relationship between fair value accounting, particularly holding losses on trading securities reducing retained earnings, which is part of Tier 1 capital, and regulatory capital maintenance. This relationship engendered considerable political influence on fair value accounting standards and disclosures, an example of the economic effects of accounting measurements, as firms may have to schedule stock offerings or hold back dividends in order to meet the equity targets set by the regulations.

It is also important to note that bank regulatory capital is similar in theory to accounting capital maintenance. In accounting, capital maintenance is concerned with sustaining the general solvency and liquidity of a firm. There are no specifics about what level of capital maintenance is desired as such measures would vary significantly across industries. Alternatively, bank regulators are specific about what constitutes capital and what level of capital are required in view of the inherent conflict between bank profitability and stability of the economy. Banks tend to be more profitable the more risk and less capital they hold. However, financial risk-taking threatens the stability of the entire business community; hence there is a need for strict bank regulation in the realm of capital maintenance. Nevertheless, financial firms attempt to circumvent the regulations by discovering new financial products that go unregulated, thus increasing risk to the firms and the economy.

Also the instructor should discuss the UK Asset Protection Scheme and the US Troubled Asset Relief Program (TARP) of the US Treasury, which involved the acquisition of investments in financial institutions in exchange for a cash infusion and guarantees of their debt, with the governments, in turn, receiving equity and constraints imposed on the executive bonuses and dividend payouts in these institutions. (Those transactions can be readily shown in terms of journal entries. See Appendix B.)

There is a moral hazard associated with the foregoing two programs. The instructor should ask the students why that is so. Big financial institutions were bailed out for their own wrongdoing. These programs were intended to prevent a meltdown of the entire economy, but it appeared as though the UK and the US governments were favoring the big institutions. Instead of focusing on the plight of individual homeowners confronting foreclosure, the governments dealt with banks and other financial institutions. Nevertheless, these plans were successful in stabilizing large banks (though many still have toxic assets on their balance sheets) and the economy, but not in spurring bank lending, nor stemming home foreclosures.

Stock Options and Earnings per Share

The instructor would include coverage of dilutive warrants in the computation of earnings per share. Warrants were involved in the UK and US bailouts of financial companies. Additionally, stemming from the controversy of paying bank executives cash bonuses for short-term performance, there has recently been an emphasis on providing such bonuses using restricted stock that vests after several years of service, emphasizing long-term performance.

Accounting Changes and Error Corrections

The instructor would cover earnings management, income smoothing, and restatements.

Statement of Cash Flows

The GFC calls for more attention to be paid in accounting to short-term liquidity and long-term solvency. Few accounting standards emphasize such concepts, apart from the statement of cash flows. The GFC highlights the importance of current and future cash flows, which should be emphasized in teaching both Intermediate Accounting courses.

Principal Lessons of the Collective Failure

The GFC was the fault of so many parties, including: the regulators (for inadequate bank capital maintenance requirements and inadequate bank disclosures), the accounting community (for lack of adequate disclosures by banks and other financial institutions), the credit rating agencies (for incorrect ratings of mortgage-backed securities), the legal community, banks, financial institutions, the Bank of England, and the Federal Reserve. London's Canary Wharf and New York's Wall Street became gambling casinos for the bond market. Unethical and illegal actions by financial firms came together to create a global credit meltdown, the likes of which history has never seen (Elliott, 2008; Ellis, 2010; Kroft, 2010; Marlin, 2009; Morgenson and Story, 2010; Riddix, 2010).

Throughout the Intermediate Accounting sequence, the instructor should emphasize the ethical aspects of accounting policy decision-making and disclosures (e.g. where financial firms were selling securities they issued to other firms and then betting that those securities would default). There was considerable deception by many parties in the GFC, including bank lenders, mortgage brokers, and credit rating agencies (Reavis, 2009). Emphasis should be placed on pressures by the European Union and G-20 Summit on the IASB and FASB, especially with respect to fair valuation of securities. The European Union and the G-20 encouraged the standard setters to provide quick fixes to the crisis by rapidly changing their accounting standards instead of going through their elaborate due process procedures. The instructor should ask the students for their perspectives on such practice. The standards issued from rushing to judgment may well be myopic. The IASB and FASB may be better advised to prepare new standards carefully with adequate due process.

Among the critical lessons stemming from the fallout of the GFC is that excessive borrowing is too risky. Governments (including Greece, the USA, the UK, Italy, Spain, Portugal, Ireland, as examples), enterprises, and individuals should act frugally, living within their means (Adams, 2009; 'Europe's PIGs,' 2010; Sorkin, 2009). Mortgages, like other contracts, should be adequately documented, including the vetting of employment history, income, and references of the borrowers, clearly reflecting an ability to pay the principal and interest in the long-term. The financial crisis also points to the desirability for considerably more transparent financial reporting disclosures (but that was a key lesson of Enron and WorldCom as well), in particular, the importance of a single set of high-quality global accounting standards. In fact, the G-20 Summit in Pittsburgh called for implementation of such standards by 2011. The Financial Crisis Advisory Group (2009) also recommended convergence of IASB and FASB standards. There is a need to break up big financial institutions, so that none of them is too big to fail. The crisis highlights the necessity for uniform, international bank maintenance requirements, enhancing the quality of bank capital, thereby lessening pro-cyclicality, as called for by the G-20 Summit in Pittsburgh. Higher capital requirements for banks are needed to guard against risky behavior. The use of SPE to avoid capital maintenance issues should be eliminated, which may be the result of UK Amendment to FRS 2, IFRS SIC 12, and FAS 167. Regulations for standardized and customized (privately-traded) derivatives such as CDS and for consumer protection, as proposed by the G-20, would be more effective if globally adopted. Another key lesson is the necessity to reform the practices of the credit rating agencies, which face no penalty when they incorrectly rate securities, owing to their freedom of oral and written expression. There is an inherent conflict of interest when security issuers pay those agencies to rate their securities; in fact, issuers can even shop around for favorable ratings on their securities. Beyond that, many financial institutions can only hold high-grade securities, making the rating agencies less likely to rate securities as low-grade. Accordingly, investors should use due diligence in purchasing securities and avoid placing sole emphasis on the credit ratings (Philips, 2008).

On 15 July 2010, the US Congress approved a final reform bill, known as the Dodd-Frank Act, the main provisions of which follow. (No such law has been passed in the UK, although the Turner Review (2009) has made a number of recommendations in this regard.) An independent consumer protection agency is to be established within the Federal Reserve to regulate financial products, including mortgages and credit cards. A resolution authority of federal agencies is to be set up to spot and wind down banks and other financial firms on the brink of failure. The SEC is to study credit rating agencies over the next two years to decide how they should function, including whether to create a special board to determine which agency will rate a particular bond issue. Companies issuing CDO must retain at least 5% of the issue on their balance sheets. Banks and other financial firms must conduct risky derivative business, including CDS, metals, and energy, through subsidiaries to be established for this purpose. Banks are permitted to invest no more than 3% of their Tier 1 capital, which currently includes common stock and preferred stock, in hedge and private equity funds. Large banks will be subject to a tax to defray the cost of this law.

Students should be asked about their perspectives on those provisions in the act, what deficiencies appear to exist in this law and about new Basel III regulations. A principal question is what steps other countries will take in response to this bill to prevent regulatory arbitrage, whereby banks and other financial firms in the USA could take their business elsewhere to circumvent this legislation (Geithner, 2010; Isaac, 2010; Volcker, 2010).

Another proposal, put forward by former British Prime Minister Gordon Brown (based on an idea advanced previously by the late Nobel Laureate James Tobin of Yale University), calls for a tax on all financial transactions since many are 'socially useless.' The instructor should ask the students: 'What are the pros and cons of this idea?' Mervyn King also wants to establish a firewall between trading and investment banking activities of big banks (Lenzer, 2010; Story, Thomas and Schwartz, 2010). In the UK, the new coalition government (elected in 2010) plans to give the power to regulate banks, financial firms, and insurance companies to the Bank of England. Additionally, a new consumer protection agency will be created to regulate financial firms offering consuming services, and a financial policy commission set up to examine financial stability issues. The instructor should elicit the students' views on the foregoing recommendations.

The FASB has issued an exposure draft, 'Accounting for Financial Instruments and Revisions to the Accounting for Derivative Instruments and Hedging Activities' ASU 825 and ASU 815, (FASB, 2010) on the fair valuation of loans, which would require banks and other financial firms holding loans to maturity to report their fair values and amortized costs, showing fair value changes in other comprehensive income. The IASB counterpart to this proposal is IFRS 9, which only requires amortized cost for those loans depending on the business model and whether the loans will be held to maturity (Rapoport, 2010b). The instructor should elicit the students' positions on fair valuation of loans.

As we have also seen, ethics, which was not only the underlying cause of the GFC but also of the corporate accounting scandals involving Enron and WorldCom earlier in the decade, cannot be legislated. Nonetheless, regulation may serve to deter fraud. The greed, deception, and fraud underlying the GFC (though there have been few legal cases brought to trial on both sides of the Atlantic) raises questions about the nature of corporate governance in banks and other financial institutions, emphasizing the well-being of their stockholders and executives at the expense of other constituents. A more suitable model for these corporations and countries would focus on how they could better serve society in terms of funding economic growth and sustainability efforts.

Summary

The main lessons students appear to derive from studying the GFC are:

(a) Accounting cannot be understood in a vacuum; accounting relates to the other business disciplines, and it should be taught with that relationship in mind. Business literacy is necessary to understanding accounting. Furthermore, accounting standard setting is too important to be left entirely to accountants.

(b) Financial and other firms need to pay careful attention to their liquidity and solvency, concepts that generally receive short shrift in accounting education and standard setting.
(c) Capital preservation in business firms is an important concept that is neglected—at least in American accounting education.
(d) Transparency in financial reporting is needed for the benefit of all the stakeholders of the firm.
(e) A single set of high quality, global financial accounting standards, uniformly interpreted and executed, would promote global credit stability.
(f) Accounting standards such as fair valuation of financial assets and liabilities can have significant economic and political consequences to the point that standard setters will be pressured by governmental bodies to amend those standards.
(g) Short-term bonuses incentivize myopic management behavior, reflecting a moral hazard.
(h) While 'caveat emptor' should prevail in any transaction, capital markets need to be regulated to deter firms from issuing securities based on toxic collateral (such as sub-prime mortgages) and subsequently from insuring themselves against the default of such securities.

Testing of the Financial Crisis Module

This approach has been tested in classes at John Carroll University (USA) during the 2009–2010 academic year in three sections of Intermediate Accounting for accounting majors and one section of a separate course of Intermediate Accounting for finance majors (the latter course, also three hours per each of 14 weeks, covering most of the topics in the two semester course but in much less depth). In those four sections, 35 students completed a questionnaire about the integration of the GFC into the accounting subject matter. (See Table 1 for the survey instrument.) This instrument was given at some point in the final two weeks of the courses at the end of the class period. Students were asked to fill out the questionnaire, but not to provide any identifying information. One student was selected to collect the instrument, and that student delivered the questionnaires in a sealed envelope to the department secretary.

The instrument provided the students with four questions about the integration of the GFC into Intermediate Accounting course. They were asked to respond to each question with either answers of 'strongly agree,' 'agree,' 'neutral,' 'disagree,' or 'strongly disagree.' The fifth question was open-ended, seeking suggestions for future implementation. For our analysis, 'strongly agree' was coded as 2, agree as 1, 'neutral' as 0, disagree as −1, and 'strongly disagree' as −2. The results are summarized in Table 2. Four returned instruments were excluded because the responses were other than the above responses[4].

All questions are statistically significant in the positive, providing support for the assertion that teaching the events of the GFC in tandem with accounting concepts adds value to the learning experience. Most especially, students felt this approach helped them to understand the relationships among accounting, banking, and finance; in fact, this question had the highest mean response at 1.39. This is particularly important as the silo nature of business was frequently a suggested cause of the GFC; departments within the financial firms did not communicate adequately among themselves, which resulted in risk mismanagement. For the open-ended question, students remarked that embedding the GFC in this course enabled them to learn not only specific dimensions of the crisis but also traditional concepts and standards in the context of corporate finance and investments. They enjoyed the real world orientation of the courses. Actually, only 20 respondents filled out the open-ended question, and eight of those specifically remarked on how integrating 'real world'

Table 1. Questionnaire instrument.

INTEGRATING THE FINANCIAL CRISIS IN THE INTERMEDIATE ACCOUNTING SEQUENCE

QUESTIONS: PLEASE ANSWER THE FIRST FOUR QUESTIONS IN TERMS OF EITHER STRONGLY AGREE, AGREE, NEUTRAL, DISAGREE, OR STRONGLY DISAGREE. ALSO PROVIDE COMMENTS IN RESPONSE TO EACH QUESTION IF YOU FEEL SO INCLINED.

1. DID THIS APPROACH HELP YOU LEARN THE ACCOUNTING SUBJECT MATTER?
2. DID THIS APPROACH HELP YOU TO RETAIN YOUR KNOWLEDGE OF THE ACCOUNTING SUBJECT MATTER?
3. DID THIS APPROACH HELP YOU TO UNDERSTAND THE RELATIONSHIPS AMONG ACCOUNTING, FINANCE, AND BANKING?
4. WAS THE TIME AND EFFORT SPENT ON THIS MATERIAL WORTHWHILE?

WHAT SPECIFIC SUGGESTIONS DO YOU HAVE FOR THIS INTEGRATION IN FUTURE OFFERINGS OF THIS COURSE?

Table 2. Questionnaire results.

Question	Mean	*n*	Std deviation	*P*-value
Learn the accounting subject matter	1.0645	31	0.7273	<.001
Retain the accounting subject matter	0.8709	31	0.8462	<.001
Understand the relationships among accounting, finance, and banking	1.3871	31	0.6152	<.001
Time and effort on material worthwhile	1.1290	31	0.8059	<.001

events helped their learning. The bottom line is that this contextualization provides a connecting theme or focus that runs throughout those courses.

The downside of instituting this framework is the work entailed in its execution. Many faculty do not feel comfortable with the inclusion of interdisciplinary topics in their accounting courses, especially if it is continually evolving as the course progresses. For them, team teaching with faculty from other areas would be desirable, assuming they can work together without significant friction. Other faculty detest the idea of sharing their classes with colleagues from other departments because it means giving up some control of their courses. There is the need to be especially judicious in time management in these two courses as the courses contain many concepts and standards to cover. In addition, once the framework is implemented, the students have to be tested on it, including the desirability of using essay questions and mini-cases, which can be time-consuming to compose and grade, as well as short-answer questions.

Our next step in this project, perhaps the hardest, is to attempt to persuade our colleagues that this endeavor is worthwhile, and should therefore be adopted. We sense inertia, if not apprehension, on their part to implement this interdisciplinary approach due to their lack of knowledge of technical financial and banking concepts and the fact that the intermediate courses are vacuum-packed as it is without adding the GFC to the curriculum. Nevertheless, we will persevere to break down the existing silos that prevail in our courses with an eye to making the courses more relevant to our students. After all, accounting played a major role in the crisis, and accounting was affected by its outcomes. Additionally, accounting has a close linkage to the other disciplines involved in the crisis. Students should be conversant with these interrelationships as they cannot be expected to understand accounting as an isolated field of endeavour. Particular faculty in our department who are knowledgeable about the GFC and are willing to experiment in curriculum change and interact with faculty from economics and finance will serve as the resource leaders in this project. As an outgrowth, a closer working relationship, perhaps a partnership, could be forged across traditional business school departments, so that the faculty can enrich not just their courses but also their research. Such ties are sorely needed in accounting where the curriculum and research tend to be especially self-contained.

Closing Comments

Achieving an understanding of the multifaceted nature of the GFC, which involves excessive bonuses and a distinctly dysfunctional risk management system in these enterprises, is tantamount to putting together a jigsaw puzzle. As faculty in this endeavour, we are attempting to walk the students through the crisis, sprinkling particular aspects of the crisis among the various topics covered in the Intermediate Accounting courses, and in specific instances reiterating those concepts and techniques for reinforcement when they apply to more than one topic area. In the process, students appreciate the interdisciplinary nature of the business disciplines (especially accounting, finance, and banking), and become motivated to read the financial press and pay attention to the other business media. In particular, students gain an understanding of the importance of capital maintenance as applied to banks and other financial institutions. Students come to the realization that, in view of the interfaces between accounting and finance as well as accounting and banking, comprehension of accounting cannot occur in a vacuum; instead, such understanding involves integrating accounting with the other business disciplines. To learn about accounting, students have to consider the needs of investors, financial analysts, and bankers—in particular, how accounting can accommodate such needs.

Acknowledgements

Thc authors wish to acknowledge the assistance of Jordan Masters, a Master of Accountancy student, and Paul Tekavec, an undergraduate accountancy major, both at John Carroll University, in editing and proofreading this paper.

Notes

[1]On 15 July 2010, Goldman settled a civil fraud case on the foregoing matter, agreeing to pay £330 million, the largest penalty in SEC history, and acknowledging that its marketing brochure failed to provide adequate information to investors about this matter.

[2]Warren Buffett, CEO of Berkshire Hathaway, has referred to 'derivatives,' which include many financial instruments such as CDO and CDS, as 'financial weapons of mass destruction' (Morris, 2008). While the subject of derivatives may be more typically relegated to the Advanced Financial Accounting course, the instructor should provide an introduction to this subject in Intermediate Accounting, the textbooks for which offer at least an appendix on this topic. A derivative is a contract with an underlying risk such as interest rates and foreign exchange rates, which can be traded on exchanges or between companies. A derivative can be used to manage the risk of oil price increases as an example, but can also be used for speculative purposes. Just as parties benefit from derivatives, so too are many harmed if oil prices fall contrary to their contractual expectations, particularly if the contract is highly leveraged.

[3]It should be noted that CDS did not require AIG to reserve capital unless the buying firm is a bank, and thus subject to capital maintenance regulation requirements. However, CDS are subject to margin calls for the issuer if excessive credit default occurs.

[4]All four of these subjects responded in the affirmative to all four questions. This could be interpreted as agreement; however, as it was not possible to determine the subjects' underlying intent, those observations were omitted from the analysis.

References

Accounting Standards Board (1998) FRS 11—Impairment of Fixed Assets and Goodwill. Available at http://www.frc.org.uk/asb/technical/standards/pub0108.html (accessed 10 November 2010).

Accounting Standards Board (1998) FRS 12—Provisions, Contingent Liabilities and Contingent Assets. Available at http://www.frc.org.uk/asb/technical/standards/pub0107.html (accessed 10 November 2010).

Accounting Standards Board (2004) FRS 26—Financial Instruments: Recognition and Measurement. Available at http://www.frc.org.uk/asb/technical/pub0654.html (accessed 10 November 2010).

Accounting Standards Board (2005) FRS 29—Financial Instruments: Disclosure. Available at http://www.frc.org.uk/asb/technical/pub0979.html (accessed 10 November 2010).

Accounting Standards Board (2009) FRS 2—Accounting for Subsidiary Undertakings 'Legal Changes'. Available at http://www.frc.org.uk/images/uploaded/documents/Amends_FRS2_6_28%20Web%20Optimised1.pdf (accessed 10 November 2010).

Adams, T. (2009) Reasons to be fearful, *The Guardian*, 4 January. Available at http://www.guardian.co.uk/culture/2009/jan/04/financial-crisis-anxiety (accessed 17 March 2010).

Basel III (2010) http://lexicon.ft.com/term.asp?t=Basel-III 7 October (accessed 10 November 2010).

Coy, P. and Reed, S. (2008) Financial crisis: how to stop the panic, *Business Week*, 8 October. Available at http://www.businessweek.com/magazine/content/08_42/b4104028030821.htm (accessed 13 January 2010).

Curtis, J. W. (Ed.) (2009) *Mark to market accounting* (New York: Nova Science).

El-Erian, M. (2009) Life after the financial crisis, *Business Week*, 21 May. Available at http://www.businessweek.com/magazine/content/09_22/b4133073646280.htm (accessed 2 September 2010).

Elliott, L. (2008) Credit crisis—how it all began, *The Guardian*, 5 August. Available at http://www.guardian.co.uk/business/2008/aug/05/northernrock.banking (accessed 21 January 2010).

Ellis, B. (2010) Feds begin criminal probe into Goldman, *CNN Money.com*, 29 April. Available at http://money.cnn.com/2010/04/29/news/companies/SEC_goldman_prosecutors/ (accessed 11 November 2010).

Europe's PIGS: Country by country (2010) *BBC News.com* Global Economy, 18 May. Available at http://news.bbc.co.uk/2/hi/8510603.stm (accessed 3 November 2010).

Ewing, J. (2010) World Panel Backs Rules to Avert Banking Crises, *New York Times*, 12 September. Available at http://www.nytimes.com/2010/09/13/business/global/13bank.html?scp=1&sq=regulators%20back%20new%20bank%20rules&st=cse (accessed 3 November 2010).

Financial Accounting Standards Board (1975) Statement No. 5: ASU 450, Accounting for Contingencies. Accounting Standards Codification. Available at http://asc.fasb.org/subtopic&trid=2155942&nav_type=left_nav&analyticsAssetName=topic_page_left_nav_subtopic (accessed 29 October 2010).

Financial Accounting Standards Board (2000a) Statement No. 166: ASU 860, Transfers and Servicing. Accounting Standards Codification. Available at http://asc.fasb.org/subtopic&trid=2155942&nav_type=left_nav&analyticsAssetName=topic_page_left_nav_subtopic (accessed 29 October 2010).

Financial Accounting Standards Board (2000b) Statement No. 140: ASU 405, Extinguishments of Liabilities. Accounting Standards Codification. Available at http://asc.fasb.org/subtopic&trid=2155942&nav_type=left_nav&analyticsAssetName=topic_page_left_nav_subtopic (accessed 29 October 2010).

Financial Accounting Standards Board (2001a) Statement No. 142: ASU 350, Intangibles- Goodwill and Other. Accounting Standards Codification. Available at http://asc.fasb.org/topic&trid=2144416&nav_type=left_nav&analyticsAssetName=_left_nav_topic (accessed 29 October 2010).

Financial Accounting Standards Board (2001b) Statement No. 144: ASU 360, Property, Plant & Equipment. Accounting Standards Codification. Available at http://asc.fasb.org/subtopicviewall&trid=2155824 (accessed 29 October 2010).

Financial Accounting Standards Board (2003) Financial Interpretation (FIN) 46(R), Consolidation of Variable Interest Entities, Available at http://fasb.org/pdf/fin%2046R (accessed 5 August 2011).

Financial Accounting Standards Board (2006) Statement No. 157: ASU 820, Fair Value Measurements and Disclosures. Accounting Standards Codification, Available at http://asc.fasb.org/subtopic&trid=2155942&nav_type=left_nav&analyticsAssetName=topic_page_left_nav_subtopic (accessed 29 October 2010).

Financial Accounting Standards Board (2009) Statement No. 167: ASU 810, Consolidation. Accounting Standards Codification, Available at http://asc.fasb.org/subtopic&trid=2155942&nav_type=left_nav&analyticsAssetName=topic_page_left_nav_subtopic (accessed 29 October 2010).

Financial Accounting Standards Board (2010) Exposure Draft—Accounting for Financial Instruments (Topic 825) and Revisions to the Accounting for Derivative Instruments and Hedging Activities (Topic 815). Available at http://www.fasb.org/cs/BlobServer?blobcol=urldata&blobtable=MungoBlobs&blobkey=id&blobwhere=1175820761372&blobheader=application/pdf (accessed 1 November 2010).

Financial Crisis: A Timeline of Events and Policy Actions, The Federal Reserve Bank of St. Louis. Available at http://timeline.stlouisfed.org/index.cfm?p=timeline#2010-1 (accessed 1 June 2011).

Geithner supports global approach to reform (2010) *The Wall Street Journal*, 27 May. Available at http://online.wsj.com/article/NA_WSJ_PUB:SB10001424052748704269204575270083043499208.html (accessed 9 November 2010).
Grunwald, M. (2010) Can bashing the banks help Obama? *TIME*, 28 January. Available at http://www.time.com/time/politics/article/0,8599,1957290,00.html (accessed 1 November 2010).
International Accounting Standards Board (1998) IAS 37—Provisions, Contingent Liabilities, and Contingent Assets. Available at http://www.iasplus.com/standard/ias37.htm (accessed 3 November 2010).
International Accounting Standards Board (2003) IAS 2- Financial Instruments: Recognition and Measurement. Available at http://www.iasplus.com/standard/ias02.htm (accessed 3 November 2010).
International Accounting Standards Board (2007) IFRS 7—Financial Instruments: Disclosure. Available at http://www.iasplus.com/standard/ifrs07.htm (accessed 3 November 2010).
International Accounting Standards Board (2009a) IAS 39—Financial Instruments: Recognition and Measurement. Available at http://www.iasplus.com/standard/ias39.htm (accessed 3 November 2010) l.
International Accounting Standards Board (2009b) IAS 36—Impairment of Assets http://www.iasplus.com/standard/ias36.htm (accessed 3 November 2010).
International Accounting Standards Board (2009c) IFRS 9—Financial Instruments. Available at http://www.iasplus.com/standard/ifrs09.htm (accessed 3 November 2010).
International Accounting Standards Board (2010a) IAS 27—Consolidated and Separate Financial Statements. Available at http://www.iasplus.com/standard/ias27.htm (accessed 3 November 2010).
International Accounting Standards Board (2010b) Exposure Draft 2010/7—Measurement Uncertainty Analysis: Disclosure for Fair Value Measurements. Available at http://www.iasb.org/NR/rdonlyres/07855A41-D0A9-4197-ADF9-15A1088E466A/0/EDMeasurementUncertaintyAnalysis0610.pdf (accessed 3 November 2010).
Institute of Chartered Accountants (1984) Statement of Standard Accounting Practice No. 21—Accounting for leases and hire purchase contracts. Available at http://www.frc.org.uk/images/uploaded/documents/A7176A%20SSAP%2021%20cover.pdf (accessed 17 November 2010).
International Financial Reporting Interpretations Committee (1999) SIC 12—Consolidation- Special Purpose Entities. Available at http://www.iasplus.com/interps/sic012.htm (accessed 18 November 2010).
Isaac, W. (2010) The inept financial reform bill, *Forbes*, 24 May. Available at http://www.forbes.com/2010/05/24/financial-reform-economy-tarp-opinions-columnists-william-m-isaac.html (accessed 13 October 2010).
Kroft, S. (2010) Wall St's delusion, *60 Minutes*, 12 March. Available at http://www.cbsnews.com/stories/2010/03/12/60minutes/main6292458.shtml (accessed 4 November 2010).
Lenzer, R. (2010) Bad news for Wall Street: Volcker has Obama's ear, *Forbes*, 21 January. Available at http://blogs.forbes.com/streettalk/2010/01/21/bad-news-for-wall-street-volcker-has-obamas-ear/ (accessed 23 September 2010).
Marlin, J. T. (2009) How the financial crisis happened, *Huffington Post.com.*, 2 May. Available at http://www.huffingtonpost.com/john-tepper-marlin/how-the-financial-crisis_b_172964.html# (accessed 7 October 2010).
Morgenson, G. and Story, L. (2010) Testy conflict with Goldman helped push A.I.G. to edge, *New York Times* , 7 February. Available at http://community.nytimes.com/comments/www.nytimes.com/2010/02/07/business/07goldmag.html (accessed 25 June 2010).
Morris, C. R. (2008) Financial Weapons of Mass Destruction. *Washington Independent.com*, 10 June. Available at http://washingtonindependent.com/1084/financial-weapons-of-mass-destruction. (accessed 17 March 2010).
Murphy, M. and Parker, G. (2010) Supertax on bankers failed, says Darling, *Financial Times*, 2 September. Available at http://www.ft.com/cms/s/0/435df6e8-b5fc-11df-a048-00144feabdc0.html (accessed 13 October 2010).
No accounting for deception (2010) *Wall Street Journal.com/Economist/Wharton.* Available at http://knowledge.wharton.upenn.edu/arabic/article.cfm?articleId=2450 (accessed 30 November 2010).
Onaran, Y. (2010) Basel Means Higher Capital Ratios, Time to Comply, *Businessweek.com*, Available at http://www.businessweek.com/news/2010-09-13/basel-means-higher-capital-ratios-time-to-comply.html (accessed 11 November 2010).
Paletta, D. (2010) White House Signals It Won't Fight to Keep Rule on Derivatives. *Wall Street Journal.com*, 26 May. Available at http://online.wsj.com/article/SB10001424052748704717004575268790976078952.html?mod=rss_whats_news_us&utm_source=feedburner&utm_medium=feed&utm_campaign=Feed%3A+wsj%2Fxml%2Frss%2F3_7011+%28WSJ.com%3A+What%27s+News+US%29 (accessed 3 December 2010).
Philips, M. (2008) Gaming the financial system, *Newsweek*, 18 November. Available at http://www.newsweek.com/2008/11/17/gaming-the-financial-system.html (accessed 23 September 2010).

Philips, M. (2010) Goldman Sachs, *Newsweek*, 16 April. Available at http://www.newsweek.com/blogs/wealth-of-nations/2010/04/16/goldman-sachs-has-the-sec-finally-grown-a-pair-under-mary-schapiro.html (accessed 29 October 2010).

Rapoport, M. (2010a) B of A, Citi made 'repos' errors, *Wall Street Journal*, 27 May. Available at http://online.wsj.com/article/NA_WSJ_PUB:SB10001424052748704032704575268902274399416.html (accessed 12 November 2010).

Rapoport, M. (2010b) Fair value proposal could cost banks, *Wall Street Journal*, 27 May. Available at http://online.wsj.com/article/NA_WSJ_PUB:SB10001424052748704032704575268962900687370.html (accessed 15 November 2010).

Reavis, C. (2009) *The global financial crisis of 2008–2009: the role of greed, fear, and oligarchs* (Cambridge, Mass:, MIT Sloan Case) Available at https://mitsloan.mit.edu/MSTIR/GlobalFinancialCrisis/Crisis-2008-2009/Pages/default.aspx (accessed 1 December 2009).

Report of the financial crisis advisory group (2009) (London, UK). Available at http://www.iasb.org/NR/rdonlyres/2D2862CC-BEFC-4A1E-8DDC-F159B78C2AA6/0/FCAGReportJuly2009.pdf (accessed 21 January 2010).

Riddix, M. (2010) Down the rabbit hole: Deciphering CDOs, *Forbes*, 17 May. Available at http://www.forbes.com/2010/05/17/what-are-collateralized-debt-obligations-personal-finance-cdos.html (accessed 10 November 2010).

Schlamp, H. (2010) Crisis Forces Europe to Unite on Financial Reform, *Spiegel Online International*, 13 September. Available at http://www.spiegel.de/international/europe/0,1518,717087,00.html (accessed 5 November 2010).

Sorkin, A. R. (2009) *Too big to fail* (New York: Viking Press).

Story, L., Thomas, L. and Schwartz, N. (2010) Wall St helped to mask debt, fueling Europe's crisis, *New York Times*, 14 February. Available at http://www.nytimes.com/2010/02/14/business/global/14debt.html (accessed 17 November 2010).

The Turner Review: A regulatory response to the global financial crisis (2009), The Financial Services Authority, March. Available at http://www.fsa.gov.uk/pubs/other/turner_review.pdf (accessed 23 September 2011).

Valukas, A. (2010) Lehman Brothers Holdings Inc. Chapter 11 Proceedings Examiner's Report. Section III.A.4: Repo 105 Jenner and Block. Available at: http://lehmanreport.jenner.com/ (accessed 10 December 2010).

Volcker, P. (2010) How to reform our financial system, *New York Times*, 30 January. Available at http://www.nytimes.com/2010/01/31/opinion/31volcker.html (accessed 2 September 2010).

Appendix A

Typical North-American Undergraduate

Accounting Program Courses (each three hours per week for 14 weeks)

Required courses:

1. Introductory Financial Accounting
2. Introductory Managerial Accounting
3. Intermediate Accounting I
4. Intermediate Accounting II
5. Cost Accounting
6. Income Taxation I (which is often individual, not corporate)
7. Auditing

Elective courses:

1. Accounting Theory
2. Government and Not-for-Profit Accounting
3. Income Taxation II
4. Advanced Managerial Accounting

5. International Accounting
6. Advanced Auditing

Appendix B

Journal Entries

Commercial Paper

Issuance

Cash	(A increase)
Notes Payable	(L increase)

Payment

Notes Payable	(L decrease)
Interest Expense	(SE decrease)
Cash	(A decrease)

Warrants

Issuance (Attachable)

Issuer

Cash	(A increase)
Convertible Bonds Payable	(L increase)

Holder

Investments	(A increase)
Cash	(A decrease)

Issuance (Detachable)

Issuer

Cash	(A increase)
Discount	(L decrease)
Bonds Payable	(L increase)
Paid-in-Capital Stock Warrants	(SE increase)

Holder

Investments in Bonds	(A increase)
Investments in Stock Warrants	(A increase)
Discount on Bonds	(A decrease)
Cash	(A decrease)

Exercise (Attachable)

Issuer

Convertible Bonds Payable	(L decrease)
Common Stock	(SE increase)
Paid-in Capital in Excess of Par Value	(SE increase)

Holder

Investments in Common Stock	(A increase)
Investments in Bonds	(A decrease)

Exercise (Detachable)

Issuer

Cash	(A decrease)	
Paid-in- Capital Stock Warrants	(SE decrease)	
Common Stock		(SE increase)
Paid-in-Capital in Excess Par Value		(SE increase)

Holder

Investments in Common Stock	(A increase)	
Investments in Stock Warrants	(A decrease)	
Cash		(A decrease)

Troubled Debt Restructuring

A. *Using an asset to extinguish the debt.*

Fair value the asset such as the investment, e.g. upward 10,000

Book Value of investment: 90,000

Investment	10,000	
Gain	10,000	

Assume accrued interest of 6000 on the note payable.

Note payable	100,000	
Interest Payable	6000	
Investment		100,000
Gain		6000

B. *Where the book value of the debt and accrued interest exceed the future value.*

Eliminate accrued interest payable. Assume the note book value is 400,000 plus 10,000 of accrued interest. Future payments amount to 15,000 in each of two years along with a final payment of 300,000.

Interest Payable	10,000	
Note Payable	70,000	
Gain		80,000
Note Payable	15,000	
Cash		15,000
Note Payable	15,000	
Cash		15,000
Note Payable	300,000	
Cash		300,000

C. *Where the book value of the debt and accrued interest is less than the future value.*

Restructure debt to lower interest rate and delay future payments. Book value of the debt 100,000 and accrued interest 10,000 are less than the future payments of 140,000.

110,000 < 140,000 assumed for two future years

Find the effective interest rate first:

110/140 = 0.7857 for n= 2, so the effective rate is approximately 13%

Interest Expense	14,300	
Interest Payable		14,300
(110,000) (0.13) = 14,300		
Interest expense	16,159	
Interest Payable		16,159

(0.13) (110,000 + 14,300) = 16,159		
Note Payable	100,000	
Interest Payable	40,000 (10,000 + 14,300 + 16,159, rounding error of 459)	
Cash		140,000

Appendix C

Lehman Brothers Repossession Transactions

In an effort to reduce its financial risk, the firm sold financial assets under a special 'repo' (repossession) agreement to buy them back shortly afterwards. Lehman took out a derivative contract to allow for the repurchase of those securities. The firm apparently debited cash along with the derivative option and credited the securities, neither affecting the income statement nor the balance sheet (no effect on liabilities or stockholders' equity whatsoever, but a reallocation of assets). Lehman used the cash inflow to reduce its liabilities, thereby improving its financial leverage ratio. Subsequently, to pay off the cash loan and reacquire the securities, the firm apparently debited the securities, credited cash and the derivative option as well as reflected any accrued interest on the actual loan. In substance, the transaction was a secured borrowing, not a sale. However, by structuring these transfers in terms of receiving £100 for every £105 for debt securities and £100 for every £108 of equity securities, Lehman was able to treat these transactions as sales rather than loans (Valukas, 2010).

Appendix D

Margin Call Examples

1. If Company A has £145 in financial leverage or liabilities (gearing as it is called in the UK) and £200 in equity, A has £345 in assets. Suppose the creditors stipulate that the equity amount cannot fall below 25% of the fair market value of A's assets; otherwise A will have to sell its assets to pay back its creditors. Assume A acquires £345 in financial securities. However, at the end of the month, the securities are marked to market (fair valued) at £260. The amount of the 'margin call' is 260 × 0.25, which equals £65. The stockholders' stake in the assets is 260 minus the creditors' stake of 145, or £115, which in this case exceeds the margin call of £65.
2. Now assume that A has £300 in financial leverage and £150 in equity. A invests £450 in risky financial securities such as CDO on subprime mortgages. At the end of the month, A attempts to mark these securities to market. However, there is no active market for these securities, so A cannot find a direct market value. Instead, A resorts to computing

the present value of these securities, a surrogate for their direct fair value, by using an investment pricing model. The present value turns out to be £225. Therefore, the margin call is £225 × 0.25, which equals £56.25. Taking the £225 and subtracting £300 in financial leverage indicates that A is 'under water' on its loan, and cannot meet its margin call. Thus, A will have to sell its assets to accommodate its creditors.

The foregoing examples illustrate a central facet of the GFC, i.e. toxic financial assets having no direct market values which financial institutions are most averse to write-down or write-off, lest they show big-bath losses and significant declines in their stockholders' equity.

Appendix E

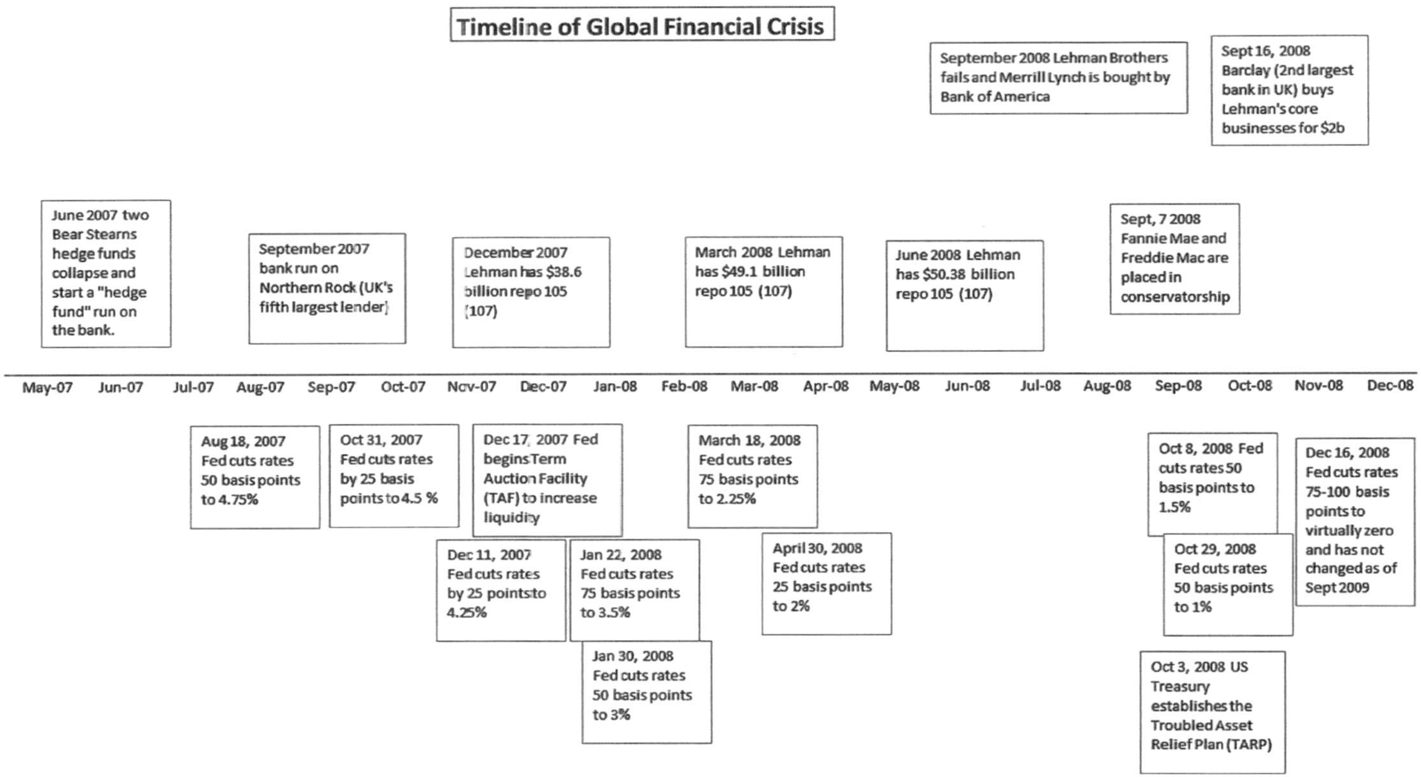

References:

Financial Crisis: A Timeline of Events and Policy Actions, The Federal Reserve Bank of St. Louis. Available at: http://timeline.stlouisfed.org/index.cfm?p=timeline#2010-1.;

A. Valukas, (2010) Lehman Brothers Holdings Inc. Chapter 11 Proceedings Examiner's Report. Section III.A.4: Repo 105 Jenner and Block. Available at: http://lehmanreport.jenner.com/

Index

Note: Tables are indicated in **bold**.